MASTER PLOTS

*Race and the Founding of
an American Literature
1787–1845*

Jared Gardner

THE JOHNS HOPKINS UNIVERSITY PRESS
Baltimore and London

© 1998 The Johns Hopkins University Press
All rights reserved. Published 1998
Printed in the United States of America on acid-free paper
9 8 7 6 5 4 3 2 1

The Johns Hopkins University Press
2715 North Charles Street
Baltimore, Maryland 21218–4363
The Johns Hopkins Press Ltd., London

Library of Congress Cataloging-in-Publication Data
will be found at the end of this book.
A catalog record for this book is available from the British Library.

ISBN 0–8018–5813–5

To Beth

CONTENTS

ILLUSTRATIONS

PREFACE

Master Plots is an examination of the intersection of racial and national discourses in the "founding" of a national literature in the United States, a national narrative that aimed to secure to white Americans an identity that was unique (not European) but not alien (not black or Indian). This study of the literature of the early national period in many ways began with my reading of late-nineteenth- and early-twentieth-century texts. There was clearly a long history to the "master plots" that helped defend and define a national identity for white Americans while proscribing those who did not "belong," so confidently could Frank Norris or F. Scott Fitzgerald, for example, call on a presumed familiarity with its conventions. And of course these plots are still narrated today, albeit often in more indirect forms. In this book I seek out points of origins for these master plots in the early national period, a period in which issues of race were repressed even as racial rhetoric was deployed in the service of narrating the nation into existence. Thus, I turn here to literary history not as a manifestation or symptom of early nationalist racism, but in order to understand the role played by early American literature—and narrative fiction in particular—in scripting stories of "origins" that imagined white Americans as a race apart, both from the Europeans without and the blacks and Indians within the new nation.

Those working to define a national literature after the Revolution certainly faced problems similar to those confronting the would-be founders of a national identity: the conventions and the very language of the literature were necessarily English.[1] Thus, it has long been a truism that literature of the early national period constitutes the "prehistory" to the fully developed national literary culture in the United States: the American Renaissance. Like other students of the early American novel, I have been suspicious of claims that necessarily relegate the works that preceded the "founding" of a "truly" American literature to the status of failed, if interesting, curiosities or experiments. This model of literary history has faced many effective challenges in recent years; nonetheless, there remains something undeniable to its central tenet: that the literature that emerges out of the remarkable productions of the 1840s and '50s influenced and continues to influence the direction of the national culture in ways that cannot be easily claimed for the earlier novel. One of the goals of *Master Plots* is to unearth some of the continuities that extend from the early novel through the first years of the American Renaissance; another is to suggest a partial explanation as to why the importance and influence of the early American novel was muted in the decades leading up to the Civil War.

Recent scholarship has helped demonstrate clearly the links between the American Renaissance and the drive toward an articulation of a "national" identity. As Lauren Berlant writes, "The American National Symbolic burgeoned during the early and mid1800s. But this cultural self-articulation did not take place 'naturally': the 'American Renaissance' emerged under widespread pressure to develop a set of symbolic national references whose possession would signify and realize the new political and social order."[2] As the fact of nationhood preceded the experience of a shared cultural or political identity among Americans, literature's place in the national culture was secured in large measure by its role in helping to provide the terms and narratives of what Berlant terms the "National Symbolic."

This book grew out of my desire to interrogate more closely what looked to be an intriguing coincidence of the *third* term that grows up alongside literature and nation: race. The same period in which American literature arrives at its "renaissance" is also the period in which race theory in the United States goes through its most profound transformations, giving rise to the "American school" of scientific racism, whose "discoveries" would help script the racialized consciousness of the second half of the nineteenth century. In the period with which this study begins, then, literature, race, and nationalism in America are all in their "prehistory," but by the period with which it concludes, all are understood to have arrived at their mature articulation. The "coincidence" of their development over a similar period of time turns out to be no coincidence at all: each of these discourses had something to offer to and something to gain from the others.

I hope to illuminate the ongoing importance of an often undervalued period of American literature, and, more broadly, to theorize American literature as not only informed by issues of national and racial identity, but informing and forming in important ways those identities and the founding stories the culture comes to take for granted. I do not make explicit here the connections and lessons this literary history might offer to our own contemporary dialogue about racial and national identity. In addressing the unique terms and conditions that first granted authority to this racialized national narrative in the early national period, I have had to relegate consideration of the legacy of these master plots to the margins of my inquiry. But I do seek to contribute to the contemporary debate by tracing the early development of narratives and metaphors that helped script and police the boundaries of the "white nation." The fantasy that still governs contemporary American identity depends on an assumption of an Americanness defined at every stage by its investment in whiteness—as George Lipsitz puts it, "as the unmarked category against which difference is constructed, whiteness never has to speak its name, never has to acknowledge its role as an organizing principle in social and cultural relations."[3] Recent scholarship has gone a long way toward forcing whiteness and white nationalism to speak its name. In history and American studies, those working out of what has come to be loosely termed "whiteness studies" have made an invaluable contribution to our understanding of the ways in which the white nation was constructed and defended. In literary studies, the work has also tended in a somewhat different but equally productive direction in recent years, toward a new literary history that documents and celebrates the mutual indebtedness of "black" and "white" literary traditions, challenging the still-dominant essentialized model of a "white" American literature.[4]

I am indebted to the work of these literary critics and historians of identity, and I work here to build on their discoveries. Investigating the intersections of race and nation in the narrative fiction of the late eighteenth and early nineteenth centuries, I seek to show how national and racial narratives helped give rise to the particular concerns of many of the texts central to the rise of the novel. I also work to explain how narrative fiction helped inform the terms of the newly articulated discourses of race and nation. This project therefore necessarily requires a historicizing approach, one that places these discourses in relation to each other at specific moments in time that witnessed significant change in their articulation. Toward this end, I rely heavily on the research of historians of the period; I also read primary historical evidence—newspapers, speeches, journals, and laws—as both product and producer of the cultural logic within which the early American novel came into its own. I do not claim to be reading as a historian; neither, for the reasons outlined, do I accept that what I am writing is not history, simply because its methodology and its primary subject is literary.

The range of central literary texts to which I devote most of my critical attention, however, is relatively narrow: a set of "canonical" texts that worked to codify and legitimate the formation of national identity in terms of race. My focus is on a specific group of novels that explicitly and in similar terms consider the construction of a national identity as bound up with theories of race. *Master Plots* traces the genealogy of this story written by several authors who self-consciously sought to found an "American literature" in an uneasy collaboration with theorists, politicians, and popular essayists of race and nation. It is a model of an "American literature" that we must necessarily understand as one among many, a fact that is made all the more obvious in that my emphasis is clearly on the novel, which played an especially large role (in ways that American poetry and drama did not) in the popularization of these terms and these narratives. Therefore, in *Master Plots* I do not focus extensively on the counter-knowledges and subversive texts that resisted these narratives and the assumptions they relied on, with the important exception of the concluding chapter on Frederick Douglass's rewriting of the literature of "American race." A fuller account of the counterliterature would constitute another project, one whose value and importance I hope this book makes clear in its literary history of these master plots.[5]

My focus on "canonical" texts is thus neither a reification of traditional literary historical models nor a debunking of texts and authors whose influence and importance are undeniable. Reexamining these texts, however, in light of the deployment of racial fantasies and metaphors toward national ends allows us to consider what is at stake not only for these authors and their own times, but also for the literary and national culture of later decades (including our own) that they helped define.

Chapter 1 examines the literature that grew out of the events of 1787, where the simultaneous origin of three discourses can plausibly be located: racial science is born with the publication of Thomas Jefferson's and Samuel Stanhope Smith's seminal essays, national identity with the pamphlets circulating around the Constitutional Convention, and American fiction with the publication of the "first" American novel. I examine the political factionalism that defined the period in terms of two conflicting narratives, both of which turned to the rhetoric of race to tell their tales. The Republicans understood the Federalists to be working with Britain to establish a nation of political slaves, a nation envisioned in terms of the slaves with which white Americans were familiar, blacks; the Federalists believed the Republicans were in league with the French to create a nation of political savages, a nation articulated in terms of the nations of "savages" Americans knew firsthand, Indians. The first three chapters focus primarily on the Federalist version of this narrative, as it is this vision that dominated national, racial, *and* literary discourse during the Washington and Adams administrations, setting many of the terms of the "story" for the first decades of the nineteenth century as well.

Chapter 2 considers Royall Tyler's *Algerine Captive,* which works to imagine a fourth term to the question of America's racial destiny: not black, not Indian, not European—but American. Set against the nation's mounting international tensions in the mid-1790s, Tyler's novel considers race both as a problem *and* a solution to the crisis in American identity his novel describes. Tyler constructs the Algerian as a stand-in for both the black and the Indian, and toward this end the novel borrows from both slave and captivity narratives. At the same time, Tyler also collapses the British and the French into the specter of the Algerian corsair, making use of the sensational accounts of European manipulation of attacks on American shipping. In the Algerian of the 1790s, then, Tyler constructs a composite threat, safely located outside the physical landscape of America, with which to confront the young nation's darkest fears. Tyler describes his hero's captivity at the hands of this composite so that he can define finally what it means to have an *American* identity.

Chapter 3 examines the debates surrounding the citizenship crisis of the Alien and Sedition Acts through the novels and later imperialist writings of Charles Brockden Brown. Examining the rhetoric of savagery in the anti-alien polemics of the late 1790s through which the problem of the alien becomes its own solution, we see how, for Brown, the threat epitomized by the Indian generates a new conception not simply of how the American might defend himself but of what the American is. Brown's equation of the alien with the savage allows his hero not only to escape becoming an Indian himself but also to come into his inheritance as an American. This novelistic treatment of the citizenship crisis brings Brown to a reconsideration both of his former republicanism and his career as a novelist, such that he abandons fiction in favor of political pamphlets calling for the active extirpation of the alien—epitomized by the Indian—and scripting the terms of the imperialism of the nineteenth century.

Chapter 4 examines James Fenimore Cooper's novels of the 1820s in terms of the widespread drive to reimagine national origins in order to distance national identity from the increasingly problematic cornerstone of race. By tracing the nation's history progressively further back to an imagined point of pure origins, Cooper works to reimagine a national identity built not on the racial metaphor of the first generation, but on the more substantial foundation of a European inheritance. Writing against the backdrop of the debates and widening sectionalism surrounding the Missouri Compromise, Cooper seeks to maintain the union by imagining the Indian as bringing about a reconciliation of the American with his lost identity, an identity now purged of race. In *The Pioneers* and *The Prairie* Cooper fantasizes scenes of compromise designed to free national identity of the burden of race scripted by the first generation.

Master Plots concludes with two chapters reading two voyages, one southward toward an ideal of ultimate whiteness and one northward toward a revised model of national identity. Reading Edgar Allan Poe's *Narrative of Arthur Gordon Pym* against Frederick Douglass's *Narrative*, the concluding chapters describe two narratives of the constitution of American race and two very different interrogations of the relationship between racial identity and problematics of writing in antebellum America. Both of these authors are writing in response to a shift in the long debate in racial theory from monogenism to polygenism—from the belief that the different races all derive from a common ancestor, to the claim that the races were in fact created separately. Poe's novel, the subject of chapter 5, serves as a culmination of the crisis narrated in the previous chapters, as he reverses the terms of Cooper's solution by having his hero abandon nation altogether in search of a southern point in which all will be ultimately white. Chapter 6 considers Frederick Douglass's own examination of the relation of writing to racial identity and his understanding, like Poe, that they are mutually constitutive. But unlike Poe, Douglass denies that this interdependence is divine, timeless, or natural. Instead, for Douglass it is through human writing—whether the racial science of the polygenists or the horrible "writing" of the slave master's whip—that white Americans inscribe the categories of race. Thus, *Master Plots* concludes with an examination of Douglass's study of racial science, in "The Claims of the Negro, Ethnologically Considered," in which he explores the history of the writing of race and places the responsibility for scripting the future of American race squarely with his contemporaries.

As with any project that spans many years and places, I have accumulated an array of debts that cannot be adequately acknowledged or repaid. This book began at the Johns Hopkins University as a dissertation in the English Department under the direction of Walter Benn Michaels and Larzer Ziff. They have been unsparingly generous with their advice, encouragement, and criticism at every stage. I must also express my deep indebtedness to the teaching and friendship of Sharon Cameron, Jerome Christensen, Jonathan Goldberg, John Guillory, and Mary Poovey. I owe to all of them the foundations for my own work. To the friends and colleagues who have read all or part of this manuscript over the years, I am eternally grateful: Catherine Jûrca, Claudia Klaver, Anthony Scott, Saadi Simawe, Joanne Wood, and most especially to Jonathan Kramnick, Cannon Schmitt, and Michael Trask, who have given more to me and this book than I ever had a right to ask for.

Funding and support that helped make this book possible has been provided by the Mellon Foundation, the Johns Hopkins University, and the Grinnell College Grant Board, which also provided me with my invaluable research assistant, Brian Jones. Many thanks go to the library staffs at the Johns Hopkins University, Grinnell College, the American Antiquarian Society, the Library of Congress, the Newberry Library, and the New York Historical Association.

A version of chapter 3 appeared in *American Literature* 66 (1994); I thank Cathy N. Davidson, Michael Moon, and their readers for their advice on this chapter, advice that helped shape the direction of all the chapters to follow. I am extremely grateful for the care and attention given to this book by Willis G. Regier and the readers and editors at the Johns Hopkins University Press, including David Anderson's masterful editing of the final manuscript.

This book owes a great deal to my experience teaching American literature at Grinnell College for the past three years, to my colleagues and students in the English Department, and especially to the students in the Race and Nation seminar (1994) and the Fantastic Voyages seminar (1995), who helped me see these texts and the issues they raise anew.

Finally I must record my deepest gratitude and love to Susan Gardner-Brooks, Bruce Brooks, Andrew Gardner, Trebbe Johnson, Natsu Ifill, Myrna Hewitt, and Jack Hewitt, for their support, refuge, and wisdom. This book is dedicated to Elizabeth Hewitt, for all I have enumerated above and for everything else.

MASTER
PLOTS

CHAPTER 1

The History of White Negroes

While Commerce spreads her canvass o'er the main,
And Agriculture ploughs the gratefull plain,
Minerva aids Columbia's rising race
With arms to triumph and with arts to grace.

Columbian Magazine (1787)

I

In 1826 James Madison wrote, "Next to the case of the black race within our bosom, that of the red on our borders is the problem most baffling to the policy of our country."[1] In many ways this diagnosis offers the terms central to this book: one "nation," two "races" threatening that nation internally and externally, and a "policy" with which to negotiate the relationship between them. The definition of a political entity—"our country"—in opposition to racial identities—blacks and Indians—has the effect of racializing national identity, and it is this formulation that gives rise to the imagination of a third "race": an American race. Concerned, on one hand, with distinguishing themselves from white Europeans, white Americans in the early national period were, on the other hand, anxious lest these distinctions should become too great. The question that resonates throughout the early national period is: What are Americans going to be? Scarcely hidden behind the question is the fear that in this undiscovered country and under this untested political system, white Americans will be either collapsed back into Europeans or else transformed into something as completely "different" as blacks and Indians. Both in the asking and in the answering of that question, racial and national identity become inextricably linked; and it is in the fledgling field of American letters that these links are forged.

The familiar paradigm for the rise of American literature commonly imagines a primal scene in which young writers struggled to define their craft in opposition to British models. However, examining the emergence of national identity in the United States through a discourse of racial identity suggests that the problem facing those who would found a national literature involved not simply cultural difference from Europe, but a complicated defensive relation to African Americans and Native Americans as well. The solution arrived at by the novel's earliest practitioners is an abstract but potent conflation of the European with blacks and Indians, such that an American literature comes to be defined not only by its cultural uniqueness but also by its defense of a model of racial purity.

This is the "master plot" reiterated throughout the early national period, with profound consequences for the development of American literature, race, and national identity. The conventions of this founding American story had unexpected costs for future Americans, including those white Americans who had presumably the most to gain from its resolutions. The story goes something like this. The American (almost always male and always white) seeks his place in the new nation, but he is opposed by a range of obstacles: lack of parental guidance, inadequate or outdated education, poverty, failure of his countrymen to recognize his claims—in short, by his lack of a clearly defined identity. This identity crisis is nationalized by the intrusion of the European and racialized by the appearance of the "other," black or Indian. The European stands as the counterclaim to the American's desires or inheritance. He is the Old World representative whose fully formed identity (parentage, education, title, and so on) promises to secure to him everything that is denied the hero. The black or Indian, however, represents the fate of the hero should his claims ultimately be unsuccessful. Denied a national identity, the white American thus risks becoming marked as racial other—in the racist imagination of the late eighteenth century, marked as uncultured, unpropertied, uncivilized, unknown, and unknowable. To fail to prove that his claims are superior to, but also significantly different from, those of the European is to be denied access to identity altogether.

All of this no doubt sounds like the plot of an early American novel, and indeed it is in some real measure the plot of several. But the story I am narrating could as easily describe the mainstream political fantasies generated as white Americans considered the nature of an American identity in the wake of the Revolution. It is a story, as I will describe at length, that can be found in one form or another in the political posturing surrounding the Constitutional Convention and in the newspapers and popular periodicals of the first decades of the nation's history. American literature did not invent the terms or manufacture the conceptions of race, nor did it generate the nationalist hysteria that fueled this story's climaxes. But the early American novel did help formulate and popularize the surprising resolution to this tale, in which a young American is rescued from his predicament and comes into his national identity (and all the rights and privileges inherent therein) by discovering and ultimately defending the equivalence of the European with the racial other.

Whether the European is British or French and the racial other is African American or Native American are questions whose answers often serve to define the particular political formulation of national identity toward which the author wishes to lead his or her hero. Ultimately, however, these political distinctions, although important to much of what follows, do little to change the larger trajectory of the plot—a story held in common in large measure by the "right" and "left" of the political spectrum. For both, the story being told is one in which the national identity crisis that faced white Americans in the years following the Revolution is racialized, raising the specter of blacks and Indians as both threat and promise. What begins as a literary attempt to define an American race by excluding all that is external to the nation turns into a widespread drive to purge the nation of an imagined internal contamination. Literature both narrates and participates in this drive, and the early history of the American novel is marked by a series of attempts to revise the meaning of an "American race."

Trying to locate an origin for the very long and complicated history of racial and national identity in the United States as it intersects with the rise of an American literature, and the American novel in particular, presents a problem. The period under discussion here—the first years of the national period—in many ways serves as the prehistory of the modern discourse of race and the prehistory of American identity. And, of course, as literary histories of the early Republic never tire of suggesting, this is the prehistory of American letters as well. Yet around 1787 we can locate what is plausibly the simultaneous emergence and codification of these three discourses in the United States: racial science is born with the publication of Thomas Jefferson's and Samuel Stanhope Smith's seminal essays; national identity is founded in the debates and pamphlets circulating around the Constitutional Convention at Philadelphia; and American fiction is inaugurated with the publication, in 1789, of the "first" American novel, William Hill Brown's *The Power of Sympathy.*

To understand how these interrelated discourses come to be defined we must revise certain conceptions of what racial and national identity look like when we encounter them in literature. In the racialist-nationalistic texts of the late nineteenth or early twentieth centuries, the problem raised by race is how to protect a white America from the physical or biological threat posed by African Americans and, later, by immigrants. But for the earlier period, the fear that is articulated through race is not in fact a fear of blacks or Indians, but a fear of becoming something like blacks or Indians. It is this identity of absolute difference that comes to be articulated in terms of race—the fear of becoming something so radically other from white Europeans that it can only be imagined in terms of blacks or Indians.

With the dangers and pitfalls of self-government that emerged with the end of the Revolution, the understanding of the potential for absolute difference begins to be formulated in darker terms. The potential effects of the political and physical landscapes that had already wrought amazing changes by 1787 are the new objects of fear. The environment was a savage one, and in it had been found "savages"—was it not logical to suspect, as some naturalists made the case, that this could be the fate of white Americans as well? As American observers looked to the violence and uprisings of the frontier, many saw there evidence of precisely such a transformation. The politics were unformed and untried; was it not possible that, unless properly defined, the nation's political identity could lead to unimaginable degeneration? Certainly, many saw in Shays's Rebellion in 1787 a manifestation of this metamorphosis. The dilemma was how best to regulate these changes, and upon the course that was chosen hung the fate of the future American: would he fulfill his millennial destiny, or would he become marked as if by race?

American millennialism had long conceived of a community in the wilderness transformed from the society of the Old World, and these scenarios, of course, date back to the earliest colonial experiences.[2] In the captivity narrative and the analogy of their condition to that of slavery, colonial Americans found the metaphors to bind community and to bring about (I crib D. W. Griffith advisedly here) the birth of a nation. What is new in 1787, however, is that after these fears are filtered through the new vocabulary of racial science, political slavery and environmental degeneration come to be described in visions of the United States as a nation of blacks or a nation of Indians. Thus, what are not necessarily, or even logically, racial fears come to be articulated in racial terms. J. Hector St. John de Crèvecoeur and William Bartram, for example, both register the changes wrought by the Revolution in racialized terms: Crèvecoeur in his description of the Revolution as an Indian war, and Bartram in his account of an encounter with four marauding blacks on his return from the South at the end of the war.[3]

Yet it is important to keep in mind that race itself has little fixed meaning at this time, and race per se (as an entity distinct from the fears of savagery and bondage) is of relatively minor political concern in this period. Later, of course, the consequences of racial fantasies and metaphors would be brought home to white Americans with the full force of Civil War. In the decades preceding that struggle, the formerly mobile rhetoric of race will become fixed and immutable in ways that many of those who continued to deploy racial categories failed to recognize until surprisingly late. In the 1820s and '30s, many American writers would have cause to reconsider the terms they helped define and the plot whose intricacies they had worked to resolve, and, as will be considered in the second half of this book, they would seek out ways to rewrite the now seemingly inevitable collapse of racial categories into the problem of national identity. As Cooper and Poe, for example, considered the central role literature had played in the writing of this "plot," they came to worry over the ways in which the definition of and justification for an American literature had become inextricably bound up in these very formulas.

But in the 1780s and '90s, there is a great disparity between the intensity of the rhetoric and the political interest in the historical African Americans and Native Americans to whom this racialized rhetoric made reference. Ultimately, novelists such as Tyler and Brown were no more concerned than the majority of their white contemporaries with the accurate definition of racial categories—and still less with the legitimate experiences of those defined as racially other. Thus, it was precisely the level of abstraction that hovered around newly charged racial categories in the 1780s and '90s that allowed for the series of substitutions binding national identity to race to take place.

Yet before beginning to trace out a literary history of the early national period in which racial and national identity are bound together, it is important first to consider briefly race and nation as discrete theoretical concerns. The abstractions and contradictions in the use of categories of racial and national identity in the literary and political rhetoric of the period demand some precision at the outset in marking the limits of these discourses and the terms of this literary history.

II

The origins of race and racial oppression in America have, at least since Edmund Morgan's seminal *American Slavery, American Freedom* (1975), been widely defined in terms of the economic and social pressures slavery both resolved and generated. As Morgan persuasively argues in his history of colonial Virginia, the restructuring of servitude as the lot of a racially stigmatized and unpaid population allowed for the development of a discourse of natural rights for white Americans, a discourse that would not fundamentally threaten the social and economic fabric of colonial society. Many subsequent writers have elaborated and expanded the forceful claims underlying this thesis to account for the rise of a formal discourse of race after the Revolution. Barbara Jeane Fields, as one important example, offers a compelling account of the ways in which the "superstition" of race found its national articulation out of the need to justify slavery in the wake of the Revolution.[4] Alexander Saxton and David R. Roediger similarly describe national definitions of race as originating from the pressing need to justify the slave trade and Native American dispossession.[5]

This recent work points to the value and potency of explanations of race as resulting from the need to defend, at all costs, chattel slavery for African Americans and the economic and political freedom for whites purchased by this slavery. The importance of such accounts cannot be underestimated, not least because they have historicized race as an ideological construction, rather than a genetic or mystical entity with a "life of its own." The limitation of such readings, however, is that they consistently read the motivations for the invention and perpetuation of race in the early national period in economic terms. The idea of race and the meanings of racial difference often circulate at this time in excess of the bottom lines of materialist history.

Many of those deploying race as a category in the years following the Revolution were not motivated by direct or indirect interest in the institution of slavery. As I describe at length below, perhaps the most shocking realization in examining the discourse of race in the early national period is how little many of those negotiating racial categories were concerned with historical slavery (and, at this time, still less with the historical dispossession of Native Americans). What, then, is motivating the currency of the rhetoric of race in excess of the explanation of economic self-interest and the defense of African American slavery and Native American removal against the paradoxical assertions of the Declaration of Independence? The answer, I argue, has much to do with literature and with narrative fiction in particular.

To suggest that literature and conceptions of race have something to say to each other is, of course, to suggest nothing new. The critical history of literary investigations into race has for some time focused on viewing literature as a repository of racial attitudes: as a mirror of the definitions of race at the time, or as a template by which to judge the racial politics of an author. More recent treatments of race in literature have considered the ways in which literature seeks to rearticulate racial problems and to imagine "resolutions." What until very recently has been less fully examined, however, is the role narrative fiction itself historically plays in the development of racial categories. I seek here to intervene in the inquiry into these issues by suggesting that the definition of racial identity was decisively informed by a perceived necessity to narrate national identity.

We exist in a theoretical moment in which the constructedness—the "fictional" nature—of identity is widely accepted. Such an understanding is not unique to our own time but resided as well, albeit in terms we would not recognize as our own, in the culture that emerged out of the Revolution. The constructedness and the textual nature of identity celebrated by post-Revolutionary writers such as Benjamin Franklin and Stephen Burroughs, for example, is well known. Far from being unique to such writers, this understanding helped inform the larger debate over national identity and the widespread understanding of the need to script mythologies that would ground the new nation in a past and a future at a time when neither was secure. Ernest Gellner reminds us that "nations as a natural, God-given way of classifying men, as an inherent though long-delayed political destiny, are a myth."[6] This claim would have been obvious to those who contemplated the problem of nation in the years following the Revolution. As Bernard Bailyn and his successors have shown, the language of nationalism was invented by the Revolutionary generation before a national identity existed in fact; the struggle for the second (and every subsequent) generation has been to make the nation as political reality live up to the imagination of a unified national identity.

Race helped provide the terms and the metaphors by which the first generations could stabilize national identity by giving it a past and a future—not because race was itself a stable and fixed category, but because the term invoked in its late-eighteenth-century definitions narratives of origins, histories of change, and fantasies about the futures of peoples. Race was a category of identity that brought with it myths of beginnings and fantasies of the future at a time when the newly claimed status of nationhood did not. Indeed, the nationhood that the United States had claimed seemed predicated on a dislocation from history and from the narratives of inheritance that had been formerly guaranteed to colonial Americans. Thus, the drive to know the origins and history of races that emerges in America at this time is not only, or perhaps even primarily, related to the need to defend slavery (which had been far too easily "defended" in the fatal compromises of the Constitutional Convention by the time the first major American treatises on race appear in print). The debate over the origins of race emerges in large measure out of the need for a category of identity that brings with it the narrative properties (of storied beginnings and fantasized destinies) that other newly defined or contested identities—national, individual, literary—cannot mine from the shallow ground of national culture. Thus, the drive to begin determining an origin for race in the late eighteenth century in the United States must be understood as being in part determined by the need to find a narrative for the modern nation "born" out of the violent unmoorings of the Revolution.

As Homi K. Bhabha suggests in the introduction to *Nation and Narration*, "Nations, like narratives, lose their origins in the myths of time and only fully realize their horizons in the mind's eye. Such an image of the nation—or narration—might seem impossibly romantic and excessively metaphorical, but it is from those traditions of political thought and literary language that the nation emerges as a powerful historical idea in the west."[7] Indeed, the modern western nation, which the United States helped define, depends on narratives that work to mask literal origins (often dealing in bloody and recent history) in favor of mythic origins, locating an origin for a people in a time and place unrecoverable save through the fantasy and defense of nation. As Bhabha's remarks suggest, the nation depends on romantic, mythic narratives of origins and on metaphorical, literary language; for the United States, race provided an important mythic narrative of "origins" to begin narrating the nation into existence. Race gave the nation the myths that would allow its disunities to be dissolved and its recent political origins lost in "time immemorial."

As Timothy Brennan argues, building on the seminal work of Benedict Anderson, "it was especially the novel as a composite but clearly bordered work of art that was crucial in defining the nation as an 'imagined community.' "[8] In defining the role of the novel in the making of national identity, he argues that nations "are imaginary constructs that depend for their existence on an apparatus of cultural fictions in which imaginative literature plays a decisive role" (49). Although Brennan's subject here is the historical links between the rise of European nationalism and the rise of the novel, this claim applies as well to the American scene in the late eighteenth and early nineteenth centuries. The turn to literature in examining the early history of "the possessive investment in whiteness" is thus not simply a search for literary manifestations or representations of the social, political, and cultural history of the interrelatedness of the rise of discourses of nation and race in the United States.[9] In other words, narrative literature is not only the site of the intersection of racial and national discourses. Rather, it offers the formal structures that make the convergence of racial and national discourses imaginable and finally so potent; that is, the discourses of race and nation in the United States are in important respects narrative in their articulation and literary in their dispersal and popularization. Thus, I suggest that the rise of the American novel (a half-century after its development in Great Britain) is due in part to demands that the newly charged concept of nation placed on imaginative literature at this time.[10]

Here, as elsewhere, I owe much to Benedict Anderson and his understanding of nations as "imagined communities." He argues that the structure of time and community put forth by the novel "is a precise analogue of the idea of the nation, which also is conceived as a solid community moving steadily down (or up) history."[11] Anderson's interest in the novel and print culture derives primarily from his argument with familiar critiques of national identity as entirely determined by a repressive state, critiques that imagine, implicitly or explicitly, true communities or identities dissolved in favor of the fabricated nation. Anderson's substitution of the term *imagined* for *fabricated* has moved the discourse of national identity away from the dichotomies of truth and falsehood and toward a consideration of "the style in which they are imagined" (6).

Despite these and similar insights that have informed my argument about national identity in the early Republic, however, there is a central point on which I am necessarily positioned against Anderson. In his chapter "Patriotism and Racism," Anderson defines what is for him a fundamental opposition between national and racial thinking:

> The fact of the matter is that nationalism thinks in terms of historical destinies, while racism dreams of eternal contaminations, transmitted from the origins of time through an endless sequence of loathsome copulations: outside history. . . .
>
> The dreams of racism actually have their origin in ideologies of *class*, rather than in those of nation: above all in claims to divinities among rulers and to "blue" or "white" blood and "breeding" among aristocracies. (149)

The opposition as he defines it is especially ill-suited to early American national context because it assumes theories that understand race as outside of time and history; this is precisely not the dominant mode of racial thought in the late eighteenth or early nineteenth century. As I discuss below, the environmental theories promulgated by the defenders of monogenism—all mankind as descending from the "original parents"—saw all racial difference as the result of the history of degeneration from the biblical source. Further, in the United States, the first avatar of polygenism—or the belief that racial difference is God-given and therefore outside of historical (environmental) time—was no defender of aristocracy, natural or otherwise (such as Anderson locates in a European context), but was instead the head of the Republican Party, Thomas Jefferson. Here, again, class does not fully explain the origins of race in antebellum America, nor does it explain away race's strong ties to nation.

Anderson differentiates racism from nationalism by describing the national community as joinable in time; thus "the nation presents itself as simultaneously open and closed" in a way that later models of race cannot (146). In the United States in the late eighteenth century, however, race was understood in precisely the terms Anderson here ascribes to nation; and accounts from the period of blacks turning white (and the fantasies of the reverse) point to the possibility of "joining" a race precisely as one would a nation. Anderson's attempt to separate the discourses of nationalism and racism holds up better in an American context when we look at it in light of the mid-nineteenth-century orthodoxy of polygenism, which did indeed seek to prove that the races were unequal as far back in time as one could possibly go. Yet, even in a polygenist context, I would question Anderson's terms, insofar as the "loathsome copulations" racism conjures are always bound up in the "historical destinies" of nationalism. In other words, racial "degeneration" is always potentially (in monogenist or polygenist terms) a part of the "historical destiny" of the nation.

The insistence on understanding race and nation as fundamentally distinct is thus not applicable to the early national period in the United States. For Anderson, "the imagined community"—the fantasy of sameness, simultaneity, brotherhood—precedes and is largely independent of the racist fantasy—the negative definition of the other. The two cannot be separated in the early United States, where the pressing need to imagine a sameness—a community after the Revolution—was always bound to the need to define a difference—from former colonial oppressors abroad and from racial "others" at home.[12] From the earliest days of the Republic, recourse was made to racial metaphors that implied both inclusion and exclusion, leading to the imagination of an "American race." Anderson is certainly correct in asserting that race and racism are not simply the products of nationalism; but neither is race a discourse whose terms can be understood independently of nationalism (any more than nation can be understood in the United States independent of race).

Indeed, a question often asked when discussing the intersections of racial and national identity in the late eighteenth century is whether the term *race* as it is understood in the eighteenth century does not more often than not refer to the older usage of *race* as *family, clan,* or *nation.* After all, it can be argued, no eighteenth-century dictionary defined *race* according to anything like contemporary usages. But, as Nicholas Hudson writes, "It is clear . . . that the dictionaries were lagging well behind the use of 'race' in science and *belles-lettres.*"[13] Hudson's useful overview of the development of a modern definition of "race" in Europe and the United States at the end of the eighteenth century underscores the fact that "the emergent concept of the 'nation' as a linguistic and cultural community was of considerable importance to the concurrent rise of a racial worldview" (256).

I would argue that the opposite is equally true and in the United States perhaps even more so: race as a developing discourse helped provide the terms by which national identity came into being. Hudson's history considers the gradual separation of race and nation as categories of investigation during the Enlightenment before their explosive recombination in the middle of the nineteenth century, but this recombination was always already under way for American theorists of race and nation in the later eighteenth and early nineteenth centuries. Even as race mutated from its earlier meanings as clan or "nation" to describe ever larger biological populations, and nation emerged as a category for describing political and linguistic communities, Americans seeking out a destiny—biological or historical—for the newly founded nation profited from the bleeding and overlap between these terms as well as between the older and newer definitions of race.

The literary history of the intersections between race and nation in antebellum America has important resonances for contemporary debates about national identity. Many on all sides of this debate invoke a notion of culture, which Walter Benn Michaels has persuasively read as a redeployment of racial logic—an essential (if ghostly) identity that must be recovered and defended.[14] The work culture performs in defining and defending national identities in contemporary discourse (writing onto the constructed nation the myth of a constantly reiterated timelessness) is closely related to what the emerging definitions of race brought to the discourse of nation in the early decades of the national period. As Etienne Balibar writes, "What is called cultural identity is constantly compared to and at the limit conflated with *national identity,* and nevertheless is in some sense 'sheltered' from the empirical existence of nations, their borders, their politico-military history."[15] Giving nations a race (in 1798) or a culture (in 1998) becomes a way of giving nations an identity that is immune to the exigencies of history, the self-determinations of individuals, or the deconstructions of intellectual analysis. Culture and race both bring to the discourse of nation an inevitability it cannot otherwise secure: as Balibar writes, "culture is . . . the name to be given to the 'essential nation'" (178). In 1787, at a time in which the new nation could in no way be understood as "essential," the need for a nationalist discourse of race was especially urgent.

III

Given what was perceived to be hanging in the balance, the degree to which factionalism defined the political landscape during the nation's first decade is not surprising. And the political factionalism of the time coded many of its darkest fears in racial terms: becoming a nation of slaves at the hands of the Federalists and their British allies, or a nation of savages at the hands of the French and their Republican minions. As Patrick Henry asks one version of the question, "Our country will be peopled. The question is, shall it be with Europeans or with Africans?"[16] For the young nation in the 1780s and '90s, phrasing the problem of national identity as a question about race allowed the future American to be imagined in terms of easy oppositions: in the case of Henry's formulation, European or African. By linking the European nations vying for America's political allegiance to the structural fears that lead toward anxieties about race, what begins to get articulated here is the notion of blacks, Indians, and Europeans as something completely different from what white America imagines itself to be. The logic of a Republican argument looks something like this: the Federalists, by reifying hierarchy, consolidating federal power, and working to reestablish the nation's former servitude to Britain, are creating a nation of political slaves, a nation envisaged in the rhetoric of the time in terms of the slaves that Americans are familiar with: blacks. For the Federalists, the Republicans, by leveling social structures, turning power over to the people, and embracing a corrupted revolutionary ideal imported from France, are working to create a nation of political savages, a nation that comes to be articulated in terms of the nations of "savages" Americans know firsthand: Indians.

The Federalist appropriation of race is most powerfully enunciated in the texts surrounding the Constitutional Convention and Shays's Rebellion in 1787. Gordon Wood characterizes the Federalists' hysterical response to republican social mobility as foreseeing a world in which everything was "turned upside down": "Against this threat from the licentious the Federalists pictured themselves as the defenders of the worthy, of those whom they called 'the better sort of people.' . . . Because the Federalists were fearful that republican equality was becoming 'that *perfect equality* which deadens the motives of industry, and places Demerit on a Footing with Virtue,' they were obsessed with the need to insure that the proper amount of inequality and natural distinctions be recognized."[17] Out of the Revolutionaries' conspiracy theories, which imagined that the British were attempting to turn the colonists into slaves, arose a post-Revolutionary generation determined to guarantee that they were not slaves. Thus, "equality" meant not only the Republican ideal of the Jeffersonians, but for a large segment of the population (and the dominant segment during the period at hand) it entailed first and foremost the preservation of a "natural" hierarchy. This idea of a natural inequality is perhaps best characterized by Jeremy Belknap in his novelistic celebration of the Federalist arguments during the Constitutional Convention:

> It is true, said they, that all men are naturally free and equal; it is a very good idea, and ought to be understood in every contract and partnership which can be formed. . . . But it is as true that this equality is destroyed by a thousand causes which exist in nature and society. It is true that all beasts, birds, and fishes are naturally free and equal in some respects, but yet we find them unequal in other respects, and one becomes the prey of another. There is, and always will be, a superiority and an inferiority, in spite of all the systems and metaphysics that ever existed.[18]

A version of natural history thus provided the justification for an inequality that had to be defended for the good of all, and racial science, as we will see, provided the prophecy (in living color) for what would happen if these distinctions were not preserved.

No Federalist literature was more influential in legitimizing this narrative than *The Anarchiad,* the most popular prounion tract of the period,

which ran in the *New-Haven Gazette* from 1786 to 1787.[19] The Connecticut Wits who wrote the satire (including David Humphreys, to whom the
Algerine Captive, the subject of the next chapter, would be dedicated)
were staunch Federalists responding to the rise in Antifederalist sentiment and to the rebellion in New England. Writing under the guise of a
scientific society that had unearthed an ancient epic in an archaeological
expedition in Ohio, the Wits used this "poem" to frame their attack on the
forces of Chaos they saw gathering around them.[20] The Wits presented
their "Antiquity" as the production of a mythical ancient civilization. In its
story of the triumph of the savage forces of "Chaos and substantial Night"
over this civilization, the Wits foresaw a similar end for the young American nation. The parallels are painfully absurd: the ancient civilization
faced a band of rebels led by one "Shays," was betrayed by cheap-money
men in a state coincidentally named "Rhode Island," and sat in "Philadelphia" at the end of their history trying to determine their response to
the forces mounted at the gates. As Hesper, sworn defender of the lost
civilization, vainly appeals to his people for union, so the reader is told
that if something is not done to reverse these uncanny parallels, the fate of
the United States will be that of the earlier civilization:

> For, see! proud Faction waves her flaming brand,
> And discord riots o'er the ungrateful land;
> Lo! to the north, a wild, adventurous crew,
> In desperate mobs, the savage state renew.[21]

At the poem's end, the narrator, despairing over the passing of his
nation, makes his descent into the "LAND OF ANNIHILATION" and records
his "theory of a race of beings, properly the denizens of that country, who,
after having mixed, undistinguished, with mankind" have corrupted civilization and brought about the triumph of Chaos at the hands of Indians
and Rebels. "What countless *imps* shall throng the new-born States!" the
poet wails. "See, from the shades, on tiny pinions swell / And rise, the
young DEMOCRACY of *hell!*" (65, 69). Thus, the series concludes by describing the factionalism among white Americans that would define the
next decade as if it were a conflict between races—a conflict in which the
forces mounted at the gates and the corrupting agents within the heart of
the nation are conceived of as so inimical and inassimilable to America's
interests as to be understandable in terms of a "theory of a race."

This appeal to race in characterizing political battles—imagining the
opposition as a rising race of savages—was a powerful one. Even maga-

zines with Republican sympathies were drawn to such allegories. The "Speech of an Indian" in Matthew Carey's *American Museum,* for example, equates Antifederalism with a defense of savagery over civilization: "Thus you see, brothers," the *Museum*'s "Indian" orator concludes, "the dangers and oppression to which you will expose yourselves by adopting the most simple form of civil government, that can be offered to you. It will destroy our heaven-born equality of rank and property. . . . Embrace once more the liberty, the independence, and the blessings of the savage life."[22] Here, as elsewhere, the nation to which the Antifederalists would give rise in their opposition to a central government and their appeals to "heaven-born equality" is conceived of as a nation of "savages," and the conflict between white Americans, a conflict that had little to do with race at all, is dramatically portrayed as a struggle for the racial destiny of the nation.

Another journalistic piece, published like the *Anarchiad* in the *New-Haven Gazette,* offers perhaps the clearest view into the logic whereby this conflation of racial and national destiny takes place. The *Gazette*'s editor, Josiah Meigs, an associate of the Wits, ran a regular column under the name of "Lycurgus," in which he proposed sardonic "arguments" in favor of disunion, poverty, and anarchy. In a long essay entitled "The History of White Negroes," Lycurgus offers a fictional account of racial transformation and the prediction of the rise of a species "rapidly increasing among us . . . likely in a short time to become the most useful of all our domestic animals."[23]

Lycurgus's history of the White Negroes unmasks the racial technologies deployed by Federalist texts. He presents the essay as a scientific treatise, playing off accounts proliferating in the magazines of the time of "white negroes," blacks who miraculously (presumably through the positive effects of fledgling democracy) had begun to turn "white."[24] But Meigs's version of the story, like so many Federalist appropriations of early race theory, shows how such transformations can go both ways: here white Americans have begun to turn into black men. After describing the devious methods whereby the British worked to produce white negroes, Lycurgus notes that in America the poor seem to be spontaneously transforming themselves into slaves: "and at a very fortunate time too," Lycurgus proclaims, "just when many of our blacks had obtained their freedom in the war, and the rest grown uneasy and unprofitable."[25] Lycurgus's "celebration" of this new race disguises with little subtlety the fear that in a nation without traditional class boundaries or strong federal government, and in a population made up of poor farmers, exconvicts, and the other dregs of Europe, there exists a potential for something like devolution: the rise of a nation of monsters. To make matters worse, the rise of this race of "white negroes" is accompanied by the first murmurings of a slave population "grown uneasy and unprofitable," murmurings that would grow to a roar with the rebellion in Santo Domingo in the 1790s and Gabriel's Rebellion in 1800.[26]

Since, Lycurgus claims, the nation can no longer blame events on British manipulations, now the source of these remarkable changes must be located in "nature": "It seems to have been the design of nature, that one part of mankind in most countries, and especially in this, should be slaves to the other."[27] As evidence of this nation's especial propensity for the production of white negroes, Lycurgus shows how the political climate (unfunded debt, fluctuating currency, the politicization of the underclass) and the physical environment have worked together to provide such "useful animals." Lycurgus ends his paean in the bleakest contemporary environmentalist terms: "Such a kind of beings [Indians] were a part of the nations of America: and it is reasonable to conclude that every soil produces things natural to it more readily, as well as in greater perfection, than those of foreign growth" (67). Lycurgus's narrative spells out the fears that other Federalist literature only hinted at. Collapsing Indians and African Americans together in his conclusion (the former aligned with environmental fate, the latter with the political), he transplants the current factionalism to a landscape on which "race" spontaneously marks those who will not consent to regulation. The notion of a pure American race thus becomes imaginable only through fierce resistance to the tendency of the Revolutionary and environmental energies to mark all Americans dark, "other."

Similar narratives proliferated in the magazines of the period, but even in more official Federalist responses to Shays's Rebellion we can see how the increasingly easy slippage between the discourse of race and fears about national identity helped dictate the government's response. In the rebellion lay the beginnings of a future of savagery, a perception that served to consolidate the elite's response to the crisis. Putting rebels in war paint made them easier to suppress. As Fisher Ames wrote, "You will behold men who have ever been civilized, returning to barbarism, and threatening to become fiercer than the savage children of nature"—a metaphor that allows for the possibility that the rebels might drag all of New England to a "rank among the savages taken somewhere below the Oneida Indians."[28] It was a metaphor that also allowed the Confederacy to utilize the guise of an invented Indian war to raise federal troops against the rebels.[29] The fears of savagery justified the bloodshed at Springfield, Massachusetts, and racial metaphors extended beyond the political fictions of *The Anarchiad* and "The History of White Negroes" into the realm of political action.

In telling these stories, the Federalists appealed to a unified national identity to contain the force of American nature and Revolutionary energy and in this way to keep Americans "white." As the revolt of 1787 became a well-known galvanizing moment in the drive toward constitutional government, we find the rhetorics of American race implicitly informing the nightmarish landscapes of insurrection Hamilton repeatedly evokes in his pleas for ratification.[30] American nature and American politics were forces to be regulated—forces capable of turning white men "black" and "red"—and it is to the scientific debate surrounding racial history as it was articulated most powerfully by the Republican Thomas Jefferson on one side, and the Federalist Samuel Stanhope Smith on the other, that writers turned for the terms of their narratives.

IV

Like other industries and disciplines, American science after the Revolution sought to prove its native genius in the fields in which it had formerly served as colonial apprentice. In 1789 Jefferson exhorted the president of Harvard University to greater vigilance in the defense of the American environment: "It is the work to which the young men, whom you are forming, should lay their hands. We have spent the prime of our lives procuring them the precious blessing of liberty. Let them spend theirs in shewing that it is the great parent of *science* and virtue."[31] Prominent among early scientific achievements were studies of racial science in its earliest manifestations: natural history, physical anthropology, and the study of Indian languages. But the flurry of scientific activity after the Revolution was not simply motivated by nationalistic pride. Behind Jefferson's chastising tone lies a belief common to American science of the period: it is from nature that the United States will receive its blessings, and it is through the ordering of nature that America will secure its identity. Bernard Sheehan describes the contradiction inherent in the approach to nature by Jeffersonian science: "[Environmentalism] offered a self-contained version of nature, essentially coherent, with its processes operating according to self-validating rules. . . . The environmentalist way of thinking gave to the Jeffersonian age a great confidence in the developing character of nature. It also imposed on the white man the terrible obligation to see that all did indeed come out as the theory seemed to predict."[32] Race theory provided both a great challenge to the identification of such an order in the American environment and a strong impetus for defending and securing that model of natural order. The American debate over race originates in large measure in the positions enunciated in 1787 by Thomas Jefferson and Samuel Stanhope Smith, both of whom looked to existing European models of racial theory and saw in them the possibility of degeneration for white Americans.

Jefferson's most important meditations on race are found in his *Notes on the State of Virginia,* which grew out of his dispute with the most famous naturalist of the time, Comte Georges-Louis Leclerc de Buffon. Buffon had argued earlier in his monumental *Histoire naturelle* that, as environment was the primary cause for all racial deviations from the white "norm," it was logical to predict that the American environment would one day turn white Americans into something resembling the Indian—savage, puny, impotent, and cowardly. Not surprisingly, Jefferson could not allow this equation to stand. In valorizing the Indian, he sought fundamentally to shift the key terms of Buffon's prophecy, ensuring that the Frenchman's future American would not come to be. By defending the Indian's virility, physical endowments, and oratory, Jefferson defended the properties and potential of the American environment.

In the course of this defense, Jefferson identified a series of contaminants posing potential danger to an otherwise pure environment, at the head of which he placed African Americans. Jefferson's extended meditations on blacks have generated much concern from his day to our own. As Winthrop Jordan writes, Jefferson's "remarks about Negroes in the only book he ever wrote were more widely read, in all probability, than any other until the mid–nineteenth century."[33] For contemporary readers, these comments expose the racist hypocrisy of the nation's "founder," his failure to follow out his own declaration that "all men are created equal." But in his own day it was the potential heresy of his suggestions that generated the greatest interest. For Jefferson here comes dangerously close to making the argument that was to become the central tenet of American racial anthropology in the next half-century—polygenism, the belief that the races were created separately: "I advance it . . . as a suspicion only that the blacks, whether originally a distinct race, or made distinct by time and circumstance, are inferior to whites in the endowments both of body and mind. It is not against experience to suppose, that different species of the same genus, or varieties of the same species, may possess different qualifications."[34]

Underwriting Buffon's explanation of racial difference had been the belief that darker skin color was the result of exposure to harsh climates. Therefore, Buffon suggested, not only might the young nation transplanted from Europe to the New World become Indians, but blacks brought to Europe might one day become white.[35] Jefferson defends the American environment through the positive example of the Indian (as well as his tables of weights and measures of flora and fauna), demonstrating the equality, even the superiority, of the country's natural resources; but he is forced at the same time to work to defend this environment against the "foreign" contaminants that he believes will spoil the system. Chief among these are blacks, and in characterizing their natural state of inequality, their inability to live side by side with whites, and advocating their removal, Jefferson was forced to rewrite the environmental model of racial science that had determined Buffon's predictions.

Jefferson saw his attack on blacks as part of his larger defense of the American environment. The primary concern in Jefferson's meditations on race is always with the purity of white America; keeping the nation "beyond the reach of mixture" poses him problems "unknown to history," especially with regard to the African American population.[36] Whereas the Indians were "vanishing" and therefore presumably posed no threat of combination (indeed, so far as one could gather from the *Notes*, the Native American was white), blacks were increasing in number (both slave and free) and mixing with whites to produce an unstable combination (a "fact" Jefferson was widely believed to know from firsthand experience). These formulations depend on the "suspicion" that the races were not all derived from an Adam and an Eve, that they might be perhaps even separate "species."

Jefferson works, somewhat disingenuously, to evade the blasphemy at the root of his arguments for keeping blacks "beyond the reach of mixture." But it was such early articulations of the possibility of polygenism that sparked Samuel Stanhope Smith to write his treatise *Essay on the Causes of the Variety of Complexion and Figure in the Human Species* (1787), which appeared in the midst of the constitutional crisis and offered itself as a defense of the unity of the human species and the stability of the entire republic.

Although Jefferson's arguments are more widely known today, it was the position articulated by Smith that dominated racial thought in the

1790s. Smith was not at this time directly arguing with Jefferson, whose *Notes* was published in English that same year, but he is doing battle with the argument buried behind Jefferson's suggestion of the possibility of different human species, a position argued openly by the British amateur naturalist Lord Kames: the belief that men "must have been originally of different stocks."[37] Smith's defense of monogenism, synthesizing biblical authority with the environmentalist explanations of Buffon and others, provided the bulwark against this first tide of polygenism. For Smith, all racial difference was the result of climate and social condition, and by properly regulating their environment, blacks could be transformed into whites, just as whites "on the frontiers . . . enter with facility into all the habits of the savages" (16). In neither of these transformations does Smith find cause for alarm; rather, he eagerly looks forward to the day when all in America will return to the racial purity of the original parents.

Although Smith's optimistic articulation of monogenism was to hold off the polygenist argument for a time, he was right in recognizing the threat posed by the popularity of polygenism in the United States. The two most important texts for early America, the Bible and the Declaration of Independence, proclaimed that all men were created equal. Yet for many observers of nature and society, the United States was a lesson in difference, hierarchy, and inequality. The foundations of the scientific racism of the next century were laid by men who earnestly sought equality and could find only difference. Over the next several decades, American scientists would move away from Smith's environmentalist model of racial difference and toward a system that promised to preserve the fixedness of the races by proving them to be separate biological species. According to Stephen Jay Gould, the polygenist school of thought, what was to be known internationally as the "American school" of anthropology in the nineteenth century, would be one of the nation's first unique contributions to science and, through Louis Agassiz's theories and Samuel George Morton's collection of skulls, the foundation for a century of scientific racism to follow.[38]

It is perhaps not immediately obvious why the leading Republican formulated a theory of the "natural inequality" of the races while the Federalists tended to line up behind Smith's monogenist defense. The answer is in large part geographic, as Jefferson and many of the Republican leaders were of course slaveholders whereas the Federalist base lay decidedly in the North. But what was at stake in these debates often had little to do with the ongoing debate over slavery (in fact, most of those involved on both sides were publicly, at least, antislavery). More important to the debate was the question of which model of nature the new nation would order itself after. For Jefferson's Republican ideal, a society in which all men were equal first demanded the definition of precisely who qualified as men to be admitted to that egalitarian society. Only if kept free from admixture with blacks, corrupting immigrants (who might turn the American system into "a heterogeneous, incoherent, distracted mass"), and foreign markets could the Republican ideal work.[39] For Smith and the Federalists, natural equality was not at issue. What was at stake was the proper ordering of society, and blacks posed no threat so long as they, like all other elements of society, remained in their proper station and so long as the Federalist leaders were given full power in guiding the organization. Thus, monogenism, with one pair of human parents, Adam and Eve, governed by a single Creator, provided a model by which Federalists conceived of their own rule.

Theorizing about race became something of a nationalist industry, and the debates were followed by the magazines as they reprinted papers and editorialized on the continuing struggle to define race in America.[40] For those struggling to transform the chaos of America's first decade into a political union (a struggle in which Jefferson figures prominently as Republican leader and Smith plays a minor role as president of Princeton and a Federalist elector), at stake in the debates over race was the very future of the nation. As Smith concludes his *Essay,* if the arguments of his opponents succeed, "the science of morals would be absurd; the law of nature and nations would be annihilated; no general principles of human conduct, or religion, or of policy could be framed; for human nature . . . could not be comprehended in any system." During the debate over the Constitution, no argument could be more forceful. "The doctrine of one race," Smith concludes, "removes this uncertainty, renders human nature susceptible to system."[41] Racial science in America, born into the crisis of 1787, became inexorably linked to the political future of the nation.

V

In 1787 national and racial identity in America emerge side by side with the attempts to found a national literary culture. Looking at the conjunction of the early novel with the twinned discourses of racial and national identity, we begin to see how the anxiety circulating around the novel in early America was not simply an extension of the moral censure of the novel in eighteenth-century Britain, but was also a response to a complicated set of American fears about the power of narrative prose to effect rather remarkable changes. As Cathy N. Davidson has argued, "The criticism [of the novel] in America may well have reached its particular level of vehemence because the novel was established here in the wake of the Revolution, at a time when disturbing questions . . . about the limits of liberty and the role of authority were very much at issue."[42] As Davidson's history of the rise of the American novel is complemented by work by Michael Warner and Larzer Ziff on the role of print culture in the early Republic, we gain a clearer sense of how, in Ziff's words, "print culture and American political culture were twins born from the same conditions and dependent on one another for their well-being."[43] Novelists of the time saw their work as intrinsic to the public sphere of economic and political production, and they worried over the effects of their productions on the young society with much the same seriousness with which those gathered at Philadelphia worried over the potential effects of their own writing.

As it was imported into the United States, the novel presented a threefold threat: foreign materials, moral corruption, and class upheaval. For most of those who considered the novel at the time, these threats came to be focused in the imagined body of the "woman reader," whom Davidson identifies as "the implied reader of most of the fiction of the era."[44] By defining the reader as a young woman, often without the protection of class or culture, novelists and critics alike conjured an image of the young nation as both full of promise and perilously vulnerable. Like this fantasy of the female reader, the nation in 1787 was perceived as fickle, excitable, and in need of protection. Thus, the debates surrounding the novel provided a metaphor for the larger question: would the young woman reader import into the bosom of the young nation the prejudices, weaknesses, and immorality of the Old World? By focusing the debate surrounding the novel on the supposedly vulnerable, and potentially explosive, force of female (and especially lower-class) sexuality, the critics of the novel—a literature devoted to seduction and gothic horrors, in which vulnerable girls are led astray by lowly Yankees or imprisoned in dark towers by licentious Old World noblemen—gave voice to the larger anxieties plaguing the Federalist imagination. What would the new nation look like? It was a question, as we have seen, increasingly formulated in biological as well as political terms, and it was a question American novelists, by their fastidious care for this imagined female reader, worked to answer.

Writing tale after tale about the disastrous effects of novel reading, the early fiction of the national period trumpeted the novel's power to corrupt, seduce, and breed, claiming at the same time a role for the American novel as the necessary protector of the female reader's virtue. Thus, after adumbrating the dangers posed by novels in general, the American novel consistently proclaimed its own unique status as white knight: *The Power of Sympathy* promises to expose "the dangerous consequences of seduction"; *Charlotte Temple* (1791) vows to "direct [its readers], through the various and unexpected evils that attend a young and unprotected woman"; and *The History of Constantius and Pulchera* (1795), dedicated "To the Young Ladies of Columbia," pledges to "inspire the mind with *fortitude* under the most unparalleled MISFORTUNES, and to Represent the happy *consequences* of VIRTUE and FIDELITY."[45] The best-selling first American edition of *The Arabian Nights* in 1795 offered an especially effective defense of the novel in its story of the woman who preserves the virtue of her countrywomen through storytelling. By hypnotizing the sultan under the spell of narrative fiction, Scheherazade becomes "the deliverer of many virgins, which but for her, would have been sacrificed to his unjust resentment."[46] Bringing about a revolution in the sultan's tyrannical government, and defending female virtue, *The Arabian Nights* validated narrative fiction's place in a democratic society.

A nation gripped with anxiety over whether it would produce a society of saints or one of monsters invested novel reading with something like a genetics. Thus, Royall Tyler's famous declaration of literary independence in the preface to his novel *The Algerine Captive* (1797)—raising the call for novels made of "American materials"—becomes more than simply a patriotic defense of an embryonic industry; these are the materials to provide the literary prophylactic to the nation. Over and over the early novel pronounced its resistance to foreign materials, manners, and morals, vowing vigilant protection (in virtuous American materials) of the female reader—the mother, for better or worse, of the new American race.

Clearly, what alarmed novelists, politicians, and racial theorists alike (and in 1787 many could claim more than one of these titles) was the unanswerable question as to what—in a nation without traditionally ordered class system, made up of people from many nations and three races—the new American would look like. In telling countless stories of seduction, illegitimate children, incest, uncertain paternity, and unrestrained female sexuality, the early novel, Federalist tracts, and racial science inaugurated in 1787 a particularly American preoccupation with breeding, and with the ordering and control of difference in the new Republic. Unknown and uncontrolled, nature would lead toward corruption and degeneration. Thus, in "the first American novel," whose tales of incest, rape, and suicide demonstrate the dangers of uncontrolled reading and uncontrolled nature, there is an allegory of the dangers inherent both in the novel and the American environment: "It is said of some species of American serpents that they have the power of charming birds and small animals, which they destine for their prey. The serpent is stretched underneath a tree: it looks steadfastly on the bird—their eyes meet to separate no more . . . it falls into the voracious jaws of its enemy. This is no ill emblem of the fascinating power of pleasure."[47]

In a novel whose subtitle is "The Triumph of Nature" and that ends with the suicides of two incestuous lovers, the lessons to be afforded by this "emblem" are obvious: the Republic's fate is bound up in the regulation and proper ordering of its novels and nature, its readers and its races, as much as in the debates over political organization at Philadelphia. As the rise of the novel converged with the formulation of racial and national identities, the narratives and metaphors these three discourses engendered came to dominate from the United States' earliest days the terms by which it colored its future and policed its present.

CHAPTER 2

The Prodigal in Chains

Chains are the portion of revolted man;
Stripes and a dungeon.

Cowper, *The Algerine Captive* (1797)

I

Royall Tyler's *The Algerine Captive* (1797) is the story of an overeducated and pompous young man, Updike Underhill, who is unable to find his place in American society. Determined that he is destined for greater things than his New England community has to offer, Updike sets off to earn his fortune, first as a teacher, then as a doctor, and finally as a surgeon on a slave ship. Fifty years earlier, Tobias Smollett's Roderick Random, also despairing of ever securing his lawful place in society, set off to earn his fortune; and like Updike, Roderick winds up as surgeon on a slaver. Tyler's debt to *Roderick Random* (1748), which was first published in America in 1794 as Tyler began his novel, has been acknowledged in describing Tyler's more general debt to the British picaresque, but the differences between the two works prove so considerable as to frustrate an extended comparison. I wish to pause over one point of divergence in particular by way of introducing the concerns of this chapter.

In each novel, the hero's mother has a dream before giving birth. Roderick's mother "dreamed she was delivered of a tennis-ball, which the devil . . . struck so forcibly with a racket that it disappeared in an instant; and she was for some time inconsolable for the loss of her offspring, when all of a sudden she beheld it return with equal violence and enter the earth beneath her feet, whence immediately sprung up a goodly tree covered with blossoms." Seeking the advice of a "Highland seer," Roderick's mother learns the dream's significance: "that their first-born would be a great traveller; that he would undergo many dangers and difficulties, and at last return to his native land, where he would flourish in happiness and reputation."[1] After the many detours that comprise the plot of the novel, this is precisely Roderick's course: cast unlawfully from his father's house, into the obscene evils of the city, he arrives finally at the recovery of his fortune and his home; and the path that leads him to his rightful end is a slave voyage from Guinea to Paraguay. The trip proves extremely profitable for Roderick, both from the sale of slaves and from the discovery of his father's lucrative plantation in South America.[2]

Updike's mother has a dream remarkably similar to that which haunted the Randoms: "My mother, some months before my birth, dreamed that she was delivered of me, that I was lying in the cradle, that the house was beset by Indians who broke into the next room and took me into the fields with them. Alarmed by their hideous yellings and warhoops, she ran to the window and saw a number of young tawny savages playing at football with my head, while several sachems and sagamores were looking on unconcerned."[3] The interpretation of this dream is far less promising than that offered to Roderick: "She was sure Updike was born to be the sport of fortune and that he would one day suffer among savages" (43). Indeed, where Roderick's is a story of a displaced aristocrat traveling through the underbelly of the empire and finally recovering his place in society through a prosperous slave voyage to America, the American hero's contact with slavery offers no such resolution.[4] Shipping aboard a slaver, Updike instead finds himself stripped naked and sold into slavery by a dark and savage race. For the American prodigal there is no title to assume, no stability of a former generation to recover, and no fortune to win that he did not possess when the novel started save patriotism—his sense of himself as an American. The lessons slavery has to teach the American hero about himself are very different from those available to the hero of the British novel. For the British novelist, slavery provides a vehicle for exotic travel and plot resolution; its meanings and effects are fundamentally economic. For the American, slavery brings with it as well other issues and anxieties: moral questions, political battles, and a more ambiguously mapped set of meanings.

The moral and political debates over slavery in the early national period have been analyzed by others in detail.[5] But, as we have seen, during this period the meanings and metaphors contained in the notion of race often have little to do with historical slavery, or with actual Indians. In addition to the moral, political, and economic debates that surround the history of race in America lie a series of landscapes, narratives, and attendant anxieties about identity that are articulated through and transformed by the language of race. It is the Federalist version of this narrative that is the focus of this chapter, a vision that dominates the period, politically and culturally; but in Tyler's novelistic reuniting of the nation we will see the attempt to synthesize and reconcile the Federalist and Republican fantasies through the composite figure of the Algerian.

It is important that the first novel to which I turn to discuss how ideas of race were called on to help construct a national identity is one that in many ways is not about race at all. Instead, it imagines racial "landscapes" upon which its hero comes to discover his "American" identity. Tyler's novel adds a fourth term to the question of his country's racial destiny: not black, not Indian, not European—but American. In his intense commitment to the idea of a uniquely American identity, Tyler uses the Algerian pirate as the composite of all the racial and national destinies he does not want for his country, and through the hero's experience of captivity at the hands of this composite he comes to define (in entirely negative terms) what it means to be an American. In so doing, the novel begins to imagine a space for something that looks like an American race. Reading the novel against the factional violence of the 1790s helps us understand what the young nation imagined this race might look like in both its ideal and monstrous forms. This, I argue, is the "profit" (224) Tyler wished his fellow citizens to reap from his hero's misfortunes in *The Algerine Captive,* the lessons to be learned from the prodigal in chains.

In 1782, while John Adams was in Paris negotiating the end of the Revolutionary War, Royall Tyler was at home in Braintree courting Adams's daughter Nabby. Tyler, who had largely missed the Revolution as an undergraduate at Harvard, had a dissolute reputation: he was rumored to have squandered the bulk of his patrimony, engineered notorious pranks, and even fathered a child with a housemaid at the college.[6] It was surely this last rumor that most troubled Adams, as one whose career was devoted to the rising fame of his nation and his family. In 1783, Adams wrote to his wife expressing his disapproval: "Your . . . letters concerning Mr. T. are never out of my mind. . . . I don't like the Trait of his Character, his Gaeity. He is but a Prodigal Son, and though a Penitent, has no Right to your Daughter, who deserves a Character without a Spot."[7] Adams's judgment regarding Tyler's spotted character was largely the meddling of an anxious father. But his concern for the family's posterity, his anxiety lest a man with a "Spot" rise from the chaos of Revolution to sire an Adams with a spot, usefully mirrors the concerns of the nation as it worried over its posterity—political, cultural, and biological. The engagement with Nabby was called off in 1785, to Tyler's great disappointment.

Although he failed to participate in the Revolution, in 1786 Tyler got something of a second chance when he enlisted as an aide-de-camp under the Revolutionary general Benjamin Lincoln. Tyler's participation in the suppression of the counter-revolution of 1786–87 allowed him to erase his "Spot" and to claim his American character; his experiences during Shays's Rebellion proved central to his conception of himself, both as a writer and as a Federalist. In the course of that service, in which he reasoned armed rebels into surrender and served as Lincoln's envoy to the governments in Vermont and New York, Tyler found his voice.[8] After his diplomatic mission to New York, he remained in the city and, in the few weeks between the end of the Rebellion and the start of the Constitutional Convention, wrote the nation's first successful comedy, *The Contrast* (1787). That a young man with no theatrical experience (indeed, he had grown up under Boston's puritanical ban on drama) could achieve such a milestone in so short a time has long delighted literary historians. Against the anxieties of his native culture about the effects of drama, Tyler created a strenuously nativist play to demonstrate the positive potential of a national drama. The encouragement of American production, the defense against foreign immorality, and the unification of a fractured nation —the play proudly claims all these as its achievements. Tyler's play translates the chaos of 1787 into a simple "contrast," one finally reducible to the pure American ideal of Colonel Manly as opposed to the corrupting Old World model of Dimple. Other anxieties troubling the cultural imagination during this time dissolve easily under Tyler's xenophobic resolution: the virtue of the American woman is protected by Manly's exposure of Dimple's stratagems, and Manly's servant, Jonathan, is reasoned out of his sympathy for Shays's Rebellion.

When, in 1794, Tyler turned to the novel for the first time, he was writing during a national crisis more apocalyptic and in a literary form more critically suspect than the one he faced when writing *The Contrast*. Setting out once again to resolve the crisis of identity facing the nation, Tyler now found the solutions not so simple as in 1787, and the contrasts no longer so comical. What to all appearances began as a comic picaresque in the style of Brackenridge's *Modern Chivalry* (1792) quickly became inadequate to his desire to define an American identity that would heal the political division that characterized the period. The local-color chapters that begin the novel give way to a series of landscapes of slavery, captivity, and degeneration—the landscapes through which the nation's prodigal son comes to understand that defining himself as an "American" is the only way to survive Algerian captivity and to avoid becoming marked himself, as if by race.

To understand the topography of these landscapes it is necessary first to examine Tyler's interaction with the Federalist rhetoric of race; an appropriate starting point is "Colon & Spondee," a regular magazine feature he initiated in 1794. A partnership between Tyler and the rabidly anti-Republican editor Joseph Dennie, the column proved immensely popular and became a leading touchstone of Federalist politics and aesthetics during the period. It was during their collaboration, and at Dennie's suggestion, that Tyler began work on his novel.[9]

In 1796 Tyler presented "excerpts" from an imaginary Indian newspaper for "Colon & Spondee," satirizing the manners of Indians and the hypocrisies of American society, a theme popular in magazine parodies of the period. But the last "items" in his "Indian paper" take the joke in a somewhat original direction: a horrified editorial on the atrocities of the French Revolution is followed by an essay, from the "Indian" point of view, on race. "The creatures," Tyler's Indian editorializes, "are whitened by disease, like the decaying leaves of the woods."[10] Tyler is referring here to theories, such as that articulated by Benjamin Rush in 1792, that the dark skin color of African Americans was a disease, related to leprosy; but of course, as did his predecessor Lycurgus, Tyler here shows that such theories can work both ways.[11] In juxtaposing the French Revolution to this "theory" of race, he voices the central tenet of the Federalist appropriation of race: like the theories of race being debated at the time, in which environment, disease, and society were believed capable of turning a man from white to brown and back again, so too can Revolution go both ways. The crucial issue for the Federalists is how to control the effects of Revolutionary change so as to protect the American from becoming implicated in such a narrative—a narrative of change imaginable in racial terms.

That Tyler understood the ways in which the concerns of American racial science were close to his own as he set out to write his distinctly "American" novel is revealed by a scene in *The Algerine Captive* in which Updike visits the Harvard museum after the Revolution to see its collection of natural curiosities. "Here, to my surprise," he proclaims, "I found the curiosities of all countries but our own" (78). When he asks to see native natural and aboriginal curiosities, the curators can supply only the most pitiful specimens: the "curious fungus of a turnip" and "a miniature birch canoe, containing two or three rag aboriginals with paddles cut from a shingle." After ridiculing the state of science, Updike concludes his chapter with a "more serious" message: "Suppose a Raynal or Buffon should visit us . . . eagerly inquiring after the natural productions and original antiquities of our country. What must be the sensations of the respectable rulers of the college to be obliged to produce to them, these wretched, bauble specimens" (78). This apparent digression in the novel serves an important function in the development of the hero's character: Updike's first moment of patriotism is born out of his anxiety lest Buffon see in the failure of American science the fulfillment of his darkest prophecies for the American race. By updating the captivity narrative in light of the headlines of the day, *The Algerine Captive* presents a nightmarish landscape on which the reader can see the consequence of such a failure. And in Updike's triumphant return at the novel's end, Tyler offers a final refutation of Buffon, as the nation is called upon to end the factionalist violence and to unite to defeat the fantastical monsters that factionalism itself had unleashed.

II

Tyler's two major literary works were both written at moments of profound crisis, when dissolution, internal faction, rebellion, and foreign threats seemed to foreshadow the end of the republican experiment. In many ways, the crisis of the 1790s was an extension of that of the 1780s, with many of the same ingredients: public debt, taxes, and disagreement over the powers of a federal government. But several additional factors coalesced in 1794, as Tyler began his novel: the entrenchment of party politics, the French Revolution and the Terror, the war in Europe, the British blockade of American trade with France and their manipulation of hostile Indian tribes, news of the revolution on Santo Domingo, a yellow fever epidemic, the Whiskey Rebellion in Pennsylvania, and, last but not least, the Algerian depredations in the Mediterranean. For a population fluent in apocalyptic interpretation, all of this contributed to a political climate unparalleled in its foreboding and its factionalism. As Larry E. Tise writes in his history of proslavery, 1787 did not bring the end of the conspiracy theories that had helped generate an "American ideology":

> Irrespective of the rhetoric of the Federalists in the 1780s, the constitutional crisis of America stood as a mere headache in comparison with the social and political convulsions of the 1790s. The latter phenomenon was probably much more crucial in determining the shape of the American sociocultural system and in establishing the permanent ideological loyalties of the American people. . . . As the perception of one conspiracy had helped launch the American Revolution in the 1760s,

another vision of subversion in the 1790s helped ignite the forces that would eventually result in a cultural transformation of America by the end of the 1830s.[12]

The crisis of the 1790s differed from that of the previous decade primarily in the prominence of the foreign threat. Both sides of the political spectrum saw evidence of foreign manipulations in the debt crisis, the uprising in Pennsylvania, the Indian wars in the West, the murmurings of slave unrest in the South, and the existence of political faction itself. As Richard Buel Jr. suggests, the foreign threat defined the factional violence of the 1790s, and the European War of 1793 moved into the public arena the internecine debate between British and French interests in Congress.[13] With warships on both sides of the Channel directing their attention toward the United States, what had been a debate between economic interests in Congress came to be figured as a question whose answer would determine the future of the nation. For the Republicans, the French Revolution signaled the glorious spread of their vision, whereas the British threatened to return the United States to its former servitude. For the Federalists in power, the British symbolized stability, but the French interpretation of the American Revolution was, horrifyingly, on the verge of spreading not only through Europe, but back to the New World as well. Buel writes, "In the Terror they saw the confirmation of their deepest doubts about the natural tendency of republican government, and in the slave rebellion on Santo Domingo they saw the logical outcome of the extremes to which France had carried republican ideals of liberty and equality. . . . The magnitude of the upheaval made a strong impression, and those leaders who were already uneasy about the prospects of republicanism began to fear that what was happening in France could happen next in the United States" (38). Of course, each side saw in the other clear evidence of corrupt foreign influence.

In her study of American millennialism, Ruth H. Bloch notes the rise in the 1790s of two opposed complaints: Republican jeremiads directed against the threat of tyranny and slavery, and Federalist jeremiads directed against the threat of anarchy and degeneration.[14] For many, the hour of judgment was at hand, and there could be no middle ground. Washington's proclamation of neutrality in 1793 only furthered the internal sectarianism: with no declared enemy, all Americans were invited, often forced, to choose sides. John R. Howe Jr. writes, "By the middle of the decade, American political life had reached the point where no genuine debate, no real dialogue was possible for there no longer existed the toleration of differences which debate requires. Instead, there had developed an emotional and psychological climate in which stereotypes stood in the place of reality."[15] The situation climaxed in 1794, as the Republicans attacked Jay's Treaty with Britain as a plot to restore America's colonial status, while the Federalists interpreted the Whiskey Rebellion as a sign of the degeneration they had long prophesied for the Republican frontier. In the eyes of the eastern elite, the western settlers were scarcely elevated above the savages at their borders, and the spread of Jacobin societies and the antitax violence (including one incident in which the rebels wore war paint) only proved the suspected connection: uncontrolled republicanism leads to savagery.[16]

On the verge of war—with the public clamoring for British blood in the wake of the seizing of 350 American ships and the publication of Lord Dorchester's inflammatory speech to the western tribes—the Federalists sought a way to delay the conflict. They found a persuasive argument in the fact that America could not fight a naval war until it was first equipped with a navy. But unwilling to raise the first American navy in violation of America's vulnerable neutrality, Congress and Washington in 1794 united in appropriating funds to battle a different threat: construction was inaugurated of "the Naval force necessary, for the protection of the commerce of the United States, against the Algerine corsairs."[17]

American sailors had first come under attack by Algerians in the Mediterranean in 1785 after losing the protection their former colonial status had afforded them. In 1793, after several years of relative calm, a British-brokered treaty between Algiers and Portugal opened up international waters to the corsairs, resulting in the capture of eleven additional American ships. News arrived in Philadelphia in early 1794, providing one more in a series of calamities befalling the young nation. But this crisis also offered an outlet for the pent-up tension of the day. All sides could unite in abhorring the pirates, and Federalists and Republicans alike used the cause to unify Congress and the public in support of the establishment of a navy.

The resurgence of Algerian piracy provided the United States with its first hostage crisis.[18] For the Republicans, the Algerian actions presented clear evidence of British conspiracy against American interests. As Madison laid the charge before Congress in 1794, the British were responsible for "the detention of the [frontier] posts, the Indians, the Algerines, and even the spoilations of our neutral commerce." Republicans frequently linked the western Indians "spurred on to war against us, by the agents or partisans of Great-Britain," with woeful tales of "the Algerine depredations" that likewise "appeared to have proceeded from the steps taken in pursuance of the views of the British government."[19] Franklin, for example, recorded a British "maxim": "If there were no Algiers, it would be worth England's while to build one."[20]

This interpretation of the Algerians as "African emissaries of England" was not opposed by the administration, which was pro-British; in fact, it was encouraged.[21] The Federalists had much to gain from public sentiment against the Algerians since the pirates distracted a nation bent on conflict with Britain and allowed Hamiltonian diplomacy room to secure Jay's Treaty and a federal navy. The Federalists recognized the advantages to be gained in rallying the nation against a foreign power conveniently coded as dark, barbaric, and savage. The Algerians made the abstract fears of the day a reality: they captured scores of American sailors and turned them into slaves. Further, the entire Old World could be shown to have conspired to augment Algeria's power. European nations had long manipulated the Algerians to secure advantage over rival powers and, through a system of tributes, had allowed the pirates to flourish. This history provided a potent symbol of Old World corruption enslaving New World innocence through savage minions, sent "to cut our throats."[22]

To understand what was at stake in Tyler's captivity narrative, it is important to recognize how fully the Algerian captives dominated the public imagination during these divided times. The progress of diplomatic efforts and the condition of the American slaves were widely reported, relief organizations were formed, and letters from the captives themselves were printed regularly.[23] When David Humphreys and Joel Barlow finally secured the treaty leading to the hostages' release in 1797, they became national heroes. At a time when the nation had much more serious threats to confront, the Algerian captive and the exotic, "oriental" background of this first American "war" united the nation in outrage and indignation. It is perhaps difficult to understand the prominence of this crisis when so many more formidable obstacles faced the nation. But as one issue not fundamentally divided by partisan politics, this international episode captured the public imagination and made "real" the abstract anxieties about "slavery" and "savagery" that haunted American politics. Referred to in the press as "Africans" and "savages" interchangeably, the Algerian of the 1790s became a dark composite of the bogeymen threatening the young nation: Indian, African American, savage, slave master, British, and French.

In the Algerians, Americans found a renewed sense of themselves as a people in chains. From Puritan times through the Revolution, the cap-

Fig. 1. Frontispiece to *The Affecting History of the Dreadful Distresses of Frederic Manheim's Family* (1794). (Courtesy, American Antiquarian Society, Worcester, Massachusetts.) This image is from the title story of the volume. It graphically portrays the imagined need to defend and define white bodies against the racialized other.

tivity narrative had provided a model for securing identity in the New World, but the 1790s saw resurgent interest in the Indian captivity narrative. With the "Manheim anthology" in 1794 (see fig. 1), the first collection published solely for profit and entertainment, and in the publication of Ann Eliza Bleecker's *History of Maria Kittle* (1797), the first captivity novel, the genre began its transformation toward the "dime novel" it would become in the nineteenth century.[24] In the rise of the Algerian captivity tale, one can see an extension of what Greg Sieminski has defined as the Revolutionary captivity narrative—imitations of the older Puritan models that substituted British for Indians so as to define the American hero through his rejection of British identity even under the most terrible trials.[25] This form of the genre, as epitomized by *The Narrative of Colonel Ethan Allen's Captivity* (1779), presents a hero suffering under the chains of "brutish, prejudiced, abandoned wretches" (here the "haughty and cruel nation" of Britain), surviving through faith—no longer in God, but in America. As Allen belligerently proclaims to his captors, "I was a *full blooded Yankee.*"[26]

Allen's *Narrative* taught the necessity of reliance on a new god: Nation. The Algerian captivity narrative (especially that of Tyler, who knew the fellow Vermonter Allen and his *Narrative*) drew its inspiration from the Revolutionary captivity narrative. The conflict with the Algerians became an extension of the Indian war, and the enslaving of American soldiers provided a new twist to the old captivity tale—now with the young nation in chains in a hostile wilderness of international relations. From the beginnings of the conflict, the Algerians provided a new dark face for the fears of the day.

The Algerian theme found its way into American letters from the earliest years of the crisis.[27] In Peter Markoe's *The Algerine Spy in Pennsylvania* (1787), an Algerian spy is sent to subvert the young United States as it stands at the crossroads of its constitutional destiny. Very much in the style of the other Federalist productions of the period, Markoe racializes the internal threats to the nation through the pirate-spy working to finance the "refractory leaders of the revolt" in order to secure Algerian dominion in America so that "their defenceless coasts . . . may be plundered without the least risque, and their young men and maidens triumphantly carried into captivity."[28] Susanna Rowson's *Slaves in Algiers* (1794) uses the fate of American captives to stage a patriotic replaying of the Revolution and a defense of women's participation in society. By fighting a second revolution to democratize Algerian tyranny, the American heroes finally recover family and freedom, and the play celebrates the conflict with Algiers as the means by which the nation finally secures the blessings of the Revolution.[29] The genre was also early on deployed in arguments against slavery, including Franklin's last published piece, which parodied proslavery arguments by equating them with an imagined Algerian defense of white slavery.[30]

Especially popular at the time of Tyler's novel were the histories and firsthand accounts of the period, including Matthew Carey's *A Short Account of Algiers* (1794), James Leach's *A New and Easy Plan to Redeem the American Captives in Algiers* (1795), James Wilson Stevens's *An Historical and Geographical Account of Algiers* (1797), and the *Journal of the Captivity and Suffering of John Foss*, which went through two editions in 1798, testifying to the continued popularity of the subject.[31] Newspapers and magazines regularly provided recycled histories, accounts of the captives, and poems and stories lamenting their fate. The genre became something of a staple of fictional entertainments, and James Butler's rambling picaresque *Fortune's Foot-ball* (1797–98) contains not one but two Barbary captivities among its many adventures.[32] By the turn of the century Algerian captivities had become almost as formulaic as Indian narratives, and the result was similar: the appearance of sensational "dime novel" Algerian fictions that emphasized gothic horrors over fact.[33] Into this subgenre came Tyler's *Algerine Captive,* a novel that embodies in its adventures the properties of both the Algerian history and the dime novel and that highlights the concerns facing the nation as it tries to imagine what an American literature, an American politics, and an American race might look like.

III

In 1795 Humphreys and Barlow finally negotiated the treaty with Algiers, and Congress financed the $800,000 in tribute for the recovery of the eighty-two surviving hostages. The *Algerian Captive* was begun in the height of the hysteria surrounding this conflict and published a few months after the return of the prisoners in 1797. As Tyler wrote many years later, "In the year 1797, when the sufferings of our unfortunate seamen, carried into slavery at Algiers, was the common topic of conversation, and excited most lively interest throughout the United States, the author . . . embodied such information as could then be obtained as to the manners, customs, habits, and history of those corsairs in a little work, entitled The Algerine Captive."[34] This passage clarifies the importance

Tyler and his contemporaries invested in the novel's long passages of Algerian "history," those chapters often denigrated or ignored by modern critics. But, of course, the Algerian adventure is only half the novel, grafted on to the adventures of the self-important hero attempting to find his place in a provincial young republic that proves fundamentally hostile to his conception of his proper place in society.

It is the local-color picaresque that has for the most part delighted the critics, while the Algerian episodes have been largely neglected as unconvincing and derivative.[35] Even those critics who try to make something of volume 2 perceive a radical disjunction between the two volumes and ignore or dismiss the many chapters of obviously borrowed Algerian history. "Among American works," writes G. Thomas Tanselle, "the first [volume] is reminiscent of Brackenridge's *Modern Chivalry*, the second of an Indian captivity narrative. . . . The two volumes must be considered separately, for they constitute essentially two books."[36] The most determined critics have failed to provide a comprehensive reading for the two volumes; for example, William C. Spengemann, while arguing against the critical tendency of "commending the local-color sketches of volume one and lamenting the vagrant exoticism of volume two," can only reconcile the two by reading the conclusion as willfully and ironically discordant: "The ending is so palpably a non sequitur, so false to the demands of the preceding action, that it seems at best a nostalgic gesture toward a world long vanished and unrecapturable."[37] Indeed, it is difficult to reconcile the novel's own early declaration of principles with its conclusion, in which the narrator celebrates the nation he had so bitterly satirized in volume 1. The novel's pleas on behalf of the virtues of union, conformity, and Federalist policies have encouraged a critical tradition focusing on its "irony." Thus, for example, John Engell argues for a reconciliation of the two volumes by reading the entire work as an ironic send-up of national identity, fundamentally pessimistic beneath its blustering patriotism.[38]

It is difficult for modern readers to understand that the Algerian captivity narrative, for both Tyler and his audience, provided a tenable, and profoundly unironic, solution to the contradictions raised by the local-color picaresque. As Larry R. Dennis points out, the novel places much emphasis on being a history written with "the impartiality of an historian."[39] A portion of this emphasis must be ascribed, as Dennis suggests, to Tyler's desire to claim a legitimated place for novelistic production; but from its first chapters of revisionist Puritan history to its concluding chapters on Algerian history and manners, this novel's interest in historical narrative exceeds such explanation. Although certainly laced with irony, it must be understood as ultimately straightforward in its commitment to defining and defending one of the most powerful inventions of the modern age, the American self. This commitment is spelled out in the Puritan history that opens the novel, chapters that offer a guide for how to read what follows.

"I derive my birth," Updike informs us at the start of the novel, "from one of the first emigrants to New England, being lineally descended from Captain John Underhill, who came into Massachusetts in the year 1630" (31). Updike is determined, he insists, to defend his ancestor's honor from the calumny of historians from John Winthrop to Jeremy Belknap (Tyler's own source for this material) who have used the historical Underhill to personify the arrogance, sensuality, and lawlessness that early jeopardized the Bay Colony. Critics have generally read these chapters for their challenge to "official" history, an attempt to subvert the official line of the day. Yet, reading this revisionist "history" of the Puritans from its proper position within Federalism, very different stakes can be located for Tyler in claiming this inheritance for his hero.[40]

Rewriting John Underhill as the champion of political independence standing against the religious tyranny of the Puritan elders, Tyler draws from a tradition begun in the Revolutionary generation, most famously by Adams himself who, in his *Dissertation on the Canon and Feudal Law* (1765), redefined the Puritans as the prophets of the Revolution. Instead of religious dogmatists, the Puritans for Adams are sworn enemies of tyranny: "It was not religion alone, as is commonly supposed; but it was a love of universal liberty and a hatred, a dread, a horror, of the infernal confederacy [of canon and feudal law] that . . . accomplished the settlement of America."[41] The Revolutionary generation reclaimed the Puritans in order to provide a genealogy and a historical justification for revolution—a precedent for resistance and an alternate heritage to keep them rooted in tradition. As Michael Warner writes, "Treating enlightenment republicanism as the latent meaning of Puritan history, and employing terms that are simultaneously world-historical and national, Adams's revisionist history became a pillar of American nationalism, and has remained so to the present."[42]

In the 1790s Tyler again reinvents the Puritan hero, now struggling to defend liberty in the face of a Puritan revolution still tainted by Old World tyranny. Updike's freedom-loving ancestor escapes political persecution at the hands of Queen Elizabeth, only to be imprisoned in America on a trumped-up charge of adultery and for his belief in religious toleration. But what is at stake for Tyler is not a vindication of Underhill but an identification of 1790s Federalism with 1630s antinomianism. After re-counting the official story, Updike presents "Brother Underhill's Epistle," found "pasted on the back of an old Indian deed," in which the hero of the Pequot War narrates the events that led to his downfall. The "govern-ment" at whose hands Underhill suffers is not the protoparliamentary democracy of Adams's imagining, but a clique of petty tyrants writing laws to suit their whims and prejudices.

The dates of this discovered epistle are significant, as is the fact that it is found on the back of an Indian deed. For in addition to his role in the antinomian controversy, the historical Underhill is also famous for being one of the first great Indian fighters and for having written one of the first "American" narratives, *Newes from America* (1638)—a history of the Pe-quot war and a justification of Underhill's vision of the individual's rela-tionship to God and the wilderness.[43] The pamphlet is an early exegesis on "American" identity, offering an account of the first genocidal Indian war, one of the first captivity narratives, and a defense of the American wilder-ness. "Thus we spent the day burning and spyling the Countrey," the first Underhill cheerily describes the slaughter of the Pequots, after which he moves easily into a real-estate tract for prospective colonists, inviting them not to the Bay Colony, but to a projected new community in the wilderness, now conveniently emptied by the extermination of the native inhabitants.[44]

These two seemingly disjunct moments of Underhill's book—the his-tory of the Indian war and the celebration of the American wilderness—provide an important clue to reading *The Algerine Captive*; they are bound together by the narrative of the "two maids captive" who discover God through their trials at the hands of the Pequots. Underhill uses this captivity narrative to explain the meaning inherent in the American experience:

> Christian reader, give mee leave to appeale to the hearts of all true affectioned Christians, whether this bee not the usuall course of Gods dealing to his poore captivated children, the prisoners of hope, to distill a great measure of sweet comfort and consolation into their soules in the time of trouble, so that the soule is more affected with a sense of Gods fatherly love, then with the grief of its captivity. . . . Better a prison sometimes and a Christ, then a liberty without him.[45]

Thus, the first Underhill exhorts his readers to come to America and bear suffering and captivity in order to discover God as one never could in

London. Similarly, Underhill's fictional eighteenth-century descendant will himself be able finally to discover America, through captivity in Algiers, as he never would have in Boston.

Clearly Tyler saw similarities between the political violence of 1636–37 and that of the 1790s. In locating the origins of his story in this first "American" crisis, one also marked by internal faction and external threat, Tyler claims for his protagonist a kinship with the hero who reduced the "alien" threat to ashes and the natural aristocrat who stood up against the (Puritan) revolutionary court. Secularizing Underhill's vision, Tyler locates his hero's origins in the first Indian fighter, and through the narrative of the first Indian war—what Richard Slotkin calls "the distinctive event of American history, the unique national experience"—he claims a pedigree for his story.[46]

"I came from England because I did not like the lords bishops, but I have yet to praye to be delivered from the lords bretherenne," Tyler's John Underhill records in his "epistle" (39–40). For the reader in 1797, the "lords bretherenne" and the revolutionary court would call to mind the Jacobins in France and their sympathetic societies in the United States. Thus, the Puritan history that begins the novel serves as an allegory for Tyler's fears that his nation has indeed just escaped from the "lords bishops" of the Old World, only to find itself imprisoned by the Republican "lords bretherenne," what he referred to in "Colon and Spondee" in 1797 as the tyranny of "mobocracy."[47] Through Captain Underhill, Tyler constructs a new genealogy for his hero, one uncorrupted by either "lords bishops" or "lords bretherenne." And beginning with the mother's dream that Updike will "suffer among savages," the author makes clear that the hero's trials at the hands of the Algerians are to be read as an extension of his ancestor's experiences among the Indians; as Updike comments, "Dear woman, she had the native Indians in her mind, but never apprehended her poor son's suffering, many years as a slave among barbarians, more cruel than the monsters of our own woods" (43–44). Tyler's fictionalized Captain Underhill ends his epistle "disappointed of libertie in this wilderness" and "ernestlie lookinge for a better countre" (40). It is this "better countre" that his descendant, Updike, now sets out to discover at the beginning of his narrative. Just as the Indian narrative of 1638 helped define the first Underhill's "American" vision, so will Updike's experiences among "savages," now removed to the coast of Africa, provide the final necessary reconciliation between the Underhill line and the people of the United States. Now, if the nation is to survive, the natural aristocrat must be reconciled to the mob.

Updike's parents, we learn, have been spared their son's inherited sense of divine election, and, baffled by his self-importance, they determine him to be destined for the ministry. Updike thus spends the years of the Revolution "labouring incessantly at Greek and Latin," believing, while the century's transformative events occur outside his library walls, "the classics [to be] the source of all valuable knowledge." His teachers contribute to this delusion, promising him that he "should be a member of congress and equal the Adamses in oratory from my repeating the speeches at the councils of the heathen gods, with such attention to the caesura," and assuring him that Washington was himself a classical scholar (47). These vain promises are the only reference the young scholar receives of the experiences that are transforming his colony into a nation. But Updike's path to Harvard is blocked when his father's fortunes fall victim to fluctuations in currency and farm values in the aftermath of the Revolution. Finding that overeducation has ruined his son for farming, Updike's father sends him off to earn his fortune. The Revolution has come and gone unrecognized by Updike, and as he enters society he finds a nation entirely alien. The novel that follows is the history of his personal American Revolution, as he learns the lessons of government, enlightenment science, and race necessary for him to take his place in the new nation.

Naturally he begins where he assumes he belongs, in "government"— here the governing of a country school. In Updike's unpreparedness for the job, Tyler provides an allegory for the Confederacy's failure to provide the nation with an identity (indeed, the fact of the new nation has not been mentioned up to this point in the novel). At first, Updike "resolved to be mild in my government, to avoid all manual correction, and doubted not these means to secure the love and respect of my pupils" (52). But his ideals are quickly shattered as he discovers his "subjects" to be a "ragged, ill bred, ignorant set." Finally, after his "throne" is "usurped in the face of the whole school" by one of the larger boys, an event that "shook my government to the center," Updike administers his first act of corporal punishment to restore order. But when the boy's father comes to school and corners him with a whip, Updike gives up all attempts at a system of central government; the class quickly devolves into anarchy and the school is burned down. In this satirical "history" of the Confederacy, Tyler points to the central ingredients leading to the crisis of 1787: the inability of the central government (Updike) to educate and discipline its subjects; the tyranny of the states (the parents) over a weak central government; and the savage ignorance and violence of the mob (the students). But more is involved here than political satire; neither students nor teacher have learned from the experience, and the deterioration described by this episode (and by the history of the Confederacy itself) serves as a warning prelude to the far more ominous landscapes of savagery and tyranny to follow.

Alienated from his country, and failing in his first attempt to take what he believes to be his proper place in its guidance, Updike celebrates the end of this period in his career: "I am sometimes led to believe that my emancipation from real slavery in Algiers did not afford me sincerer joy than I experienced at that moment" (55); and his mother, hearing about his experiences, "said she had no doubt that her dream about my falling into the hands of savages was now out." Although her optimism will prove unfounded, the mother's interpretation of these events makes clear that Updike's suffering at the hands of the ignorant mob in volume 1 is meant to correspond directly to his suffering under Algerian tyranny in volume 2.

As Updike sets out on the next stage in his career, it is here that his education properly begins. He decides to become a doctor, despite his father's wry disapproval in noting that "he did not know what pretensions our family had to practice physic, as he could not learn that we had ever been remarkable for killing any but Indians" (57). He apprentices himself to a doctor who has learned how to make the blind see, a man devoted to practical knowledge and good works who, much to Updike's initial dismay, is devoid of the pretensions of classical erudition that he had been led to believe were crucial to success. This is the first example the novel offers (Benjamin Franklin, the model American, will be the other) of the natural aristocrat who uses his talents not to lord over an ignorant mob but to help them see, to lead them to the light. The doctor is the embodiment of rational science: "In him were united, the acute chemist, the accurate botanist, the skilful operator, and the profound physician" (76).

At his mentor's hands, Updike learns the skills that will enable him to see his nation for the first time, and, at the novel's end, to raise himself out of captivity.[48] "I now applied myself sedulously to my studies," Updike declares, "Cullen, Munroe, Boerhaave, and Hunter, were my constant companions" (74). These eighteenth-century pioneers of chemistry, anatomy, and pathology include in their ranks the prominent contemporary British physician and anthropologist John Hunter, whose carefully hierarchized "gradation of skulls" provided a foundation for several theorists on race.[49] Thus, a racial theorist serves as one of the cornerstones of Updike's Enlightenment. Upon completing his studies, he immediately goes to Cambridge to visit the museum where, as we have seen, he laments the want of a proper organization of American natural and racial sciences. As Updike's adventures are about to begin in earnest, we see how important this scientific education is to be in the development of his American identity, for the scene at the museum is the first moment in the novel where he discovers his patriotism. Studying Enlightenment science under his teacher, and learning to order human difference, Updike now has cause to worry where "a Raynal or Buffon" might place America in the great scheme.

Updike, however, has not yet learned all his lessons, and in the comic encounters that follow Tyler widens the gulf that divides the people from their would-be leader. Reading the *Iliad* to a gathering of young people, for example, Updike is only able to secure an audience so long as they believe he is reciting Indian poetry (65). He writes one young lady a panegyric, "assimilat[ing] her to the ox-eyed Juno" (66), and is promptly challenged to a duel for what is perceived to be an insult. These episodes, highly prized by critics for their satiric portraits of everyday life in late-eighteenth-century America, work for Tyler to expose the ignorance of the majority and the blinding pretensions of the elite. As episode after episode delivers these lessons to Updike, he begins to outgrow his pedantic foibles, but far from embracing his fellow New Englanders, he grows more severe in his abhorrence of their society until finally he abandons New England altogether. Disgusted with the local doctors, the boorishness of his countrymen, and the dubious morality of the women besetting him at every turn, Updike heads south in search of fortune and romance: "I set out in the stage for the southward, condemning the illiberality and ignorance of our own people, which prevented the due encouragement of genius. . . . I intended, after a few years of successful practice, to return in my own carriage and close a life of reputation and independence in my native state" (89).

Updike sets out on his journey after a brief visit with Benjamin Franklin, the model American, who like the doctor offers a model of compromise between the arrogance of Updike and the ignorance of the mob. But his misadventures only serve to drive him further still from the young nation. Tyler's New England is characterized by a fatal division between the elite and the masses; the South's society of masters and slaves is depicted as the first in a series of nightmare landscapes of the potential consequences of such division. The division of the elite and the masses in New England will lead to the degeneration of both, and in the brutality of slave society Tyler offers dark prophecy for the possible fate of his America (always northern) if true union is not achieved. Each of these nightmarish visions offered by Tyler's novel describes a potential circle of hell for an unreformed New England, and each takes an unreformed Updike Underhill farther from home.

Unable to make his fortune and hounded by debt in the South, Updike finds himself rapidly declining toward a condition that he once again compares too easily to slavery when he is forced to consider returning to teaching. In the South, he says, "to purchase a schoolmaster and a Negro was almost synonymous," and he proudly insists he "preferred laboring with the slaves in their plantations, than sustaining the slavery and contempt of a school" (97). But Tyler's hero is clearly not yet ready to learn the lessons of his own racial metaphors, and he flees from the horrors of southern slave society and his fears of becoming himself a "slave" by signing aboard a slave ship, *Freedom,* as a surgeon.

Sailing to England on his way to Africa, Updike visits in London the novel's second nightmare landscape. Escaping the South, in which he was almost forced into a condition "synonymous" with that of the blacks, he arrives in a nation dominated by hereditary slavery, yet another vision of the potential future of New England society. Here, as Lycurgus had declared, the British have indeed learned to "make white negroes." Instead of an imagined order and purity, Updike finds "a motley race in whose mongrel veins runs the blood of all nations," who "rotting in dungeons" boast proudly of the "GLORIOUS FREEDOM OF ENGLISHMEN" (99). In the two grotesque creatures he finds walking the London streets, the "mongrel" poor and the "hereditary senators," Tyler presents another vision of New England's fate if it continues on the path of faction. As he maps out these visions of his nation's potential future, he is also engaged in defining—always in negative terms—precisely what the American is not to be: not slave, not slave owner, not British hereditary senator, and not mongrel poor.

These lessons narrated, but still somehow unlearned, Updike sails for Africa to pick up his cargo of slaves. What he expected to find aboard a slave ship is certainly difficult to imagine, given what he has already seen, but his experience of the slave trade puts an end to his blindness once and for all. The chapters devoted to the slave trade, loosely borrowed in part from Olaudah Equiano's *Interesting Narrative* (1789), preach against the evils of slavery:

> When I suffered my imagination to rove to the habituation of these victims to this infamous, cruel commerce, and fancied that I saw the peaceful husbandman dragged from his native farm; the fond husband torn from the embraces of his beloved wife; the mother, from her

babes; the tender child, from the arms of its parent; and all the tender, endearing ties of natural and social affection rended by the hand of avaricious violence, my heart sunk within me. I execrated myself for even the involuntary part I bore in this execrable traffic. I thought of my native land and blushed. (109)

The scene is deliberately reminiscent of an Indian captivity narrative, only here it is white Americans, and explicitly southerners, who author this assault against the "peaceful husbandman" and "his beloved wife." The graphic portrayal of the brutalities endemic to the slave trade demonstrates Tyler's genuine horror.[50] But without diminishing his antislavery sentiment, even here his concerns are primarily with his native New England. Updike is horrified by the "involuntary part" both he and his nation bear in this traffic, and he swears he "would sooner suffer servitude than purchase a slave," a vow he has now made once too often. Through this act of fictional servitude, Tyler will purge his hero and his nation of the stain of slavery.

When volume 1 ends, Updike finds his world turned upside down as he is captured by Algerian pirates and loaded in chains while the former black slaves are given free run of the ship. In Algiers, the final rung in his descent into the novel's prophetic circles of hell, Updike is valued lowest among the slaves at the market and sold for hard labor. Forced to accept the camaraderie of his fellow slaves (the dregs of society, with none of the Noble Slaves as promised by Aphra Behn), he has finally entered the American history he had missed during his earlier captivity to classical education—that is, as a slave in Algeria, Updike is able to relive the founding dramas of American history. Reduced to the lowest station in life, that of slavery, he finally becomes a man of action and attempts to lead a revolution.

After receiving a blow from the overseer, Updike discovers for the first time his American spirit:

This was the first disgraceful blow I had ever received. Judge you, my gallant, freeborn fellow citizens, you who rejoice daily in our federal strength and independence, what were my sensations. I threw down my spade with disdain, and . . . upon his lifting his whip to strike me again, I flew at him, collared him, and threw him on his back. Then setting my foot on his breast, I called upon my fellow slaves to assist me to bind the wretch and to make one glorious effort for our freedom. (130–31)

Updike's revolution, however, is a failure, and yet in the course of his failed call to action, he learns his identity: "They could not comprehend my language. . . . I spoke to slaves, astonished at my presumption, and dreading the consequences for me and themselves." As the lone American, Updike's revolution fails because his fellow slaves, bred in the Old World to be slaves, cannot understand, as only an American can, the meaning of independence. Although he fails to bring about his revolution, the experience provides for his final conversion to the spiritual calling that Tyler believes an American identity to be:

> How naturally did the emaciated prodigal in the Scripture think upon the bread in his father's house. Bountiful Father of the Universe, how are the common blessings of thy providence despised. When I ate of the bread of my father's house and drank his refreshing spring, no grateful return was made to him or thee. It was amidst the parched sands and flinty rocks of Africa that thou taughtest me that the bread was indeed pleasant, and the water sweet. Let those of our fellow citizens who set at nought the rich blessings of our federal union go like me to a land of slavery, and they will then learn how to appreciate the value of our free government. (132)

Updike's newfound faith in his nation and in his identity as an American transforms the narrative voice of volume 2 and serves as the precondition for his slow rise in society, from abject slave to an American hero.

But first his new faith is sorely tested by the Mollah, a renegade who attempts to convert Updike to Islam by offering freedom, wealth, and position. Like Gulliver and his Houynhnhnm master, Updike and the Mollah argue the merits of their opposed systems of belief on a rational level, and the Mollah's skills and education defeat every justification that Updike can raise for his own faith. The strength of the Mollah's claims on behalf of Islam and the weakness of Updike's defense seem to demand the latter's conversion. Indeed, as a defender of Christianity, Updike is a failure, all but powerless in the face of the Mollah's arguments, so persuasively presented that some contemporary readers even charged Tyler himself with apostasy. But what pulls Updike through this most severe trial is not his Christianity, which has ceased to be the grounds for identity it had been for Mary Rowlandson, but his faith in America.

As his Puritan forefather had counseled, Updike embraces captivity as a way of claiming his identity, seeking "safety in my former servitude" (143). The Mollah is the Algerian stand-in for the Jacobin Thomas Paine,

whom Updike had met earlier in London, and from his experience with
Paine he had learned the lesson that ultimately saves him from the Mollah's snares: that the only proper response to the devious rational arguments of heresy is silence. If rational debate, epitomized in the novel by
Paine, had been necessary for the success of the Revolutionary generation, what is demanded now for the future well-being of the nation is the
rejection of pure reason in favor of a new faith. Now, safely distanced
from America's shores, the Algerian captors become the bearers of the
sophistry and seductive argument that have led the American people
astray from their national purpose. Here Updike, as the American captive, becomes empowered by a faith that extends beyond the reach of
argument. Embracing his captivity, he preserves his identity and prepares
himself for independence.

It is at this point, and much to the dismay of many twentieth-century
readers, that the novel gives way to history and guidebook. Borrowed
chapters of information about the language, history, government, and
habits of the Algerians appear at the very moment when the narrator
seems doomed to a life of perpetual servitude. It is important to remember that these chapters, deprecated today by even the most appreciative
critics, were very much in demand in 1797. Further, this material allows
the voice of the "slave" to be succeeded by that of the historian, and while
this history is being narrated, as we learn after the fact, Updike begins his
miraculous rise in Algerian society through his ability to give sight to the
blind. Offering natural science to a barbarous society that "had no theory
nor any systematic practice" (152), he earns more and more liberty to
begin amassing money toward his freedom. Thus, the novel awkwardly
establishes a correlation between the science that leads Updike to freedom and the history chapters' careful dissection of Algerian society.

It is in this context that the guidebook chapters serve centrally in the
resolution of the novel: they provide the ammunition with which Updike
and the United States finally defeat the Mollah and Algerian tyranny. By
fixing the Algerians into their correct place in the order of things, Updike
wins. As he himself explains the importance of these chapters:

> This dry detail of facts will probably be passed over by those who read
> for mere amusement, but the intelligent reader will, in this concise
> memoir, trace the leading principles of this despotic government; will
> account for the avarice and rapacity of a people who live by plunder;
> perceive whence it is that they are thus suffered to injure commerce
> and outrage humanity; and justify our executive in concluding what

> some uninformed men may esteem a humiliating and too dearly pur-
> chased peace with these freebooters. (167)

Updike cautions the reader to draw from the history chapters the novel's
most important lessons, both for dealing with Algiers and for the future of
the nation. Here are the roots of savagery and despotism, bound up in
race, corruption, and partisan politics—the very roots that must be extir-
pated from American soil if the nation is to survive.

The "History of the Algerines," the longest chapter in the novel, re-
duces this people to its proper place: vassals to the Turks, a mongrel
nation of Arabs, Moors, and "the miscreants and outcasts of other nations" (166), "this barbarous race" has for centuries been the bane of the
civilized world. But instead of working to put this upstart race back in its
place, Europe, at war with itself, has unnaturally fostered the rising power
of these pirates. "The narrow politics of Europe seek an individual not a
common good," the narrator tells us, as do the partisan politics of America
in the 1790s—and with potentially similar results. Embodying simultaneously the slave master and the slave of the South, the "savage" of
America's frontiers, the "mongrel" of England, and both the "hereditary
senator" and the satanic Jacobin, the Algerian becomes a composite of all
the threats to an American identity. The corruption of the Old World has
let loose the Algerians against the United States and has fatally divided
the nation against itself. To drive the warning home, the novel's history
concludes with short chapters cataloging the dominance of faction, foreign corruption, and competing philosophies of government in Algeria.
This places the nation in its proper place, and it serves as a warning similar
to that of *The Anarchiad* as to the potential futures that face the United
States. However dull and digressive these chapters might appear today,
for Tyler they served as the climax of the novel. Their story told, Updike's
subsequent triumph over his situation is all but effortless.

After finishing his extended history of Algeria, Tyler returns to the final
episodes of his hero's story in which Updike meets a wealthy Jewish mer-
chant named Adonah Ben Benjamin who promises to help him secure his
freedom. Updike works to purchase his independence, saving all he can
earn with Benjamin's help. But on the eve of his liberation Benjamin dies,
and his son disavows knowledge of the plan, claiming Updike's money for
himself. Ben Benjamin, as the Algerian stand-in for Ben Franklin, had
led Updike toward freedom through frugality and industry. But Benjamin's son, the representative of the second generation, betrays his father's ideals, just as, Tyler implies, the heirs to the Revolutionary genera-

tion have betrayed their responsibility to the people, selling them, as the younger Benjamin does Updike, into slavery once again with "the gratitude of a Jew" (220).

This new servitude does not last long, however, for the novel's lessons are finally at their end; at the last second Updike is fortuitously rescued by a Portuguese ship. Suddenly the world is turned right side up again, with the Algerians in chains and Updike returning to America. The year is 1795, at the height of the crisis that was dividing the United States against itself. In place of a reformed society, all Tyler can offer is a transformed Federalist prepared to fight the natural tendency he has observed in his travels of a divided society to degenerate into tyranny and slavery. Having resolved the impasse of the first volume through the captivity of the second, Tyler still cannot portray his hero's return to American society. He can only promise that Updike is now ready to serve as a "worthy FEDERAL citizen." Updike ends his narrative with an extended meditation on the blessings of these United States:

> My ardent wish is that my fellow citizens may profit by my misfortunes. If they peruse these pages with attention, they will perceive the necessity of uniting our federal strength to enforce a due respect among other nations. Let us, one and all, endeavor to sustain the general government. Let no foreign emissaries inflame us against one nation by raking into the ashes of long extinguished enmity. . . . Our first object is union among ourselves. For to no nation besides the United States can that ancient saying be more emphatically applied; BY UNITING WE STAND, BY DIVIDING WE FALL. (224)

In 1796 Joel Barlow wrote a letter of recommendation to the secretary of state on behalf of the former Algerian captive Captain Richard O'Brien, promising that "the University of Algiers is better for certain purposes than New Haven."[51] So it has proven for Tyler's Updike, who had to go far from his home, as the novel has had to go far from its avowed purpose, in order to discover "America." The novel began, in its famous preface, with an early call for the cultural liberation of the American novel from the imported models of the gothic and exotic adventure, and it set out in good faith to portray American society and manners in the lighthearted tone of *The Contrast*. But in the course of the first volume, the author, like his character, reached a stalemate with his nation and his narrative. Having failed to achieve his nationalist aims for his novel, and much against his original intentions, Tyler found himself writing a gothic adventure in the second volume. Yet, it is only in the course of this generic "servitude" that the novel discovers its nationalist voice. Only by putting his novel in chains to the conventions, as he himself describes them in his preface, of the English novel does Tyler discover how to write an American novel, just as Updike first had to experience slavery at the hands of a dark and mysterious race to learn how to be an American citizen.

Updike, shielded from the Revolution by a false education, could not reconcile himself to his new nation; he had to undergo his own captivity and his own revolution—in effect, replaying the nation's recent history—in order to embrace his national identity. He went off in search of fortune, but what he found were landscapes that staged the fate of the nation if it continued to be divided by faction—the fate of being marked (by tyranny and slavery) as if by race. It is these landscapes that teach hero and reader alike the need for patriotism. The story is of an individual's captivity, but the experiences, Tyler insists at the end, belong to the nation as a whole. By the conclusion of the novel, the issue of chattel slavery has entirely given way to the threat of "foreign emissaries," internal faction, and corruption; the first volume's critique of New England society has been canceled by the landscapes of the southern United States, Britain, France, and Algiers; and the impassable gulf dividing Updike from his nation has been negotiated by his experiencing firsthand the savagery and slavery his fellow citizens feared: "I had been degraded to a slave, and was now advanced to a citizen of the freest country in the universe. I had been lost to my parents, friends, and country; and now found, in the embraces and congratulations of the former and the rights and protection of the latter, a rich compensation for all past miseries" (224).

The Algerine Captive portrays the education of an upper-class colonial into true citizenship in the new republic, what Davidson describes as a more moderate and democratic Federalism; but for its project to be successful it must also imagine achieving precisely what it cannot show, the education of the people.[52] Toward this end, Tyler read his novel-in-progress to his own maid, who "had imbibed the common prejudices against the 'horrid Algerines' and felt greatly interested in Dr. Updike Underhill," and he delighted in the fact that she believed the story to be factual.[53] This is the imagined female reader, "the farmer's daughter," Tyler worried over in his preface, here reading a novel of virtuous American "manufacture" and believing it to be "founded on FACT," so as to gain a proper "idea of the world in which she is to live." He asks his reader to see in volume 1 the world in which she lives, in volume 2 the fate that could be hers, and to join with Updike (the representative of the elite) in seeking out Captain Underhill's "better countre," "the world in which she is to live" (28–29).

For Tyler, as for many of the first decade of the national period, the metaphors of race allowed him to picture society at its potentially most degenerated state, at the same time fantasizing a race uniquely American. The novel's use of the landscapes of racial encounter, in Spengemann's terms, "offers, at once, benign reassurance and a dark prophecy."[54] The metaphor of Algerian captivity provided a chance at resolving the conflicts of American society through the invention of a composite threat that would both chastise and unify the nation through the dichotomous metaphors of race: dark and pure, corrupt and chosen. Those confronting the problem of defining a national identity found recourse in the metaphors and narratives of race to embody what it was they did not want the American to be. In 1797 the Federalist literary imagination could summon forth the darkest scenes of slavery and savagery in the service of a united defense of an American identity.[55] At the end of the decade, however, the lessons to be afforded by race would no longer be so easily learned, nor the resolutions so effortlessly imagined.

CHAPTER 3

Edgar Huntly's Savage Awakening

The States of America form a complete sovereign nation, in their *united* not in their severed capacity; most especially in their relations with foreign powers and foreigners. There can be no complete sovereignty without the power of removing aliens; and the exercise of such a power is inseparably incident to the *nation*.

Charles Lee (1798)

I find it hard to forbear commenting on your rashness in no very mild terms. You acted in direct opposition to my council, and to the plainest dictates of propriety. Be more circumspect and more obsequious for the future.

Edgar Huntly (1799)

I

Few bodies of criticism surrounding a work by a major American author are so insistently uniform in their concerns and conclusions as that devoted to Charles Brockden Brown's *Edgar Huntly; or Memoirs of a Sleepwalker*. The critical tradition grows out of Leslie Fiedler's seminal reading of *Huntly* as "an initiation story, the account of a young man who begins by looking for guilt in others and ends finding it in himself."[1] Although arguing over the particular terms applied, most critics after Fiedler have reasserted that this is fundamentally a novel about a boy's initiation into experience and the primal conflict with the Father. In these readings, the landscape is internal, the shadows and doubles are projections of the divided self of the narrator, and the Indians are figures for the "dark" (uncivilized, savage) nature with which Edgar must do violent battle in order to claim his civilized self.[2]

I argue, instead, that the treatment of Brown's Indians as representations of an essentially internal personal struggle—whether between father and son or between civilized man and his "dark side"—universalizes a conflict that Brown himself understood as local and psychologizes a project that Brown understood as essentially political. In other words, the question of identity in *Edgar Huntly* is importantly national rather than (generally) human or (particularly) individual. Examining the novel in the context of the fiercely fought identity debates of the early national period, we are able to see the ways in which Brown's Indian adventure is not simply a shadowy progenitor of Cooper's nineteenth-century tales; for Brown the threat of the Indian has less to do with questions of what it means to be civilized than with the question—newly urgent in the United States in 1799—of what it means to be American.

Brown suggests that the originality of his novel lies in its depiction of the Indian.[3] In a "Fragment" published in his own *Monthly Magazine,* Brown points to the Indian battle scenes as the novel's best advertisement and insists upon the realism of his representation of the Indian, calling attention to the "minuteness" of his descriptions and to the historical "Truth of these incidents."[4] He returns to the Indian in the preface to *Huntly,* one of the most aggressive declarations of literary independence in the early American novel, staking his claim to a uniquely American writing via his portrayal of the Indian:

> One merit the writer may at least claim; that of calling forth the passions and engaging the sympathy of the reader, by means hitherto unemployed by preceding authors. Puerile superstition and exploded manners; Gothic castles and chimeras, are the materials usually employed for this end. The incidents of Indian hostility, and the perils of the western wilderness, are far more suitable; and, for a native of America to overlook these, would admit of no apology.[5]

Although critics have for the most part suggested that the Indians, like the wilderness they inhabit, are finally best read as projections of Huntly's divided self and repressed guilt, for Brown the Indian is the primary justification of the novel's nationalist project. At the same time, however, it is essential to realize, as Larzer Ziff reminds us, that "Indian-white relations are not the theme of *Edgar Huntly.*"[6] Rather, the Indian (and, more generally, the savage) embodies here (and in the broader political discourse of the period) a whole array of threats to the new nation—from the alien to, most troubling of all, the un-American American. It is this aspect of the Indian's presence in the novel that is left unaccounted for by the familiar critical binaries. By positioning "Savagism" not against universalized notions of "Civilization," but against conceptions of the American particular to 1799, we see how the tropes and metaphors of race serve the political and literary project of constructing national identity. Deriving its terms from the debates surrounding the Alien and Sedition Acts, *Edgar Huntly* describes how the act of exorcizing the alien (be he Indian or, as we shall see, Irish) from the land allows American identity to come into existence. In staging an Indian war thirty miles outside the nation's capital, Brown leaves his young hero, unguided by family, religion, or any authority higher than his own self-conceived notion of benevolence, to meet single-handedly the crisis of identity facing the nation as a whole.

Edgar Huntly was Brown's last important novel, and critics have long been frustrated in their efforts to identify the connection between the young Republican novelist and the passionately Federalist pamphleteer he would become in the following decade. But by reading *Huntly* in terms of the question of national identity and by looking forward briefly to the first of his political pamphlets, we can begin to see the continuity of Brown's career. After public neglect led Brown to abandon writing novels in the early 1800s, the concerns raised by *Edgar Huntly* became his primary focus, and in a series of political pamphlets he called for an aggressive defense of the nation against all alien forces.[7] His first pamphlet, *An Address to the Government of the United States on the Cession of Louisiana to the French* (1803), which Alan Axelrod suggests "can be considered Brown's most ambitious piece of fiction," was the most popular and influential work of his career.[8] The first edition sold out quickly, an abridged version was published less than two months later, and newspapers throughout the country abstracted and commented on its contents.[9] The pamphlet became, in the words of one paper, "a political event of importance" for a few weeks, and the Republican papers expended much energy in attempting to expose the identity of its author and refute its claims.[10] Brown, for the first time in his career, had the nation's attention.

The pamphlet consists primarily of an invented letter from a French minister of state advising Napoleon to give up the conquest of Santo Domingo and turn instead toward the much more profitable United States. As the Republican paper, the *Aurora,* complained, "The object of this pamphlet we believe to be to plunge this country into a war with France and Spain," and indeed this is precisely what Brown hoped his fictional document would encourage.[11] Brown's invented minister catalogs the many weaknesses that leave the United States vulnerable to foreign conquest, especially "their form of government, and the condition and habits of the people" that expose it to factionalism, as best evidenced by the fact that the French "faction" "has lately gotten the mastery" of the nation's government: "Was there ever a people who exhibited so motley a character; who have vested a more limited and precarious authority, in their rulers; who have multiplied so much the numbers of those that govern; who have dispersed themselves over so wide a space; and have been led by this local dispersion, to create so many clashing jurisdictions and jarring interests, as the State of America?"[12]

The minister then pulls out the trump card by which he claims he can all but guarantee the success of French aspirations in America—race:

> When *war* becomes the topic of discourse, this people will turn their eyes to the calamities of St. Domingo, and then to their own provinces, where the same intestine plague exists in a degree equally formidable, and where their utmost care is requisite to prevent the struggling mischief from bursting its bonds. . . .
>
> With what prudence can this nation attack a neighbour, who can fan at pleasure, the discontents of this intestine enemy; who can give union, design, and arms to its destructive efforts at revenge? (44)

He points toward the threat of slave revolt that hangs over the young nation and cites the ability of the French to "fan at pleasure, the discontents of this intestine enemy"; but in addition to the slaves at the disposal of the French, Brown's fictional minister promises "there is still another reign . . . by which the fury of the States may be held in at pleasure . . . by an enemy placed on their western frontiers. The only aliens and enemies within their borders, are not blacks. . . . The INDIANS are, in many respects, more dangerous inmates" (44–45).

With the deployment of specifically racial anxieties to epitomize the anxieties surrounding the more amorphous category of the "alien" threat, the fictional French minister concludes his letter. Brown devotes the remainder of the pamphlet to refuting in his own voice the "charges" brought against his nation. He undermines them one by one, proving the nation to be more unified, more determined to protect its borders and its identity than the minister suggests. Only one charge is left unanswered, the assertion that the United States remains vulnerable through the existence of "aliens and enemies within their borders"—this alone Brown grants as being worthy of consideration (48). But in deploying racial fear in his fictional plot of French conquest, Brown also demonstrates how by raising the specter of race, the minister gives the lie to his claim that America has no unified identity as a nation:

The American war supplies us with an eternal confutation of the slan-
der. It was evident that the ploughman and mechanic at either end of
the continent, could recognize a common interest with each other. . . .
Mutinous slaves in the heart of the country; hostile garrisons and for-
tresses on one side; numerous and tumultuous savages around us; the
ocean scoured by the fleets of our enemy; our sea ports open to their
inroads . . . all these affrighten not the men of that day from the pursuit
of an end most abstracted from personal ends. (47)

Race, conceived as the most perilous threat to American identity, thus
becomes at the same time a cornerstone in the myth of nation-building: it
is the presence of "aliens"—and blacks, Indians and Europeans alike are
here enveloped by this denomination—that allows Americans to recognize
common interests in each other, to recognize each other as Americans.[13]
Brown's first political tract—a call for the government to take a preemptive
strike against France by seizing the Louisiana Territory and decisively
ridding the nation of its enemies—borrows much from his earlier novel-
writing career in its depiction of a powerful villain, a "discovered" document, and a gothic tale of rape and conquest. Most important, it has
learned the lessons of *Edgar Huntly*'s engagement with the logic of the
Alien and Sedition Acts: constructing and exorcizing the alien is the precondition of a national identity; without the alien, there is no American.

II

The Alien and Sedition Acts grew out of the debates that had framed
attempts to define the nation's identity since the Constitutional Convention, debates that generated fantasies of an internal enemy—often rhetorically painted in warpaint or blackface—directed by an external power
seeking to undermine the very foundations of the young nation. But
under the divided administration of Adams and Jefferson, and with the
nation in undeclared war with France, the factionalism that had characterized the political landscape came to be frighteningly embodied in the
fact of a nation literally divided against itself. The immediate impetus for
the Alien and Sedition Acts was the infamous XYZ Affair of 1798, in which
France's representatives made it understood that unless certain "loans"
were made available, American shipping would be captured and the nation isolated. But the more explosive information revealed by the XYZ

dispatches was their boast of American agents ready to act on the Directory's command at a moment's notice. Not only were alien forces at work within America, but Federalists now were able to identify the enemy literally at the heart of the nation, in Vice President Jefferson and his Republican opposition.

During the XYZ Affair the problem of defining a national identity took on newfound urgency. In the press, the cry was raised against the nation's internal enemies. As one Federalist paper put it, "To be lukewarm after reading the horrid scenes [of the XYZ dispatches] . . . is to be criminal— and the man who does not warmly reprobate the conduct of the French must have a soul black enough to be *fit* for *treasons stratagems* and *spoils.*"[14] The French are coded as corsairs, while those who support the French have "black" souls, graphically linked with the Algerian corsair and the African American (see fig. 2). But the logic here goes further, because it is not just open conspirators who are so identified, but anyone who can read these dispatches and remain "lukewarm" is marked as "criminal"—identified, in terms of the legislation to follow, with the alien. In this passage we have something like a history of these acts in miniature.

The crisis led to what was, in effect, a battery of tests designed to determine who was the alien. Beginning with the Naturalization Act of 1798, the Federalists worked to close the gates against aliens by making citizenship more difficult to obtain.[15] This was followed by two other laws directed at aliens: the Alien Enemies Act, giving the administration power only over the citizens of nations at war with the United States, and the Alien Friends Act, which bolstered the legislation to include the more dangerous population of aliens who had disguised themselves as friends of America. But in the very justification for the Alien Friends Act, a problem emerged for those responsible for its enforcement: the alien in America could not be discovered by physical appearance, genealogy, or any of the signs upon which nations traditionally could rely. This helped motivate the drafting of the Sedition Act, which made seditious writing a crime against national identity and allowed for a visible sign of the alien in disguise to be located in acts of writing, even if the "alien" happened to be "disguised" as a citizen.

What lies at the center of these acts is an erasing of America's own immigrant past through the scapegoating of a class of aliens who can be identified, pursued, and expelled. No longer the land of Crèvecoeur in which immigrants come together and are transformed by the magic properties of the land, the nation is now imagined as immaculately conceived.

Fig. 2. "Cinque-tetes, or the Paris Monster" (1798). (Reproduced by permission of the Huntington Library, San Marino, California.) The image portrays the XYZ Affair as an encounter with a multiheaded "monster," explicitly coded as an Algerian corsair. In the background Mme. Guillotine presides over a "Civic Feast," at which sit a Jacobin, a devil, and a black man.

The logic of this fantasy is perhaps best exemplified by Humphrey Marshall's "The Aliens: A Patriotic Poem" (1798), a celebration of the administration's policy of aggressively rooting the alien from "our land within":

> For Aliens, who've cross'd the seas,
> In language strong, and firm accost them;
> The innocent—be they at ease,
> The guilty—make haste, and arrest them.[16]

As in Crèvecoeur's earlier account of Americanization, Marshall's America serves as a magnet to Europeans born to lowly station who wish to escape their "condition," "like slaves of base bred" (6). Here, however, citizenship is a vicious testing ground through which aliens attempt to "become like one of us": "You have only to do, thus, and thus" (8). The "thus" by which immigrants can become "like one of us" (never precisely one of us) is significantly not spelled out, but Marshall does allow that some will pass the test—learning "love of country" and "virtue"—and these are invited to become citizens. But this narrative, he continues, does not tell the whole story:

> One class only, do I sing thus,
> For of Aliens, there are e'en two;
> It is proper to distinguish those,
> From the other; a malignant crew.
>
> . . . .
>
> At home involv'd in horrid war,
> And all the vices, that curse the mind;
> Conspiracy—dark fiend, was there,
> Foe to themselves, and to all mankind.
>
> . . . .
>
> From hence, till now, our land within,
> Has been a troop, of venal wretches;
> Whose greatest object, it has been,
> To poison our minds, with false speeches.
>
> To make us hate, each the other,
> They bid us fear, the men who rule us;
> They would arm, brother, 'gainst brother,
> Of freedom, and our peace, to fool us. (11–14)

There is another "class" of alien that plagues the nation, "poison[ing] our minds, with false speeches," one that demands an aggressive and participatory method of surveillance to distinguish more accurately one kind of alien from the other. And the hunting of aliens itself provides the means for citizen and friendly alien alike to prove their Americanness:

> The stranger then, within thy gates,
> Shall bless the justice, of equal laws;
> And rise up to defend the States,
> Where merit, give safety, and applause.
>
> The wicked, they will hunt around,
> And with the citizens, they will join,

Until all those, are surely found,
Who against the common weal combine. (18)

Thus, these laws serve as proving ground not only for immigrants who would become "like one of us," but equally, and perhaps more significantly (the poem's subtitle is, after all, "A Patriotic Poem") for citizens as well. Calling on all to forsake the bitter divisions of party that make them vulnerable to alien machinations, Marshall replaces ideology with identity, proclaiming a new standard for the nation: "AMERICANS! be your, [sic] party call" (16). It is not America (the abstract nation) but "Americans" (the body of its citizenry) that is the site of "patriotism," and it is to the defense of the purity of this identity—an identity founded on the purgation of aliens—that all must rally, bringing to bear an artillery of laws, surveillance, and vigilance.

Brown's most improbable plots pale in comparison to those offered by the Federalists in justifying their repressive measures. Most prominent among these were a series of conspiracy theories focusing on the elusive Bavarian Illuminati who were said to be working to pervert the citizenry and institute anarchy. Contemporary with the Alien and Sedition Acts and the XYZ Affair, pamphlets were circulated documenting Illuminism's authoring of the French Revolution and its deadly inroads into America's institutions.[17] The anti-Illuminists identified national unity as the means to salvation from the plague infecting the land from within and without. The leading Federalists were drawn to the theory of alien conspiracy and to the antidote of national identity, as Timothy Dwight, for example, in *The Duty of Americans* (1798), preached that irreligious philosophy and subversive politics would only be exorcized if the citizens united as a nation against the corrupting forces leagued against them.[18]

Brown himself was fascinated with the Illuminati, and they figure in several of his works, including *Ormond* and *Arthur Mervyn*. But especially useful for our discussion is the way in which the hysteria surrounding the Illuminati highlights Federalist attempts to answer the question: Who is the alien? In the accounts of this invisible conspiracy, we see how anxieties about aliens were conflated with anxieties about race. And the repertoire of faces the alien wore in the Federalist imagination provides insight into how giving to the alien a racial identity becomes a way of making the invisible threat visible.

In the Abbé Barruel's popular history of the Illuminati, the Federalists were told two of the forms the alien would take: the rebellious black and the conspiring Irishman:

As the plague flies on the wings of the wind, so do [the Illuminati's] triumphant legions infect America. Their apostles have infused their principles into the submissive and laborious negroes; and St. Domingo and Guadaloupe have been converted into vast charnel houses for their inhabitants. . . . [T]hey are still sufficiently numerous to raise collections and transmit them to the insurgents of Ireland; thus contributing toward that species of revolution which is the object of their ardent wishes in America.[19]

Figuring the alien conspiracy as a black uprising was a pervasive narrative. Anxieties about the French and their minions were collapsed in the Federalist press into fantasies about slave revolt or an invasion from Santo Domingo—prophecies, painted in vivid racial metaphor, of what would happen if Americans failed the test of true citizenship: "Remove your wives far from the Internal Fraternal embrace, or you may prove witness of their violation and expiring agonies, or if reserved for future infamy, may increase your families not only with a spurious, but a colored breed. Remove your daughters . . . unless you would be silent spectators of their being deflowered by the lusty Othellos."[20] Here occurs a crucial but familiar slippage from the threat of an alien conspiracy to a phantasm of black violence.[21] This nightmare of slave revolt spectacularizes that which remains invisible (the Illuminati—"the Internal Fraternal embrace"), the apocalyptic but concealed threat of the alien made visible through the imagination of marauding blacks and the white bodies they leave in their wake.

It was the Irish-Americans, however, a highly politicized Republican community, who came to epitomize the alien for the Federalists. Many of those active in the 1798 Irish Rebellion were believed to be in exile in the United States, and the professed affinities between the United Irishmen there and the pro-French revolutionaries in Ireland sparked widespread hostility toward this immigrant population. The Irish were linked with the alien conspiracy and set up as the primary targets for both the Alien Friends and Sedition Acts.[22] Even Congress was not safe from this anti-Irish vehemence, as Matthew Lyon of Vermont, infamous for having spit in the face of a fellow congressman, was himself prosecuted under the Sedition Act.

One Federalist, "griev[ing] that the saliva of an Irishman should be left upon the face of an American & He, a New Englandman," saw in Lyon's actions a savagery unparalleled even by the Indians themselves and determined that Lyon should be sent to Kamchatka where he would be at home "among the furred tribes."[23] In such rhetoric we can see how the Irish in

America, as they had been in Britain, came to be coded as savages. In the United States, however, this abstract metaphor invoked a unique and highly charged concatenation of anxieties, ambitions, and fantasies surrounding a people with whom white Americans had long shared a troubling coexistence. Thus, in the use of the rhetoric of Indian-hating to describe the "Irish conspiracy" we see the third face the alien wore in the Federalist imagination. So when William Cobbett, in *Detection of a Conspiracy, Formed by the United Irishmen* (1798), wishes to characterize the Irish as France's minions in the United States, he employs the imagery of the resurgently popular captivity narrative to mobilize against the Irish a particular set of fears related to the experience and imagination of the Indian: "Real, sincere, villainy, . . . without property, without principles, without country and without character; dark and desperate, unnatural and blood-thirsty ruffians; these were what [the French] wanted; and where could they have found them with such certainty of success, as amongst that restless, rebellious tribe, the emigrated UNITED IRISHMEN?"[24]

Cobbett's sensational effort to prove that the Irish were conspiring to lay the groundwork for a French invasion plays on the connections between the "unnatural and blood-thirsty" Irish and the Indian. Like the tribes in the western territories long suspected of leaguing with European nations against the United States, the Irish are described as a secret nation-within-the-nation, and Cobbett calls for their violent extirpation. And as in Marshall's poem, the persecution of the alien for Cobbett becomes the litmus test for true Americanness: "If any American, *native* or *adopted,* is in possession of the means of producing such proof, and neglects to produce it, he is to all intents and purposes a TRAITOR," whereas "the man, who shall bring the leaders of this conspiracy to the halter, will deserve as well of his country as those who shall shed their blood in its defense."[25] In uncovering and punishing the Irishman—in proving, that is, the implicit homology between the Irish and the Indian— the citizen proves himself an American. As we have already seen, Brown himself will explicitly cite the Indian as the most dangerous of the nation's "aliens and enemies" in the first of his political pamphlets, but it is in *Edgar Huntly* that he literalizes to the point of equivalence the association implied by Cobbett and others between Irish and Indian.

In the characteristic invisibility of the alien threat we see the difficulty facing white Americans who would expel them from the land. The efforts of the administration to enforce these short-lived laws were far from successful, but their failures illuminate the severity of the problem at hand and the vertigo that those who considered the implications of the laws must have experienced, Brown himself among them.[26] A problem immediately arose in attempting to put this law into practice: if an alien is in disguise, what does he look like? He looks like an American, of course. And what then does an American look like? Here the more profound problem is exposed, the very problem the Alien and Sedition Acts had been designed in some measure to resolve. A positive description of what it meant to be an American was not easily arrived at; clearer was what the (white) American hoped he was not: he was not black, red, British, or French. But of course, Americans look like Europeans, so what was needed was a way to make the alien look like something else. Without recourse to physical description as a technology by which to extract him from the citizenry, those responsible for enforcing the laws had to turn to what he said and wrote for signs of the alien.

It is for this reason that there were no successful prosecutions under the Alien Friends Act during its brief tenure. The force of the prosecutions came to fall predominantly not on aliens, but upon citizens, those who had disguised themselves as Americans and were supposedly conspiring with external powers to overthrow the legitimate institutions of the nation.[27] In thus extending to citizens the forensic technologies invented for aliens, the Sedition Act allowed for the imprisonment of anyone found guilty of writing or speaking against the government so as to undermine the faith of the people in their rulers. It became the "duty of Americans" to hunt down such writing, and in the law's defense the administration encouraged the formation of a network of amateur Jacobin and sedition hunters. Although the majority of those prosecuted under this law were Irish, none was tried under the Alien Friends Act; using the Sedition Act, it was upon their writings that the government based its prosecution. In the history of these acts we see how language becomes linked to identity; to speak openly against the government—be one technically a citizen or not—is to prove oneself an alien.

But if you identify the alien by what he writes, as the history of the Alien and Sedition Acts suggests, what implications did the logic of these laws have for America's first professional novelist? As removed from political debate as his novels may appear to us today, it is important to remember, as Michael Warner has demonstrated, that Brown conceived a public role for his novels from the start, even sending a copy of *Wieland* to Jefferson in vain hopes of official endorsement.[28] And theorizing the alien and his relationship to American identity is elemental to much of Brown's fiction. In the unfinished sequel to *Wieland*, "Carwin the Biloquist," and *Ormond* (1799), he deploys the threat of the Illuminati in two charismatic and powerful aliens plotting against the virtue of the Republic; in "Stephen Calvert," Brown's unfinished novel of doubles, the alien threat is the hero's degenerate twin brother, raised under the influence of the European papal conspiracy.

But where among all these aliens lies the American? Brown's novels are highly concerned with lineage and inheritance; it is a standard moment in his fiction for the hero to catalog his or her ancestry, and far from fixed, national borders in the novel are crossed and recrossed almost obsessively in search of identity, inheritance, and asylum. Yet these novels remain fundamentally, if confusedly, committed to the idea of an American identity; Brown's first novel is subtitled "An American Tale," and all of his major work specifically grounds its action in the United States. Thus, by the time Brown arrives at *Edgar Huntly,* the necessity of fully tackling the still unanswered question "What is an American?" comes to prominence among all the questions raised by his fiction, as it had also come to dominate the imagination of the press and public.[29]

III

Following Sydney J. Krause's conjecture that the composition of *Huntly* began in February 1799 and William Dunlap's reliable firsthand information that the novel proceeded "rapidly" after the publication of the first volume of *Arthur Mervyn,* I want to suggest that the writing of *Edgar Huntly* led, in an important sense, to the rewriting of *Arthur Mervyn* itself.[30] David M. Larson argues that the apparent contradictions of *Mervyn* can best be understood by placing *Edgar Huntly* between the two volumes, where it was, in fact, written.[31] Characterizing *Arthur Mervyn, Second Part* as "less a sequel to the first part of the novel than it is a rewriting of it," Larson's reading of *Edgar Huntly* as reflecting changes in Brown's thinking at the time and motivating, by its conclusions, the rewriting of *Mervyn* is very useful. Both novels, as Larson points out, test the limits of benevolence and personal judgment as guiding principles for individual action.

But the meaning of these limits cannot be fully understood without placing the novel that effected Brown's own transformation against the larger political and cultural crisis of the time, a crisis that brought Brown to where he could no longer follow through on the principles of *Arthur Mervyn, First Part.* When Brown rewrites the story, he turns on his hero— exposing him as the duplicitous, self-serving, and conspiring agent that he had been accused of being (and wrongly so, by the terms of the first volume); in the second volume Arthur abandons his American farmgirl for an older European Jewess, abandons writing for luxury, and, finally, abandons America itself for the Old World. The interrogations, suspicions, and legal proceedings directed against Arthur in the first part by a society presented as distrustful, petty, and irresponsible are now shown to have been judicious.

The contradictions of the two parts of the novel are understood only by following out, as Brown did, the consequences of the unregulated individualism represented by both Arthur and Edgar. In the first part, Brown ends by siding with his protagonist against the institutions of his city—an innocent youth beleaguered by a society that cannot trust his success or the benevolence of his intentions. But after writing *Huntly* Brown begins the story again, having himself moved to a position in which the institutions of the nation must be valued over the philosophies of the individual.[32] He offers a first-person narrative that reveals the machinations Arthur had successfully hidden from the narrator of the first part, Dr. Stevens—a man, like Edgar Huntly, who believes supremely in the power of his benevolence to effect the most remarkable transformations and to determine character independently of society.

Edgar Huntly is a detective story about a young rural Pennsylvanian's search for the murderer of his friend, Waldegrave, a search that is deflected into a series of explorations that lead him seemingly far from his original purpose. The story is told, for all but the last three short letters, as a first-person account from Edgar to his former fiancée, Mary, sister of the murdered Waldegrave. It is a narrative that begins utterly paralyzed by its task:

> Am I sure that even now my perturbations are sufficiently stilled for an employment like this? That the incidents I am going to relate can be recalled and arranged without indistinctness and confusion? . . . Yet when I shall be better qualified for this task I know not. Time may take away these headlong energies, and give me back my ancient sobriety: but this change will only be effected by weakening my remembrance of these events. In proportion as I gain power over words, shall I lose dominion over sentiments. (5)

Here, in the opening pages of his long letter to Mary, the nightmare that will be narrated is characterized as a literary crisis. What Edgar has experienced, at the expense of his "ancient sobriety," has made it all but impossible for him to tell an orderly narrative. But at the same time the recovery of his former sobriety would be at the expense of his ability to describe the experiences themselves. This fundamental incompatibility between his experiences in the wilderness and traditional narrative structures is a dilemma related in important ways to that which Brown describes in his preface. The "ancient sobriety" of British literary form is seen as inimical to the narration of these adventures—the "emotions" of his New World experience are irreconcilably opposed to narrative "order and coherence." This may be read as a justification for the irregularity that characterizes much of this plot; but even so, it is a peculiar kind of excuse, one that finds its terms in the exceptionalist nature of an experience that demands new forms, new structures, new energies.

Edgar must first find words and forms to describe the apparition he discovers while staking out the site of Waldegrave's murder:

> The shape of a man, tall and robust, was now distinguished. Repeated and closer scrutiny enabled me to perceive that he was employed in digging the earth. Something like flannel was wrapt round his waist and covered his lower limbs. The rest of his frame was naked. I did not recognize in him any one whom I knew.
>
> A figure, robust and strange, and half naked, to be thus employed, at this hour and place, was calculated to rouse up my whole soul. (10)

Edgar, in the true spirit of the Alien Friends Act, sets out to determine the identity of the mysterious figure he had seen the night before. He is quickly led to his man: "I perceived that the only foreigner among us was Clithero. Our scheme was, for the most part, a patriarchal one. Each farmer was surrounded by his sons and kinsmen. This was an exception to the rule. Clithero was a stranger, whose adventures and character, previously to his coming hither, were unknown to us." To all appearances Clithero is a model alien, "a pattern of sobriety and gentleness" (14). But in making "this man the subject of my scrutiny" with "minute inquiries" and "seasonable interrogations" (15), Edgar begins to uncover a hidden side to this stranger's character, a side that has exposed itself in his nightly sleepwalking. Clithero's employer and fellow laborers testify to his suspicious "musing and melancholy deportment" (25), and Edgar's investigations throughout the neighborhood provide him with evidence to confirm his suspicions about the Irishman's character.

Determined to solve the mystery, Edgar trails his suspect on his nightly wanderings through the woods, "resolv[ing] . . . not to lose sight of him till the termination of his career" (18). But the task becomes increasingly difficult as Clithero, despite having been in the United States only six months, proves able to negotiate the forest with an agility worthy of a native, a skill that threatens Edgar's pride: "I disdained to be outstripped in this career" (23). Edgar imagines the Irishman early on to occupy a rivalrous position, and what is at stake in the "career" this novel will narrate is a competition for the privileges of the wilderness, a right Edgar has claimed as his own: "Perhaps no one was more acquainted with this wilderness than I" (97). When, later in the novel, he again voices this rivalry, it is explicitly marked as if it were a competition with the Indian: "I had delighted, from my childhood, in feats of agility and perseverance. . . . I disdained to be out-done in patience under hardship, and contention with fatigue, by the Mohawk" (212).

Despite his many claims to superiority, however, Edgar is routinely baffled by an unfamiliar landscape and by the uncanny ability of Clithero to navigate an impassable wilderness. At one point, having lost Clithero in the valley below, Edgar stands atop a precipice that affords a view of the surrounding landscape, and he determines that "since the birth of this continent, I was probably the first who had deviated thus remotely from the customary paths of men" (103). This pioneering boast will be disproved when he awakes the next day in the cavern above which he now stands and encounters his predecessors in the form of a band of Indians. But the challenge is raised more immediately when, looking down on the water below, Edgar spots "an human countenance" (103) that turns out to belong to Clithero. And the Clithero he finds has become a savage indeed: "His scanty and coarse garb, had been nearly rent away by brambles and thorns, his arms, bosom and cheek were overgrown and half-concealed by hair. There was somewhat in his attitude and looks denoting more than anarchy of thoughts and passions" (104).

From our first introduction to Clithero, Edgar has consistently been drawn toward the imagery of the Indian narrative, and though Clithero is no Indian, he will justify these first impressions, proving the correspondence that the novel hints at in its opening pages. Over the course of the novel, Clithero has grown closer to becoming the savage Edgar initially imagined him to be—closer, that is, to the Indian with whom Cobbett and others would have linked him. And in making his wilderness home in the secret den of the Indians conspiring to attack Solesbury, Clithero will prove the connection stronger still. Edgar searches for the alien through the woods with the most benevolent of avowed intentions, but the narrative of his hunt describes a process of alienization whereby the Irishman is increasingly made equivalent to the Indian, and with the darkest savagery of the wilderness: "His grey coat, extended claws, fiery eyes, and a cry which he at that moment uttered, and which, by its resemblance to the human voice, is peculiarly terrific, denoted him to be the most ferocious and untamable of that detested race" (124).

Out of the cave into which Edgar had seen Clithero descend emerges a horrible and ravenous beast. The panther described in this passage serves to forge the connection between Clithero and the Indian in two important ways. First, the panther points toward "Abraham Panther's" popular captivity narrative, convincingly cited by Richard Slotkin as a source for Brown's novel.[33] More important, the panther—referred to almost exclusively as the "savage"—has emerged from Clithero's den, suggesting the Irishman's transmutation into this "savage" form. This encounter provides Edgar with the first of many opportunities to avow his horror of "carnage and blood" (124) as well as his first chance to boast of his innate abilities as a destroyer of "savages": armed with a "tom-hawk," he describes how he had "often . . . cut the sinews of a cat-o'mountain, at the distance of sixty feet" (125). But in hunting Clithero into the woods, Edgar had left his trusty tomahawk behind, believing the forest cleared of these "savages."[34]

This is Edgar's first crucial error: failing to recognize, as Clithero's seeming metamorphosis into the panther has demonstrated, the link between the alien and the "savage." It is a mistake Edgar is doomed to repeat, and here he escapes with his life only through the fortuitous collapse of the bridge that provided the sole access to Clithero's lair. Edgar returns home vowing "never to traverse the wilderness unfurnished with my tom-hawk" (129). That night he undergoes his own first bout of somnambulism and begins the series of adventures that lead him deeper and deeper into the savage landscape from which Clithero never again will return. If the first half of the tale describes the attempt to redeem the alien, the second half describes Edgar's own experience of and redemption from Clithero's disease and the savagery that it has brought upon him.

Going to sleep in his own bed, he wakes to find himself literally in another world:

> My return to sensation and to consciousness took place in no such
> tranquil scene. I emerged from oblivion by degrees so slow and so faint,
> that their succession cannot be marked. When enabled at length to

attend to the information which my senses afforded, I was conscious, for a time, of nothing but existence. . . .

I attempted to open my eyes . . . but the darkness that environed me was as intense as before. (159–60)

What follows is an excruciating scene of rebirth, as Edgar attempts first to see, then to move, and finally to determine where he is. He is half-naked, covered in blood and bruises, and barely conscious—reborn into a primitive state. And the first object he finds as he searches his new prison is "an Indian tom-hawk" (161). Armed with this familiar weapon, he staggers through the cavern gripped with a bestial hunger that craves nothing less than warm blood: "My hunger speedily became ferocious. I tore the linen of my shirt between my teeth and swallowed the fragments. I felt a strong propensity to bite the flesh from my arm. My heart overflowed with cruelty, and I pondered on the delight I should experience in rending some living animal to pieces, and drinking its blood and grinding its quivering fibres between my teeth" (164). Edgar is granted his wish, as a second panther attacks him when he stumbles upon the spot "where [the] savage was lurking." Killing this "savage" with his tomahawk, Edgar finds himself devouring its body raw. The American, in his hunt for the alien, has become the savage his narrative had made of Clithero. Having spontaneously degenerated to this lowest state of savagery, a state that even now he "review[s] . . . with loathing and horror" (167), Edgar turns in disgust and begins his long journey back to civilization. It is the project of the second half of the novel to bring Edgar back to his rightful place in society and to demonstrate how and why he can make this journey of return while Clithero cannot.

At the mouth of the cavern, he discovers a band of Indians sleeping around a fire, and it is this spectacle that allows Edgar to begin anew, shaking off his savage state for the role he finds himself to have been born for: not that of the Indian but of the Indian fighter. Although this transformation is triggered by the sight of the Indians, it is an identity that Edgar retroactively traces back to his father and a primal scene of frontier violence:

My father's house was placed on the verge of this solitude. Eight of these assassins assailed it at the dead of night. My parents and an infant child were murdered in their beds; the house was pillaged, and then burnt to the ground. . . .

Most men are haunted by some species of terror or antipathy, which they are, for the most part, able to trace to some incident which befel them in their early years. You will not be surprized that the fate of my parents, and the sight of the body of one of this savage band . . . should produce lasting and terrific images in my fancy. I never looked upon, or called up the image of a savage without shuddering. (173)

The father's claims to the forest led to his murder by the Indians he had displaced, and it is Edgar's role—as son of the murdered pioneer—to reclaim his father's rights for himself. Whereas the genealogy of the Old World, epitomized in this novel by Clithero's Irish tale, brings down upon the sons the sins of the fathers, this American lineage preserves Edgar from Clithero's savage fate. Despite the persistent pleas of pacifism that punctuate each of the novel's scenes of violence, from this moment on Edgar becomes the most improbably effective Indian fighter until Natty Bumppo and Nathan Slaughter.

Edgar's competition for the rights to the woods is clarified by this scene of primal violence. But the novel has also already shown, even before this childhood trauma is narrated, the degree to which he is motivated by a competition for the rights to a father. Waldegrave is not the only surrogate father Edgar has found and lost since the death of his own parents. In Clithero's confession to Edgar of the "murder" of his Irish benefactress, Mrs. Lorimer, a crucial coincidence had come to light: the man who was Clithero's father figure in Ireland, and the man who was to marry Mrs. Lorimer, is the same man who a few years earlier had served as Edgar's own surrogate father in Pennsylvania: Sarsefield. Thus, the competition between Edgar and Clithero is made even more resonant, and when Edgar breaks into Clithero's ingenious wooden box an important detail is occluded by his justification of his trespass on the basis of his benevolent intentions "to restore [Clithero] to peace" and his curiosity as a fellow "mechanist" to "know the principles on which [the cabinet] was formed." It was Sarsefield, we know, who instructed Edgar into the artistry of secret cabinets; and it is from Sarsefield, Edgar knows, that Clithero has learned the same skills. Edgar, therefore, in looking at (and ultimately destroying) the box "with the eye of an artist" is setting himself in competition with Clithero for mastery of this father's teachings.

Edgar emerges from the cavern onto a landscape devoid of all signs of civilization: "No marks of habitation, or culture, no traces of the footsteps of men, were discernible. I scarcely knew in what region of the globe I was placed" (182). Coming to a ramshackle hut, he discovers how far he still has to travel. A rude log structure with no window and no furniture, this habitation merits from Brown one of the more precise descriptive passages in a novel that is notably devoid of vividly defined landmarks and characters (183).[35] His attention is explained by the fact that this is the home of Queen Mab, self-proclaimed defender of the Indian "nation" against the white invaders and, as Edgar discovers at the story's end, the force behind all the novel's action, from the murder of Waldegrave to the attack on Solesbury.

When the Delawares had abandoned their lands to the settlers, Queen Mab alone had remained behind to defend their claim, establishing a home for herself and three dogs "of the Indian or wolf species" (207). This curious family comprised a nation unto themselves, ruled firmly by Queen Mab and protecting its borders fiercely: "To the rest of mankind they were aliens or enemies. . . . They would suffer none to approach them, but attacked no one who did not imprudently crave their acquaintance, or who kept a respectful distance from their wigwam. That sacred asylum they would not suffer to be violated" (208). These are the principles upon which Queen Mab has founded her own nation-within-a-nation, even going so far as to set up a system of taxation whereby the alien invaders provide her subsistence for their use of the land: "The English were aliens and sojourners who occupied the land merely by her connivance and permission, and whom she allowed to remain on no terms but those of supplying her wants" (209). Edgar was the one "alien" whom Queen Mab allowed into her "nation," and as it is Edgar who will single-handedly foil her plans for the conquest of Solesbury, she will have reason to regret opening her borders to even one "alien," just as Edgar himself will be forced to learn the consequences of his own weakness for his alien, Clithero.

Mab had taught Edgar her language, and he condescendingly gave her her name (209), a name that links the Indian to Old World nobility as well as to the European literary tradition against which Brown has positioned himself. But now Edgar must reconsider his humoring of Queen Mab's pretensions to royalty and national identity, as he is able to make the frightening connection between her absence from the hut and the Indian war that has been unleashed on Solesbury. Queen Mab is the only Indian who merits characterization in this novel, and her role is a vital one to the project at hand. What began as a search for and implicit competition with the alien now becomes open confrontation with the Indian, epitomized by Queen Mab, for the rights to this frontier "nation." The hunt for the

Irishman has been absorbed in and made equivalent to the hunt for the Indian, and both lead, inexorably, to the solution Edgar first set out to find: the murderer of Waldegrave.

Just as the uncovering of the alien led, through the contagion of somnambulism, to the alienation of our detective, so here does the discovery of the Indian at the heart of the matter bring with it the recognition of the Indian at the heart of Edgar himself. Brown's interest in racial cross-dressing was of long standing: in his earlier fiction there had been several such scenes deployed for sensational effect, such as Ormond's disguise as a black chimney sweep, Carwin's discovery of his powers of biloquism through imitating "the shrill tones of a Mohock savage," or Stephen Calvert's self-imposed exile to the frontier to live with the Indians.[36] In the *Weekly Magazine,* the repository of so many of Brown's hobbyhorses, we find an account of the famous Henry Moss, who, through the ameliorative effects of American institutions, had supposedly "changed" from black to white. Although borrowing most of its facts from the many articles about Moss's miraculous transformation published earlier in the decade, the *Weekly Magazine* account focuses not so much on the positive transformation, but on the instability of racial identity the change itself reveals:

> The lines dividing the black from the white, are not regularly defined, but indented and insulated, the borders appearing as islands and peninsulas, as are represented on the chart of a sea coast. . . . As the change from *white* to *black* must be admitted as equally possible with the reverse above stated, it may be well for the white slave dealers, and their *fair* abettors, whether legislators or others, to consider how far they may be *personally* interested in perpetuating such a criterion: as by it, they may ultimately be doomed to the wretchedness, to which they are now devoting millions.[37]

Moss's story is here used as an argument against the slave system, but one that plays on the anxiety highlighted by the logic of the Alien and Sedition Acts: if a black man can turn white, so too can a white man turn black.[38] As we have seen, the fear that Americans will be transformed by contact with the alien into something other than Americans lies behind the Alien and Sedition Acts and their defense—and it is this fear of contamination that Brown deploys as the central nightmare of his novel. It is only by aggressively exorcizing the Indian from the land that Edgar will be able finally to exorcize the Indian from himself.

Severely wounded during a fierce battle at Queen Mab's hut, Edgar is left for dead; he wakes, reborn once again, to find himself painted red: "My head had reposed upon the breast of him whom I had shot in this part of his body. The blood had ceased to ooze from the wound, but my dishevelled locks were matted and steeped in that gore which overflowed and choaked up the orifice" (197). In this state—stained red with blood, half-naked, and covered with bruises—he finds himself mistaken for an Indian by those he encounters along the way. Edgar cannot shed his red skin—his "native hue exchanged for the livid mark of bruises and scarifications" (236)—and the consequences of this transformation are made frighteningly manifest when he finds himself fired upon by a band of men (his long-lost "father," Sarsefield, among them) who take him for an Indian and whom Edgar likewise believes to be Indians themselves. This is the novel's nightmare: a nation plagued by aliens and Indians demands a unified defense of identity; otherwise it is transformed into a world where citizen fires upon citizen, father upon son, and none can tell the American from the savage, the citizen from the alien.

The meaning of this encounter is driven home when Edgar arrives at a house to all appearances the "model of cleanliness and comfort" (226); he believes he has at last found his people again: "Methought I could claim consanguinity with such beings" (226). But behind the facade—"painted white," with all the "tokens" signifying "not only rural competence and innocence, but . . . beings, raised by education and fortune, above the intellectual mediocrity of clowns"—Edgar finds an interior ravaged by violence. Here the proper home—"painted white"—masks a scene of savage destruction that clarifies the connection the novel has etched between the alien and the Indian. For not only has the house been vandalized by marauding Indians, but the violence here is also explicitly located in its resident: Selby, raised in Europe, had come to America to inherit his father's farm and had degenerated into drunkenness and dissipation. When Edgar discovers Selby's wife hiding in the barn, she is seeking refuge not from the Indians, but from the threats of her husband to "cut your throat" (228). In the scenes of violence Edgar discovers outside the house, a scalped girl and a dead Indian, it becomes unclear indeed whether the massacre was committed by the drunken farmer or the invading Indians. The alien and the Indian are now truly one.

If you cannot tell your fellow citizen by his appearance, Edgar has a dilemma on his hands as he approaches his home. How will he prove himself to be a citizen of Solesbury, and not the Indian he appears to be? To make matters worse, Huntly has received from a passing farmer confirmation of his wildest fears (that later prove to be unfounded) that his family has been butchered and his home destroyed by the Indians, and he is now ready to give up all as lost. His property was all that remained to mark him as distinct from the savage he had almost become and, indeed, for which he is now frequently mistaken; as he bemoans his fate, without "my chamber, my closets, my cabinets . . . my very cloathing. . . . Why should I survive this calamity?" (235). What is there left to distinguish him from the Indian? Or, to rephrase the question raised earlier by the Alien Friends Act, how do you identify yourself as an American when you are disguised as an alien? Edgar hits upon the answer: "I must trust to the speed with which my voice and my words should disclose my true character and rectify their mistake" (236–37). It is through language alone that Edgar can identify himself as an American, just as in the history of the Alien and Sedition Acts identity came to be grounded finally upon what the subject wrote and said.[39]

Indeed, this is primarily what comprises the rest of the novel—a series of storytellings and scenes of writing. Coming at last to an apparently deserted house on the edge of Solesbury, Edgar lets himself in and discovers none other than Sarsefield himself, his long-lost father who has come to America to give to his adopted son the inheritance that would have been Clithero's. Recovering here his "father" and Waldegrave's misplaced letters (the radical past Edgar proved unable to let go), Edgar also receives a material inheritance beyond his wildest expectations: not only will Sarsefield be his father, and Mrs. Lorimer (who survived Clithero's attack) his mother, but Clarice, Clithero's own betrothed, is now to be Edgar's as well (259).

So father and son tell each other their stories—Edgar proving himself to be truly himself, and Sarsefield telling of his own adventures and explaining away the loose ends that remained tangled by Edgar's ignorance of his own somnambulism. But father and son's narratological reunion is violently interrupted, poisoned by the mention of the one thing this newly reconstructed family cannot absorb: Clithero, who has emerged from the wilderness, mangled by Indians, an incurable madman. Edgar's naive insistence on Clithero's potential for redemption is defined by Sarsefield as outright treason, but Edgar perseveres despite this fierce opposition. His continuing appeals on Clithero's behalf force an open rift between Edgar and his new family, and Sarsefield leaves to await Edgar's submission to his will. There will be no Clithero, no alien, in Sarsefield's America: "I will not occupy the same land, the same world with him" (263).

Edgar trusts in his ability to cure Clithero of his savagery because he himself, having lived a parallel experience in the wilderness, has been reborn, a new man with a new family in a new society. Edgar still mistakenly shares Crèvecoeur's belief that any man, under the influence of American soil and experience, will "feel the effects of a sort of resurrection," casting off "his European prejudices" to be reborn a member of "that race now called Americans."[40] For Crèvecoeur in the 1770s, and for the agrarian Republicans who followed, this process was an organic one, like transplanting "a sprout growing at the foot of a great tree" so that "it will become a tree bearing fruit also." But the process, as we have seen, is no longer imagined to be so simple, the metaphors no longer so organic. It is this sentimental model of Americanization and the deism of the Jeffersonians, the youthful intoxicants of both Edgar and Brown himself, that must now be rejected in order to confront the crisis facing American identity at the turn of the century.

Edgar and Clithero, as critics have demonstrated, undergo parallel experiences, marking them as the first in a long tradition of psychological doubles, out of which will be born the masterpieces of Poe, Melville, and Hawthorne. But Edgar and Clithero's doubleness is crucial in the end primarily insofar as it makes explicit their differences, differences from which Edgar (and the reader) is expected to draw vital lessons. Becoming an American, Edgar learns, proves to be something more than simple transplantation or even passive submission to the machinery of citizenship. What in the novel seems to be a competition for the right to be an Indian—to claim an Indian inheritance, as Richard Slotkin puts it—is in fact something significantly different. Edgar claims his ownership of the forest, and the rights, skills, and qualities of the Indian, not by becoming an Indian, but by killing Indians; and it is the alien—who does himself fatally become the Indian—who allows Edgar to achieve this. Aliens become Indians; Americans become Indian killers. Indeed, it could be suggested that Edgar is in fact not especially successful at anything else in this novel. As a detective, as a woodsman, and as a maker of secret boxes, he finds himself continually bested by Clithero's superior skills. In the end it is only as an Indian killer that Edgar proves superior to his Irish counterpart. But this proves, for the novel, the crucial difference.

The American is distinguished from the alien by his ability not to become an Indian, and it is Brown's perception of the alien's equation with the savage that allows Edgar to escape becoming an Indian himself. Collapsing the Indian and alien together allows for the killing of Indians to bring the American his proper inheritance. Edgar's hunt for Clithero does then become a "hunt for himself," as the critical line has run, not because he and Clithero are doubles, but because it is his misguided

attempt to redeem the contagious alien that secures their crucial difference. It is despite his naive benevolence, indeed, quite despite himself
entirely, that Edgar discovers what it means to be a true defender of
America: it is he who identifies the dangerous alien in the garden, it is he
who destroys him—just as (and the equivalence is deliberate) it is he who
single-handedly puts down the Indian threat to his native community.

With Sarsefield's proscription of Clithero from his "land" the first long
letter ends, and what follows are three short letters describing the consequences of Edgar's inability to learn his final lesson from his experiences
by submitting to Sarsefield's judgment. Edgar discovers Clithero in resi-
dence in Queen Mab's hut, living the life of an Indian, heir to the throne
Mab has abdicated after her unsuccessful war. Whereas Edgar has reen-
tered society and claimed his inheritance, Clithero has renounced civilization for a savage existence. Edgar comes to redeem him, telling him
that Mrs. Lorimer is not dead after all, only to provoke the subject of his
benevolence into setting off to complete her destruction. Writing fran-
tically to Sarsefield to warn him, Edgar pleas, "I have erred, not through
sinister or malignant intentions, but from the impulse of misguided, indeed, but powerful benevolence" (290).

The last two letters recount the effects of this "misguided benevolence" directed toward the alien: Clithero is captured at last by Sarsefield,
only to drown himself while being transported to the insane asylum; but
Edgar's letter of warning, falling accidently into the hands of Mrs. Lorimer, leads to the miscarriage of her child (292). Edgar's language, which
earlier proved him to be an American, here reveals its darker potential in
fulfilling Clithero's deadly intentions. Edgar's murder of Mrs. Lorimer's
baby is a standard scene straight out of the tales of Indian atrocities
popular in the 1790s, in which the savage tears the unborn infant from its
mother's belly. It is important that Edgar is still marked—indeed, always
will be—as potentially a savage, for stasis is not achieved in this model of
citizenship: the line between Indian and American is always provisional; it
must be redrawn daily. Here it is through irresponsible and unregulated
writing that Edgar's savage potential is realized.

Indeed, what remains in excess of the novel's resolutions is writing.
Earlier in the novel, immediately before his own somnambulism began,
Edgar had received a visitation from his dead friend, Waldegrave, who
chastised him for not destroying, as promised, the radical letters Waldegrave had written him in his youth. The novel suggests that Edgar's contamination with the "disease" of somnambulism is due not only to the
alien sleepwalker, Clithero, but in some measure to Edgar's continued

attachment to Waldegrave's earlier radicalism as well. At the end of the novel, Edgar remains infected despite the fact that his sentimental model of benevolence, his belief in his ability to transform the degenerate Euro-pean into an American, has been belied again and again. It is this belief that leads to all his dilemmas, making him vulnerable to the contagion of both the alien and the Indian, as he inherits first Clithero's disease and then, more terrifyingly, the savage's skin. Yet even after fighting through the darkest woods and seemingly countless enemies, Edgar still has not learned his lesson. He remains sufficiently contaminated to fulfill, uncon-sciously, the hostile aims of both the Indian and the alien in his unwitting murder of Sarsefield's child through an irresponsible act of writing that falls into the hands of a vulnerable reader.

By curing himself of his vulnerability to aliens, Indians, and dangerous writing—a cure that can only be effected by submission to authority—Edgar will finally arrive at his proper station in the new nation. His disobedience makes him susceptible to the contagion of alien and Indian alike, and this disobedience must be disciplined. Thus, Sarsefield's final reprimand, startling in its dispassion, becomes the most important lesson the novel has to offer reader and hero alike: "I find it hard to forbear com-menting on your rashness in no very mild terms. You acted in direct oppo-sition to my council, and to the plainest dictates of propriety. Be more circumspect and more obsequious for the future" (292). Sarsefield, now Edgar's father and the locus of authority in the community, has arrived to teach this very simple lesson, a lesson it cost him his natural-born child to teach: "Be more circumspect and more obsequious *for the future.*"

IV

It was a lesson Brown himself had been reluctantly learning for many years: his family had repeatedly advised him to restrain his passions and his pen and give up literature for a responsible office in the family's mercantile firm. Caution and circumspection was also a lesson that the author's closest friends, William Dunlap and Elihu Hubbard Smith, had been trying to teach Brown since his writing career began. As Smith chastised him in 1796:

> That the example of J. J. Rousseau had too many charms in your eyes not to captivate you and incite you to imitate him, and that you were pleased to have others believe those misfortunes to be real which you

knew how so eloquently to describe. The transition is natural, to a mind
of sensibility almost unavoidable. You began to fancy that these fictions
were real; that you had indeed suffered, enjoyed, known, and seen all
that you had so long pretended to have experienced; every subsequent
event became tinctured with this conviction and accompanied with this
diseased apprehension; . . . and you wandered in a world of your own
creation.[41]

Smith's image of Brown as the diseased man of sensibility wandering in
a world of his own creation is an apt description of both Clithero and Edgar. It is in defining the difference between them—rescuing Edgar from
Clithero's fate and teaching him the restraint Brown himself is learning—
that Brown puts an end to his novelistic career that brought him to this
point. Writing in 1800 to his brother James, Brown sounds like a man who
has fully learned his lessons, turning his pen over to the public will: "Your
remarks upon the gloominess and out-of-nature incidents of *Huntly,* if
they be not just in their full extent, are doubtless such as most readers will
make, which alone is sufficient reason for dropping the doleful tone and
assuming a cheerful one, or at least substituting moral causes and daily
incidents in place of the prodigious or the singular. I shall not hereafter fall
into that strain."[42] Brown took his family's advice so far to heart as to
largely give up novel writing altogether, with the exception of two unsuccessful minor novels, models of obsequiousness and circumspection.[43]

At the end of his career, Brown's creative energies were directed, as we
have seen, toward political writing. His first pamphlet was one of the most
influential pieces of Federalist propaganda during Jefferson's administration and was for some time debated as a legitimate transcription of a
secret French document. In it the Federalists believed they had at last
found conclusive evidence of an alien conspiracy directed against the
United States, and papers across the nation cited the pamphlet as providing the same kind of litmus test for Americanness reserved five years
earlier for the accounts of the XYZ Affair. As the *New-York Evening Post*
editorialized, "If anything can arouse the government and the people of
this country to a proper sense of the dangers which menace their peace
from the magnificent and alarming projects of a towering, ambitious foreigner, it will be the perusal of this pamphlet."[44]

Two months later, Brown followed up with his second pamphlet, *Monroe's Embassy* (1803), taking Jefferson to task for failing to move decisively against French and Spanish schemes in the western territory. Here
his imperialistic rhetoric is all but identical to that of the French minister

Fig. 3. William Charles, "A Scene on the Frontiers as Practiced by the Humane British and Their Worthy Allies" (1812). (Courtesy of the Library of Congress, Washington, D.C., LC-USZ62-5800.) Charles plays off the earlier images and fantasies of the 1790s in this portrayal of the British and their Indian "allies." The Indians and British are linked visually in their similar complexions (especially when compared to the "whiteness" of the martyred Americans) and in the insert on the lower left, which shows them dancing arm-in-arm.

he had ventriloquized in his first political tract, and now Brown even confesses admiration for the French insofar as they have demonstrated the true love of country and clear national purpose that Jefferson, in his diplomatic half-measures, has failed to inspire in Americans. Brown's rhetoric here is also very similar to that found in another Federalist pamphlet, in which the reader is reminded "that every Frenchman bears with him every where a French heart, and so he ought. . . . O! that Americans had always an American heart!"[45] It is only because "the French are aliens to me, and the citizens of these states are my brethren" that Brown announces he must stand against them: "I deprecate, with all the fervour which self-preservation produces, the arrival and neighbourhood of those, who cannot but check the progress, disturb the peace, and endanger the concord and the safety of the brotherhood of which I am one."[46]

Brown admires the French for their strong national identity, but as aliens the French constitute a threat to his nation, and it is to the defense of this "brotherhood"—the brotherhood of all those who are not aliens—that Brown rallies his countrymen. And despite the manifold dangers posed by the French presence in the West, Brown concludes his pamphlet with a declaration of his faith in an American victory in the ensuing war: "Fate has manifestly decreed, that America must belong to the English name and race" (54). In his gothic portrayal of the alien, his spelling out of the equivalence of the threat of the alien with that of race, and his narrative whereby the conflated threat of alien and race provides the ground on which American identity is born, Brown brings fully to light the concerns of *Edgar Huntly*.

Thus, Brown has arrived at nineteenth-century imperialism, the lessons of *Huntly* having brought him to an early formulation of Manifest Destiny. As Attorney General Charles Lee said in defending the Alien Acts, "There can be no complete sovereignty without the power of removing aliens; and the exercise of such a power is inseparably incident to the *nation*."[47] Thus, there is no nation without aliens and the ability to remove them, and this nation of immigrants finds itself in the tenuous position of founding its national identity on the alienation of a class of people from whom the nation must in turn be protected. Defining and exposing the alien becomes in this period fundamental to the machinery of citizenship; the citizen distinguishes himself from the alien he so closely resembles by hunting the alien from the nation. To be an American is to be always almost an Indian, almost a European, and in this dilemma lies the solution: collapsing Indian and alien together and clearing both from the land, a unique national identity is born.

In *Edgar Huntly* it is not the frontiersman who becomes the Indian, as writers from Crèvecoeur to Dwight had prophesied, but the alien—and this transformation becomes finally the way you identify the alien (see fig. 3). What does an alien in disguise look like? asks the novel—the question that framed the Alien and Sedition Acts. Like an Indian. The recovery of the alienated hero's identity necessitates, and is coincident with, the destruction of the Indian and the purging of the alien who together had authored the novel's violence. Cleansing the nation of aliens becomes a form of Indian warfare, and in his proclivity for the hunt Edgar proves himself an American.

CHAPTER 4

Cooper's Vanishing American Act

If I were as drunk with enthusiasm as Swedenborg or Westler, I might probably say I had seen Armies of Negroes marching and counter-marching in the air, shining in Armour. I have been so terrified with this Phenomenon that I constantly said in former times to the Southern Gentlemen, I cannot comprehend this object; I must leave it to you. . . . What we are to see, *God* knows, and I leave it to him, and his agents in posterity. I have none of the genius of Franklin, to invent a rod to draw from the cloud its Thunder and lightning.

John Adams to Thomas Jefferson (1821)

I

"To make a long story short," Washington Irving writes toward the end of his famous tale, "the company broke up and returned to the more impor-tant concerns of the election."[1] Rip Van Winkle "resumed his old walks and habits," taking "his place once more on the bench at the inn door and was reverenced as one of the patriarchs of the village, and a chronicle of the old times 'before the war.'" But if Rip has at last found his proper role in his community as the chronicler of life before the war, he is also the teller of his own strange tale of revolution. While the change in govern-ment is reflected in the well-known changing of the tavern sign from King George to General George, for Rip the significance of the Revolution lies in his liberation from the "species of despotism under which he had long groaned and that was petticoat government." Thus, Rip's story, which he tells to all who arrive at Mr. Doolittle's inn, can be read as a revolutionary story—of how he threw off his former servitude by escaping to the woods to join a band of pioneering men. Yet even in the hands of this innocent old man, the tale remains, as Irving characterizes it, a dangerous story, for it is now "a common wish of all henpecked husbands in the neighborhood, when life hangs heavy on their hands, that they might have a quiet draft of Rip Van Winkle's flagon" (784).

Here is a problem facing those who would write of America's origins: the fear that revolutionary stories have the power to spark revolution anew. How does one tell a Revolutionary history without—to put the problem hyperbolically—starting a revolution? Irving's solution is clear: tell the story allegorically, and clearly mark the protagonist a member of a vanishing race. As Irving goes to some lengths to assure the reader, Rip's indigent and revolutionary stock will die out with the succeeding generations, as prophesied by the fact that his son "evinced a hereditary disposition to attend to anything else but his business." Rip's daughter, on the other hand, marries an industrious Yankee farmer and is promised a successful assimilation. Thus, Irving's Dutch go the way of all "vanishing Americans": fading away through sloth and fatalism or marrying successfully into post-Revolutionary America. In either case—whether maintaining their native traits or adopting those of their new nation—the Dutch community of Irving's tales vanishes and becomes part of the nation's nascent mythology, in precisely the same way that the Indians and Indian mythologies of the tale's postscript have themselves vanished in favor of the Dutch.

But the concerns facing American fiction writers in the 1820s were not limited to anxieties about Revolution. In the preface to his own tale of the Revolution, *The Spy*, James Fenimore Cooper catalogs the problems connected with writing an American novel, citing Charles Brockden Brown's *Edgar Huntly* as the primary example of the failures of the previous generation. Cooper's invocation of Brown at this juncture in his career, as James D. Wallace has argued, demonstrates his general anxieties about beginning a career as a novelist with Brown's recent failures as precedent.[2] But it is also significant that it is to *Huntly* that Cooper calls our attention, and to that novel's Indian adventures in particular. After itemizing the many reasons for writing American novels, Cooper confronts the many "contras," "removing all reasons in favor of the step" with the example of Brown:

> [When] the English critics not only desire, but invite works that give an account of American manners, we are sadly afraid they mean nothing but Indian manners; we are apprehensive that the same palate which can relish the cave scene in *Edgar Huntly*—because it contains an American, a savage, a wild cat, and a tomahawk, in a conjunction that never did, nor ever will occur—will revolt at descriptions here that portray patriotism as more than money making—or men and women without wool.[3]

I pause over this preface because it shows how the example of Brown hovers over the origins of Cooper's career, for reasons directly related to that earlier author's exploration of intersections between national and racial identity. As we saw in chapter 3, the cave scene that Cooper derides here was *Huntly*'s central scene: the point at which the alien and the Indian were collapsed into each other so that the hero might discover a uniquely American identity, an identity defined in terms of a difference that is simultaneously political and racial. Cooper's dismissal of the scene for containing a conjunction of elements—panther, Indian, American— that "never did . . . occur" is a very purposeful act of literary back- stabbing. In *Edgar Huntly*, the fact of racial difference was crucial to the definition of American identity as a racialized identity; in Cooper's novels we see an effort to remove the question of different races, to turn what seem to be conflicts between races into quarrels between American and European whites. In the Leatherstocking Tales, Cooper rewrites the equation of national identity that Brown inscribed in 1799 so as to prove that Americans, savages, and aliens really do not belong together at all.

But there is more in this paragraph worthy of attention. Cooper belit- tles the critical penchant for American novels that portray not only In- dians, but also men and women with "wool," that is, African Americans. To make certain his readers understand his meaning here, Cooper con- tinues, "We write this with all due deference to . . . Mr. Caesar Thomp- son," the name of the African American character in the novel.[4] What is odd here is the slippage in Cooper's tirade from Indians to blacks, a slippage that makes no sense in terms of the literary conventions against which he claims to be rebelling. For African Americans seldom appear in early American fiction, and almost never as central characters; and no- where does one find a discourse on either side of the Atlantic in which American stories are equated with stories about blacks. In fact, as Kay Seymour House wrote thirty years ago, only mildly overstating the case, "Cooper was the first American author to characterize repeatedly . . . the American Negro."[5] For Cooper, as we will see, this slippage from the Indian tale to the fact of African American men and women is a crucial one, one at the heart of his invention of the Vanishing American and Cooper's novels of the 1820s.

There is a critical tendency to assume that the Revolution itself serves as the model for all revolutionary moments in Cooper's novels, or that the Revolution was the only moment in the history of national identity with which Americans were concerned at the time.[6] Cooper himself was certainly preoccupied with the Revolution in the 1820s, as evidenced by *The Spy, The Pilot,* and the gothic *Lionel Lincoln,* and these works have been examined in great detail for what they have to say about the Revolution and the dangers and responsibilities of writing revolutionary tales.[7] But the historical specificity of his greatest works, the Leatherstocking Tales, has been largely evaporated by a critical tradition that insists on treating these novels as engaged in ahistorical myth-making, allegorizing the "progress" of man from primitive to civilized.[8] *The Pioneers* (1823) and *The Prairie* (1827) do not provide simple archetypes of a general history of civilization or allegories of the Revolution itself. Although they are set in historical moments not easily recognizable as transformative periods, these novels do indeed examine revolutionary moments in the nation's identity and demonstrate that the Revolution was not the only moment when radical change occurred.

As I have argued in the previous chapters, the decade from the mid-1790s through the debates surrounding the Louisiana Purchase was marked by national crises that brought about fundamental changes in the ways in which national identity was formulated. *The Pioneers* and *The Prairie* focus on these crises that first put into play a rhetoric of race that had by the 1820s proved both increasingly inseparable from and problematic to national identity. It is this national history that Cooper is rewriting in these tales, precisely at the time in which the nation begins to recognize the potential for a more cataclysmic factional crisis in its future.[9]

In the preceding chapters I described the formulation and dissemination of a rhetoric of an "American race," a way of defining and defending the national body as if it were a race. The 1820s mark the beginning of the end of this conception of national identity, as the rhetorics of "slavery" and "savagery," which had long served the cause of nation-building, were brought for the first time to confront the hard facts of slavery and the real dangers—physical and moral—slavery had brought upon the white nation. Writing in a decade that witnessed the first national crisis surrounding slavery and the earliest premonitions of disunion, Cooper devoted his early career to reimagining national origins so as to negotiate a reconciliation between New and Old World. If Brown came to depend on the threatening presence of the racial other for his conception of a national identity, then Cooper staged its disappearance in order to reimagine national identity reunited to its "natural" relation to the Old World. As race emerged as potentially divisive, we begin to see a desire to remove it as a crucial factor in American life. In the service of this project, Cooper turned—seemingly counterintuitively—to the Indian, "inventing" the "vanishing American" to bring about this reconciliation.

I argue that a subtext of Cooper's novels is a response to the Missouri Crisis and to the eruption onto the national scene of the repressed problem of black slavery. The beginning of Cooper's career is coincident with this crisis and its "Compromise," and his own insistence on telling stories of reconciliation over and over helps us see the problem he and many of his contemporaries faced: if national and racial identity were proving increasingly incompatible, they also proved to be troublingly indivisible. Jefferson's letter describing the shock that accompanied the Missouri Crisis—"like a fire bell in the night"—characterizes as well the more abstracted crisis of American race: "We have the wolf by the ears, and we can neither hold him, nor safely let him go."[10] Cooper's novels of this period narrate and negotiate scenes of conflict in an attempt to erase race from national identity—to solve the dilemma described by Jefferson by making the wolf disappear altogether.

We see Cooper's consideration of the question of black slavery most clearly in *The Prairie,* which explicitly considers issues of enslavement, union, and law against the backdrop of the Missouri Territory itself. But before we can begin to make sense of the fantasy Cooper indulges in this novel, we must turn to *The Pioneers* and the first appearance of Cooper's Vanishing American. Only in coming to understand the significance of this novel's resolution—in which the Indian turns out to be a British nobleman—does the logic of Cooper's Indian tales begin to reveal itself. It is precisely this dénouement that has been widely dismissed by the critics as unconvincing or forced, as has been the corresponding turn in *The Prairie,* in which the "slave" turns out to be a Spanish noblewoman. But these twists are the center of Cooper's project, not merely weak narrative devices. As Jane Tompkins rightly points out in assessing the "apologetic tone" of Cooper criticism, there is a long-standing tendency by his readers to "posit a distinction between the 'surface' and the 'depth' of Cooper's work, a distinction which enables them to discard as superficial what they find most embarrassing (often the entire plot) and to declare significant those features that satisfy their critical expectations" or to "substitute . . . a contrast between center and periphery, according to which the main plot (the apparent center) distracts attention from what is truly valuable in Cooper (the real center)."[11]

If precisely those aspects of the tales that have suffered this neglect are interrogated and the plot—the "apparent center"—taken seriously, the reasons for why what, in *The Pioneers*, looks like a conflict between white and Indian comes to be transformed into a conflict between American and British whites becomes understandable. More astounding still, this fantasy is taken to its extreme in *The Prairie* such that what looks like it should be a story about black slavery—a tale that has at its core the bringing of a slave into the Missouri Territory—is itself transformed into a conflict between whites.

II

Long regarded as Cooper's first great work, *The Pioneers; or the Sources of the Susquehanna* has received more than its share of biographical and psychological interpretation. Of all his works, this was the one to which he would be forced to return again and again, working to distance his own story from the seemingly autobiographical one recorded in the novel. As Stephen Railton puts it, "By locating its action in Cooperstown he prompts the reader to look for autobiographical elements in it, by using the word 'sources' in the title he encourages an analysis of the way in which it was influenced by the unconscious impulses and desires fixed in his childhood."[12] Yet, insisting in his title on a plurality of "sources," Cooper also invites the reader to search beyond the obvious pioneer (his father, William Cooper) and the river's geographical source (Cooperstown) for alternate sites of signification. This invitation, however, has not been widely accepted by many readers of the novel who have chosen to focus on the Oedipal drama it explores at the expense of the historical transformations with which, I argue, Cooper is more centrally concerned.

Many of the background details of the novel are notoriously grounded in Cooper's family history. Judge Cooper had purchased the lands that were to become Cooperstown from a bankrupt British loyalist, George Croghan, in much the same way that the novel's Judge Temple obtains his lands from the Tory Effinghams. Like Temple, William Cooper was a poor Pennsylvania Quaker scrambling his way up the young nation's economic ladders. But it is the differences between the two figures that have most interested the novel's readers. Whereas Temple is portrayed as supposedly holding the lands in trust for his loyalist friend, William Cooper had aggressively wrested the patent for his lands from William Franklin and the Croghan heirs through a protracted legal battle that carried on into the nineteenth century. Temple improved the lands in Effingham's absence that they might be restored to their rightful owner with interest, but the elder Cooper settled his town by selling off parcels during the trial in order to complicate any restitution to the original patent holders. By establishing a community of settlers with rights to the land, Judge Cooper protected his own interest and provided his claim with a base of supporters. Thus, the Croghan patent became Cooperstown. If, in *The Pioneers*, Judge Temple is wrongly condemned for greed and thievery, Judge Cooper was precisely the man Temple was suspected of being.

These differences in character and history between the novel's Judge Temple and the historical Judge Cooper, far from supporting Cooper's persistent claims for their distinction, have led to a series of ingenious interpretations of *The Pioneers* as an Oedipal drama in which the son of the pioneer exposes his father's legacy as a fraud, displacing him as the founding father of the community that bears his name. On one level, this is what happens, as the judge's claims to the land are negated in the end in favor of those of a young, well-bred Englishman. But there are reasons beyond the personal and the psychological why Cooper would have wanted to revisit and revise this scene of origins. As William P. Kelly reminds us, "The particular tensions Cooper experienced as the son of William Cooper . . . only intensified the broadly defined generational pressures of his age . . . the unresolvable longings of Cooper's contemporaries to be free from, and bound to, the past."[13] Cooper's revisionism is both specific to his own troubled relationship to his pioneering father and also part of a larger social project to revise and reconsider national origins in the 1820s in the wake of the passing of the Founding Fathers and the fiftieth anniversary of the Declaration of Independence. Thus, we do well to take seriously the 1832 introduction to *The Pioneers*, in which Cooper made a distinction between "how much of its contents is literal fact and how much is intended to represent a general picture."[14]

Although Cooper is borrowing heavily from family history, he is writing first and foremost a historical tale. In later years he expended much effort reiterating the claim that Templeton and Judge Temple were related "no more to Judge Cooper, of Cooperstown, than . . . to Judge Sanger of Sangersfield."[15] That the novel and novelist are struggling under the burden of generational guilt and competition is undeniable: having survived four elder brothers who died in the shadow of one of America's earliest success stories and having himself lost in a few short years almost everything his father left behind, Cooper had reasons to struggle with his father's legacy.[16] But it is important to recognize that Cooper had in mind something more ambitious than an act of literary parricide. As America's pioneer novelist, he is working to found an alternate genealogy with him-

self as the "founding father." He does so not—or not only—out of competition with the father, but because of the perception that his father, and his
father's generation, had founded the nation on quicksand. It becomes the
task of the novelist to rewrite the nation's identity upon a more solid
foundation.

In the opening chapter of the novel, Cooper describes Otsego County
as it appears to him in 1823, but this vision of an organic society ruled by
wholesome laws is not what we are presented with in the novel that
follows. There we see an aggregate of individual wills, of religious and
nationalistic parties, of ineffectual laws and repressive and incompetent
officers. The Templeton of the 1790s shows clearly how much remains to
be done. How this remarkable transformation took place turns out to be a
story not of the pioneering father, but of a mysterious stranger, in redface,
who came into Otsego County, claimed the lands on behalf of his "Indian
blood," and in so doing brought about the restoration of order to the
wilderness.

The plot of *The Pioneers* centers on questions of identity and inheritance, questions that are continually presented as if they were questions
about Indians, but that turn out, in the novel's resolution, to be something
else entirely. The novel opens with the well-known scene, a debate between two hunters over who is entitled to a deer: the owner of the land,
Judge Temple, or the judge's predecessor, the landless Natty Bumppo.
This scene has been read by many as offering the central terms for the
novel to follow: Natty's nature versus the judge's civilization. Indeed, the
debate seems to be setting up precisely these concerns as the judge carefully presents his legal claims to the kill while Natty lectures on the effects
of settlements on hunting populations. But at the point at which the two
contestants appear destined for a more serious conflict, Natty dismisses
the case out of hand as having been tried on false premises. The deer,
Natty reveals, belongs to neither of them, and the mysterious Oliver Edwards is summoned from behind a tree, where he has been stoically nurs-
ing the bullet wound that proves beyond question his claim to the deer.

This is indeed the novel in miniature, and what for the rest of the novel
is presented as a debate between Natty's radical republicanism and Temple's staunch Federalism is shown from the beginning to be a false fight—
false in precisely the same way as is the subsequent debate over Oliver's
racial identity. The novel is punctuated by a series of such debates in
which rhetoric is shown to obscure the "real" issues. The chief issue
driving the plot is land rights, but the real meaning of the dispute is buried
beneath the rhetoric of Indian claims, claims that the characters treat as if

they were the main concerns of the debate. The plot's effect is to prove these fights to be false by exposing as empty the rhetoric of race around which they so often revolve.

The novel's central plot line involves speculation as to Oliver's racial identity. From the start, hints are dropped that Natty's defense of Oliver's claims to the deer are somehow related to the hunter's familiar arguments on behalf of the rights of the Delaware to Temple's land. A curious combination of hauteur, rebelliousness, and high polish makes it difficult for the other characters to place Oliver. That he is so difficult to decipher proves troubling to the town of Templeton, which itself is a composite of many nations, traditions, and interests, with Temple's "castle"—a hodgepodge of architectural forms and styles—as emblem of the "composite order" (43) that defines the town. All "character and nations" make up the "motley . . . dramatis personae" of the novel (96). Even Natty and Chingachgook are described as composites, admixtures of two races: the habits of the hunter were "nearly assimilated to those of the savages," while "the habits of Mohegan, were a mixture of the civilized and savage states" (85).

Everyone in this community is so marked by this composite nature that at first the town finds it easy to accept Oliver himself as a "half-breed"—as, in a sense, one of their own. But he continues to inspire curiosity and suspicion because in manner he reveals himself to be too "pure," too refined. We are told he bears the blood of a "chief," but also that he is the purest Episcopalian in the state—the only one who has "arrived at manhood, in this country, without entering a dissenting meeting-house" (134). If he is indeed a composite like everyone else, he bears none of the marks of degradation that are supposed to determine the character of the half-breed. "When did you ever know a half-breed . . . who could bear civilization? for that matter, they are worse than the savages themselves" (204), the judge's officious cousin Richard Jones proclaims.

Although common rumor at first determines him to be Natty's son, Oliver and his friends—Natty and the Delaware chief, Chingachgook—work to encourage the perception that Oliver is actually of Indian descent, true heir to the land on which Templeton now stands. Oliver's Indian identity rests primarily on Chingachgook's pronouncement: "The 'Young Eagle' has the blood of a Delaware chief in his veins: it is red, and the stain it makes, can only be washed out with the blood of a Mingo." As Eric Cheyfitz writes, "If we take Chingachgook at his word, then along with the settlers of Templeton we will be surprised at the end of the novel when we discover that we have been reading Chingachgook . . . wrongly, according to the conventions of the white community of the pioneers. For within these conventions, which Chingachgook's speech appears to question by using the metaphoric literally, Oliver is not a literal Indian, but a figurative one."[17]

This account, in which the reader is surprised by race, is precisely the point Cooper wishes to make in this novel, although not for the reasons Cheyfitz would have it. For Cheyfitz, Oliver is metaphorized as an Indian "to mask the white man's dispossession of the red" (87). But nothing of the kind is being masked in this novel, as from the opening pages attention is being drawn to precisely this act of dispossession. Because this act of dispossession is such a nonissue for Cooper (and his presumed audience) he can deploy it as a plot device masking what is for him the more pressing burden of white guilt—the dispossession of the British. Oliver is set up as the novel's metaphorical Indian because Cooper is working out of the tradition described in previous chapters in which Indians came to serve as metaphors for disputes between white Americans. Here Cooper stages the Indian masquerade so that in the end all the tension that seems to have gathered around the issue of Temple's claims versus those of the Native American gives way before the civilizing claims of the Tory Effinghams.

Oliver plays his extended role in red face to claim his proper title to the soil, a title that for most of the novel is presented as if it rightfully belonged to the Delaware. In fact, a second reading of the novel with Cooper's redface game in mind reveals how much fun Cooper is having with the joke throughout, namely that no one in the novel really cares about Indian rights, even as everyone pays court to the idea that such rights merit consideration. It is part of the project of this novel to get all the characters to acknowledge these rights without anyone being required actually to turn anything over. Much of the plot revolves around the judge trying to coax Oliver into his home in recompense for his wound, and the ensuing debates between the members of Temple's family as to how "improvable" the supposed half-breed might be. Richard sees in Oliver "the natural reluctance of a half-breed to leave the savage state" (202), while the judge believes him to be highly amenable to the fruits of civilization. But as Oliver's role in the novel is finally to improve rather than be improved—to bring law rather than be subjected to it—there is a counterscene in which Oliver (still playing the redface game) and his companions speculate as to the improvability of Temple and his subjects as they plan for Oliver's ascension to his rightful place in society.

Before Oliver can claim this rightful place, however, he must first be accorded his proper place in his new family, which Elizabeth phrases by asking, "In what table is he to be placed?" (204). The members of the Temple family all have different notions of where he belongs in the household: Elizabeth would have him placed with the blacks; Richard places him farther up the social ladder with the white servants ("the natives hold the negroes in great contempt"); whereas the judge wishes him to be taken in as a member of the family. This debate over the proper ordering of household and society is for Cooper the proper subject of consideration, but here it is turned into farce because it takes seriously Oliver's redface game and the issues of race that are raised by his "Indian" claims.

For his own part, Oliver's expresses growing anxiety about his identity once he has accepted a place within Temple's family:

> Who could have foreseen this, a month since! I have consented to serve Marmaduke Temple! to be an inmate in the dwelling of the greatest enemy of my race! Yet what better could I do? The servitude cannot be long, and when the motive for submitting to it ceases to exist, I will shake it off, like the dust from my feet.
>
> . . . I will forget who I am. Cease to remember, old Mohegan, that I am the descendant of a Delaware chief, who once was master of these noble hills, these beautiful vales, and of this water, over which we tread. Yes, yes—I will become his bondsman—his slave! (206)

Oliver's metaphorical (and manic-depressive) Indian lament collapses effortlessly into the rhetoric of political slavery familiar to the period in which this narrative is set.

As we have seen, the first decade of the national period was marked by an intense factionalism that produced two competing fantasies: one of a future of "savagery" at the hands of the Republicans, the other of a fate of "slavery" at the hands of the Federalists. Cooper grounds his tale at this point in the nation's history; and Oliver's anxieties about being a "slave" to the Federalist landowner, and the anxieties on the part of Temple's family about their new intimate's potential "savagery," are all part of the elaborate play Cooper is staging. Replaying the factionalist conflict of the 1790s, Cooper has everyone talk about race when what is at stake has nothing to do with race at all.

On the one hand, *The Pioneers* works to expose the origins of the ways in which metaphors of race became linked to the language of partisan politics and national identity. But on the other hand, Cooper himself is able to use the slippages inherent in such racial language on behalf of the larger project coming into shape as he writes this novel. Oliver's ability to con-

THE PIONEERS.

Miss Temple did not, or could not move. Her hands were clasped in the attitude of prayer; but her eyes were still drawn to her terrible enemy.

London, Published by H. Colburn & R. Bentley, 1832.

Fig. 4. Robert Farrier, "The Panther Scene" (1832). (Courtesy of the American Antiquarian Society, Worcester, Massachusetts.) The frontispiece to Richard Bentley's Standard Novels edition of Cooper's *The Pioneers*; the scene was one of the most popular images from the novel.

ceive of himself as a "slave" refigures slavery as an "Indian" problem rather than an African American one; but this displacement is only preparation for the crucial one—not to be fully followed through until *The Prairie*—in which slavery will be transformed into a white American problem.

Once it is shown that all the talk of race has nothing to do with racial difference, the seeming opposition between Temple's Federalist elitism and Natty's republican lawlessness is itself exposed as a nonissue. Natty, far from the anarchic republican he appears to be for most of the novel, turns out to be the most feudal citizen of all. It is he who recognizes "the true blood" in Oliver, and it is he who vows to "support it, to the face of Judge Temple, or in any court in the country." Much of the novel focuses on Temple's struggle to bring law to the settlement and Natty's resistance to this law. But, in fact, there really is no resistance to law, on the part of Natty or anyone else, once the novel has resolved two very important changes in the racial makeup of the community. After Cooper restages Brown's panther scene—rescuing Elizabeth from the "savage" in the woods (see fig. 4)—the last of the Delawares, Chingachgook, dies, and his "grandson" is revealed to be the true British heir to the land. Natty finally recognizes the validity of the law, not on behalf of Temple's rule, but in the name of Oliver's inheritance.

The struggle between Indian and American is dissolved, as the Indian turns out to be a Briton and the American turns out to be dedicated to preserving rather than usurping his rights. Cooper's subplot (and the critical center for so many of his readers) of the conflict of forest freedom versus the sovereignty of the law turns out to be an attempt to romanticize a very unromantic, if not downright un-Americanist, plot. Temple's goal of imposing order on the pioneers is fulfilled not by reason or by force, but by the accession of a new leader, raised and educated in Britain, who establishes his rights to the land not through speculation and pioneering, but through ancient, immemorial claims. These claims prove by the end so strong and "natural" as to be all but equivalent to what they appeared to be throughout the novel: Indian claims.

Just as the opening scene resolved the dispute between the judge and Natty through the appearance of a mysterious third claimant whose presence nullified the arguments of both Federalist landlord and radical republican, so the removal of Oliver's Indian mask resolves a similar, albeit more violent, impasse. On the verge of a full-scale civil war, the proper order of things is at last restored. Major Effingham, the mad old Tory whom Natty and Chingachgook had served all along, is revealed to be the true owner of the Temple lands, and Oliver Edwards, the "half-breed," is revealed to be the major's grandson, heir to the disputed lands, lands granted to the major when he was made an honorary Delaware. "This, then, is thy Indian blood?" the judge asks. "'I have no other,' said Edwards, smiling." In sharing this final joke, all the novel's conflicts are resolved. The displaced British heir is united with the well-bred American woman, curing the hereditary madness of one family and legitimizing the dubious claims of the other. The Indian blood that flowed through Oliver's veins is now drained from the land once and for all, and Natty heads for the uncharted West where he will reappear in *The Prairie*, "the foremost in that band of Pioneers, who are opening the way for the march of the nation across the continent" (456).

Thus, one of American literature's first Vanishing Americans turns out to be a Briton in red face. But if the noble savage turns out to be no Indian at all, merely a highly educated young Briton, he is not the only one shown to have been claiming an identity that was not truly his. The whole town, in fact, is revealed to have been engaged in a kind of elaborate masquerade, playing at precisely what they had no business being. Judge Temple was ennobled a "duke" by his cousin Richard; Richard in turn was given the role of sheriff as a Christmas present from Temple. Playing at "squires," "major-domos," and "dukes," the rude ruling family of Templeton is shown to have been involved in their own costume party, claiming titles of gentility and nobility they were not entitled to. It is precisely this pretense on the part of Temple and his family that can be said to have precipitated Oliver's charade. Installing himself as the leader of Templeton, Oliver puts everything back in its proper order: the "savage" is shown to be noble, while the "nobles" are shown to be—if not savage—certainly not the proper rulers of a civilized society.

With the vanishing of Oliver's redface and the death of the "real" Indian, Chingachgook, society reorders itself, as if by magic.[18] The reordering of the "composite order" of Templeton extends even to the lower rungs of the society, as Mr. Le Quoi, who had fled the West Indies in the wake of the French Revolution to become a shopkeeper in Templeton, now "emerge[s] again from his obscurity into his proper level in society" (397). But of course, the Frenchman finds not simply his proper place in society, but his proper society as he leaves Templeton for the West Indies. Oliver's succession has indeed worked wonders on the town. Even the corrupt architect and self-interested officer of Temple's law, Hiram Doolittle, pulls up his stakes and heads west at the novel's conclusion as he discovers that "the composite style" that he had brought to the town was not "quite suitable to the growing wealth and intelligence of the settlement" (446). With Effingham's succession, the unifying roof is finally provided to the "composite order" of Templeton and Temple's "castle."

Richard Jones complains toward the end of the novel, "What the devil has gotten into you all? More things have happened within the last thirty-six hours than in the preceding six months." The conclusion of the novel has been criticized as an improbable and forced resolution; everything that had complicated the novel is domesticated for the young lovers, ordered to such an extent that it all becomes somewhat surrealistic. Donald A. Ringe, for example, rejects the ending: "The return of the lost heir to claim the inheritance . . . is obviously a stock element and may be dismissed as a concession to the popular taste of the time."[19] But there is nothing generic about the return of this "lost heir" for the national history that Cooper is here rewriting. Restoring the title of a Tory family in a novel set in the 1790s cannot be dismissed as conventional—as the conflation of European and Indian in *Edgar Huntly* made manifest. In that novel, as we saw, the Irishman was made equivalent to the Indian so that the American could claim his identity. Writing in the 1820s, Cooper can work to rewrite the unlikely "conjunctions" of Brown, so that now the Indian is made equivalent to the Briton only to restore ultimately to America its European inheritance. Nor are Cooper's efforts to return British breeding to republican America limited to this one novel. In other novels from this period he can be seen to be working toward precisely this resolution, erasing race and installing the displaced British heir in its place.[20]

In the 1820s, there was a marked shift in the literary Indian away from the captivity narrative and toward the romanticized Vanishing American, a shift commonly located in the publication of Heckewelder's Indian "history" and Cooper's "pioneer efforts" on behalf of the genre in 1823.[21] The usual explanation is that, inspired by Scott's Waverly novels, Americans turned toward the Indian in search of their own mythology, their own literary "monuments." But the transformation of the literary Indian from oppressive captor to vanishing martyr has as much to do with a shift in social and political anxieties as with the inordinate pressure of the example of Scott; and those anxieties have as much to do with the problem of black slavery as with the policies toward Native Americans, a relationship that has been closely studied.[22]

Historians of the Native American have demonstrated the inadequacy of a purely literary account of the rise of the Vanishing American myth, exposing the intersections between the romantic trope and the concerted policy of Removal that was begun in the 1820s. Brian W. Dippie usefully describes the interrelations between the literary and the historical Indian during this time:

> Extermination as policy was unthinkable, but a fully rounded version of the Vanishing American won public acceptance after 1814. By its logic, Indians were doomed to "utter extinction" because they belonged to "an inferior race of men. . . ." A popular convention, premised on moralistic judgment, had become natural law. Romantic poets, novelists, orators, and artists found the theme of a dying native race congenial, and added those sentimental touches to the concept that gave it wide appeal. Serious students of the Indian problem provided corroboration for the artistic construct as they analyzed the major causes hurrying the Indians to their graves. Opinion was virtually unanimous: "That they should become extinct is inevitable."[23]

Thus, the literary invention of the Vanishing American was connected in vital ways with the new pressures toward Removal and the discovery of a justification for such policy in the desire to "save" the Indian from devastating contact with civilization. We have come to see how a newly articulated national policy of extermination—beginning with General Andrew Jackson's genocidal war against the Seminoles in 1818 and John Quincy Adams's justificatory interpretation of this race war (a "savage and negro War," as Jackson called it)—went hand in hand with the romanticization of the exterminated.[24]

But if the literary invention of the Vanishing American cannot be separated from the social and political pressures of historical Indian policy, for many of the northern creators of the myth (Cooper being the most prominent and influential), the Vanishing American had less to do with historical Indians and fantasies of their preordained extinction than with a new set of anxieties about slavery and African Americans. In 1827 Cooper returned to the Vanishing American and Natty Bumppo for the third and what he thought was the last time, staging his disappearance in the Missouri Territory at the site of the nation's first great conflict over slavery.

III

At the time he began his Leatherstocking Tales, in 1821, Cooper was watching his state play a central role in a factionalist dispute that threatened to divide the nation in two. Today we would presume that the rhetoric of race that circulated around the Missouri Crisis had concrete reference to the facts of American slavery, but these facts quite surprised many at the time. Like the crises surrounding the Constitutional Convention and the Alien and Sedition Acts, this one too revolved around long-standing distrust between Federalists and Republicans and apocalyptic fantasies painted in racial metaphors. Thus, when New York Representative James Tallmadge proposed an amendment forbidding the extension of slavery into Missouri, both sides made recourse to the familiar rhetoric of the past decades.

As with earlier factionalist debates in the nation's history, the Missouri Crisis was built upon a series of imagined conspiracies. For northern leaders the fatal compromise of 1787, whereby slave representation was fixed at three-fifths of a person, was increasingly understood as a pact with the devil, not because it perpetuated the enslavement of African Americans, but because it bargained away the political rights of northern whites. Thus, after a long succession of Virginian presidents, northerners began to conceive of themselves as political slaves to the South.[25] They imagined a conspiracy to further erode their already diminished power, and the South's blocking of legislation aimed at giving protectionist relief to the northern states seemed to support this idea. As a New Jersey paper put it at the time, "It is undeniable . . . that the slave holding states to the Southward originate and uphold this pernicious system [of dependence on foreign manufactures], which must ere long reduce us (unless corrected) to a state more wretched than colonial servitude."[26]

Southerners, on the other hand, responded to the amendment as a conspiracy against their constitutional rights, and like their northern counterparts, they took refuge in the by-now routine rhetoric of political slavery and forebodings of racial apocalypse. Jefferson, for example, in a letter to his former ally Albert Gallatin, argued that if the North succeeded in limiting the expansion of slavery, it would only be a matter of time before they set all slaves free, "in which case all the whites South of the Patomak and Ohio must evacuate their States; and most fortunate those who can do it first."[27]

The Missouri delegation responded to the House's narrow approval of the amendment by threatening disunion, and over the next two years threats of civil war were commonplace.[28] Both sides responded to the political debate by once again making recourse to the rhetoric of political slavery or the fantasies of political savagery: both conceived of themselves as the minority fighting for their representation, both imagined night-marish scenes of disinheritance and violence in the event of failure for their side.

It would be wrong to ascribe entirely political and cynical motives to the players in the debate. Serious abolitionist efforts were behind, if not the initial political maneuverings in the House, then certainly the lobby-ing and pamphlet war that followed. But throughout the crisis the rhetoric of political slavery on the part of both the North and the South, and not the confrontation of the institution of slavery, dominated the debates. The rhetoric of the "equality of rights" that the northerners trumpeted through Congress had little to do with the rights of African Americans, and everything to do with the rights of northern whites. As the Federalist veteran, Rufus King, made the case, "The equality of rights . . . is a vital principle in our theory of government . . . ; the departure from this princi-ple in the disproportionate power and influence, allowed to the slave holding states, was a necessary sacrifice to the establishment of the consti-tution. The effect of this concession has been obvious in the preponder-ance which it has given the slave holding states, over the other states."[29]

William Hillhouse staged the northern case elaborately in a satirical pamphlet, *Pocahontas: A Proclamation* (1820), a pretended call—not un-like that of Brown's fictional French minister in 1803—to the people of the South to rise and defend their rights and privileges, privileges con-ferred by the princess Pocahontas. Here are equated the expansion of slavery and the South's "domination" of the North, as the pamphlet's fictional southerner insists that the North be made to recognize the natu-ral order of the "body politic," which "depends on the subordination of the inferior members to the head"—a model "most happily illustrated by the subjection of the slave to his master."[30] The northern states are chas-tised for their "rebelliousness" and warned that Virginia will brook no further challenges to its "imperial claims" (9). The pamphlet ends by describing in apocalyptic terms the northern fantasy of the ultimate ends of the expansion of slavery:

> Then shall the eyes of the people of the slave holding states be con-stantly gratified with the sight of children torn from their parents, and parent from their children, and wives and husbands from each other . . . which sights, by habit, and their constant repetition, are become neces-sary to their gratification and happiness, even as the sight of the tor-tures inflicted on captives, who were to be sacrificed at their council

fires, and their dances of death, were necessary for the savage gratifica-
tion of the subjects of our red progenitor, and of his contemporaries,
and predecessors. (13)

Here the metaphor of southern slavery is used to describe both the
historical enslavement of African Americans and the North's perception
of its own growing political servitude to the South. The iron chains of
slavery are made equivalent, even rhetorically subordinate, to the phan-
tasmic chains of political domination. In affixing "the royal name of Pocahontas" to the pamphlet, Hillhouse slyly suggests that the inheritance the
South has "received" from the Indian lies not in Pocahontas's royalty but
in the Indian's "savagery."

There is, of course, nothing new in this rhetoric—or in the way it
collapses historical slavery with rhetorical slavery and metaphorical savagery—and with only a little editing the pamphlet could have been made
to serve Federalist agendas of the previous decades, whether directed
against Antifederalists, aliens, Illuminati, or Jeffersonians in general. In
all previous paper wars, the recourse to charges of "savagery" and fantasies of "slavery" were not only a familiar but, as I have argued, an
essential element of the debate over national identity. What has changed
here, however, is that the terms of the opposition are no longer Federalist
and Republican, but regional. Instead of being used to forge a national
identity, racial metaphors now became the tools of regional identifica-
tions. That the North imagines itself in these terms is evidenced in an
appeal by Robert Walsh on behalf of his newly coined term "The Universal Yankee Nation": "The Virginia race have unhesitatingly proclaimed
and invariably pursued the maxim of being 'true to themselves'—the race
of New England cannot be blamed for imitating their example."[31] In
Timothy Dwight's *Travels in New England and New York* (1821) there is
an underlying concern with the Yankee as a "race" particular to that
region, one whose qualities, "exhibited by their descendants of every
generation," needed to be defended against the onslaught of immigration
and internal migration.[32]

Thus, political and geographical distinctions between North and South
came to be translated into the familiar rhetoric of race. Once again the
rhetoric was not first and foremost a defense of the men and women
subjected to slavery, but, to focus on the North, a defense of the white
northerners made into "slaves" at the hands of the slave-holding states.
Thus, growing regional divisions between North and South prompted

metaphors of race to describe distinctions that were regional, political, economic—anything but racial.[33]

What remains unclear is why passions became so heated upon the introduction of a bill expected to excite little interest; or, from our position of hindsight, why anyone thought the issue of the expansion of slavery would not explode the Era of Good Feelings. What makes the scene so important to the larger narrative here is that it offers a telling vision of the extent of the national repression of the real horrors of African American slavery that lay behind the rhetoric of race. In the desperate moves that followed on both sides to work out a compromise, we see the attempt to put under the rug once again the monster—Jefferson's "wolf"—that had been released. It was almost as if the lawmakers of the North, living in increasing isolation from the facts of slavery, were unprepared for the fact that their amendment would spark a debate about real slavery. With the unleashing of the abolitionist lobby and the resulting threats of disunion, Congress began looking for a way to make the whole issue of African American slavery vanish, like Indians.

This fantasy lies in important ways behind Cooper's myth of the Vanishing American. In *Notions of the Americans* (1828), written in Paris while he was completing *The Prairie*, the third of his Leatherstocking Tales, Cooper considers at length the meaning of the Missouri Crisis and the dispute over slavery it had inaugurated. The book is devoted in large measure to disproving the works of European travelers to the United States, such as Henry Bradshaw Fearon and Frances Wright, writers who had written about America in terms Cooper found either too critical or too idealistic. Writing as an Englishman traveling through the States, Cooper covers the traditional topics of the American travelogue, from the qualities of American women to the details of an election. Since the problem of slavery looms large in most British accounts of America, Cooper's narrator first attempts to erase the issue of slavery out of hand by insisting on its fundamental irrelevance to his subject, which is "Americans": "It is manifestly unsafe to found any arguments concerning the political institutions of this Country on the existence of Slavery, since the Slaves have no more to do with Government than inanimate objects."[34] But toward the second half of the book, as he approaches the South, the narrator is forced to consider the problem of slavery, and it is here that Cooper performs the Vanishing Act that gives new meaning to the central "myths" of his Tales.

After first executing complicated arithmetic whereby he attempts to show that, far from presenting a growing threat to white Americans, blacks themselves are quite literally vanishing, the narrator concludes with this observation: "One must remember how few marriages take place among these people, their moral condition, their vagrant habits, their exposure, their dirt, and all the accumulated misfortunes of their race."[35] If the rhetoric here sounds familiar, it should, for it is the rhetoric of the Vanishing American—a vision of the American Indian that Cooper himself had popularized. But here the race that is vanishing is not the Indian (who for Cooper had long since vanished), but blacks.[36] "Freedom," the narrator continues, "is not favorable to the continuation of the blacks," thus "nothing remained, but to give them all their freedom, in order to render the race extinct. . . . Blacks, like the aborigines, gradually disappear, before the superior moral and physical influence of the whites."[37]

In making explicit the equation between the "fact" of the Indians' "disappearance" and a projection of a similar fate for American blacks, Cooper offers new meaning to his myth of the Vanishing American. His is a white America, one in which blacks follow the Indians, bowing before the overpowering force of white civilization and breeding, a fact "proved" by the fictional experiences of his British narrator: "Nor is a traveller who has witnessed the immense number of white-headed and chubby little urchins he sees all over the Country at all disposed to suspect [this conclusion]" (243).

If blacks are a vanishing race, Cooper's narrator goes on to argue, then the whole Missouri Crisis becomes a moot issue. The compromise itself becomes proof of the genius of the government for recognizing the fact that slavery is in truth a nonissue and working to preserve union at all costs (440). Having made free blacks and the Missouri Crisis disappear, Cooper then sets out to make the institution of slavery vanish from the scene as well. His description of the South is devoted to a discussion of slavery and a critique of those who would make an issue out of race. Again, he juggles a complicated series of figures to demonstrate that even though the slave population appears to be growing, natural forces are actually at work to rid the nation of slavery:

The danger of slavery, so far as it is connected with numbers, has its own cure. . . . I think, that the free black population . . . does not increase, or at least not materially; and that the proportion between the white and the blacks is steadily growing in favor of the former; that in the future it will even grow faster; that emigration, the Navy, Commerce, and unsettled habits will tend to repress the increase of the blacks and to consume their numbers; and that the time of the inter-mingling of the races to any great extent is still remote. (477, 481)

Left to deal with the "intimate" issue of slavery with "discretion," the slave states will begin the process of emancipation at which time natural forces in the nation will begin to do their work, bringing about the even-tual disappearance of the former slaves through environment, coloniza-tion, and what Cooper terms "black nature."

It is an unusual argument, to say the least, as so much of the rhetoric on both sides of the slavery debate was focused on the perception that the black population was increasing and fantasies of an army of blacks march-ing on the capital (as Adams, for instance, offers in this chapter's epi-graph).[38] But Cooper's blacks go the way of all Vanishing Americans: "As a rule the red man disappears before the superior moral and physical influ-ence of the White, just as I believe the black man will eventually do the same thing, unless he shall seek shelter in some other region."[39] Thus, in the Leatherstocking Tales, which spectacularized the myth of the Vanish-ing American, we might now recognize a new meaning to the myth: a fantasy of the vanishing not only of Native Americans but of black Ameri-cans as well. *The Prairie*, I argue, is founded on the logic made explicit in *Notions of the Americans*, in which the myth of the Vanishing American brings about the vanishing of slavery, the state of Missouri, and the very fact of racial difference altogether.[40]

IV

About a third of the way through *The Prairie*, we are introduced to two of the novel's main characters: Hard-Heart, the noble savage, and Mid-dleton, the representative American hero. In the way each is introduced, we begin to see what is at stake for Cooper in the writing of the third of the Leatherstocking Tales in 1827. We are first introduced to the Pawnee chief as a complex conglomeration of racial types, as he is discovered hiding in a thicket: "It is difficult to describe the shape or colors of this extraordinary substance, except to say in general terms that it was nearly spherical and exhibited all the hues of the rainbow intermingled, without reference to harmony and without any ostensible design. The predomi-nant hues were a black and a bright vermillion. With these, however, the several tints of white, yellow, and crimson, were strangely and wildly blended."[41] Hard-Heart, the novel's noble savage, wears his "pie-bald" mask so as to vanish from the white man's eye.

In a structurally similar scene, we are introduced to Middleton, the novel's noble American. Middleton too is a racial cross-dresser, like Oliver before him, and he is introduced to the reader as overburdened with the masks that had bedecked Cooper's heros of the 1820s. But Middleton's cross-dressing never threatens to obscure, as it does so powerfully and anxiously for Natty, his fundamental racial identity:

> His body was enveloped in a hunting shirt, of dark green, trimmed with the yellow fringes and ornaments that were sometimes seen among the border-troops of the Confederacy. Beneath this, however, were visible the collar and lapels of a jacket, similar in colour and cloth to the cap. His lower limbs were protected by buckskin leggings, and his feet, by the ordinary Indian moccasins. A richly ornamented, and exceedingly dangerous, straight dirk was stuck in a sash of red-silk, net-work; another girdle, or rather belt, of uncolored leather, contained a pair of the smallest sized pistols, . . . and across his shoulder was thrown a short, heavy, military rifle; its horn and pouch occupying the usual places, beneath his arms. At his back he bore, a knapsack, marked by the well known initials [of] . . . the Government of the United States. (108)

If Hard-Heart wears many colors on his skin so as to vanish into the landscape, Middleton wears the costumes of all of Cooper's earlier novels —costumes previously worn in attempts to hide the hero's true identity— so as to make himself profoundly (if not ridiculously) visible. Here we have the redface and buckskins of the *Pioneers,* the dirk and sash of Wilder's pirate costume in *Red Rover,* the kerchief of Harper/Washington in *The Spy,* and the coat of John Paul Jones in *The Pilot.* Middleton comes to the desert wearing all the costumes by which the novels' previous heroes had hid their true identity, and—much as we might be prepared by Cooper's own precedent to find him to be other than he seems—he turns out to be truly who he first appears to be: an American who need not hide his true identity. Middleton's elaborate wardrobe defines him as the man who can wear many hats at once. His character is entirely defined by his ability to absorb all these identities (as indeed, the novel's conclusion promises, he shall absorb Inez's Spanish Catholicism as well). Cooper is performing an elaborate display of his own artifice with the character of Middleton, exposing his props to the audience as if to announce that they are no longer needed.

The novel works to explain how Middleton can serve to embody all of these competing identities. Middleton and his family, we are told, have literally absorbed all the conflicting characters and identities of the first two tales and made them cohere into one ruling family. Grandson of the blundering British commander, Duncan Heyward, in *The Last of the Mohicans*, Middleton bears as his middle name the identity of American literature's most famous Vanishing American: Uncas. Others in the family, he tells his new friends, are named after Natty. Middleton absorbs the energies that Cooper's novels had released, energies that the author found to be in excess of his own abilities to reel them in. The Vanishing American and the pioneer are absorbed into the Middleton line and brought back to the Senate so that Middleton will reclaim his rightful place in society, here as a leader of the nation. This act of absorption seems almost effortless. But more than simply the Indian and the Pioneer must be made to vanish if such a resolution is to come about. Other excesses, the excesses of slavery and the Missouri Crisis in particular, remain unresolved, unvanished. It is Cooper's aim, in this novel, to perform the ultimate act of vanishing.

The Prairie is a difficult novel for several reasons, justly criticized for its unrealistic portrayal of the West, its absurd plot devices (not the least being the convergence of the novel's actors in the prairie in the first place), and its somewhat cardboard characters. But although it was the least popular of the tales because it lacked the qualities for which the others were admired, *The Prairie* was Cooper's personal favorite. For him, it was the culmination of his exploration of the American pioneer experience. The first two tales dealt with the New York woods and history that Cooper knew so well; the third deals with the relatively unexplored territory of the Purchase, which Cooper did not know at all, save through written accounts. The first question to be asked, then, is why Cooper takes the pioneer from the New York forests to the Missouri Territory?

One easy answer would be that in light of growing interest in the territory in the 1820s, Cooper saw the need to assimilate this vast region into his myth. As James P. Elliott suggests, *The Prairie* was in large measure a response "to the ever-increasing public interest in Jefferson's Louisiana Purchase."[42] But such an answer does not account sufficiently for the ways in which Cooper deploys the territory here. The year after publishing *The Prairie*, Cooper wrote in *Notions*: "The purchase of Louisiana, was the greatest masterstroke of policy that has been done in our times. All the wars, and conquests, and cessions of Europe for the last hundred years, sink into insignificance, compared with the political consequences that are dependent on this increase of territory."[43]

Cooper imagined the territory as bringing to an end the factionalism and instability of the nation's early history and inaugurating a new period of national consensus. In a novel set in the first year of the possession of the territory, and specifically in the part of the territory that would become the focus of the Missouri Crisis, Cooper devotes the earliest pages to fixing his historical background quite precisely. The language of the opening pages could have come right out of one of the political pamphlets generated by the debates of 1803–4 to which Cooper makes explicit reference:

> Much was said and written, at the time, concerning the policy of adding the vast regions of Louisiaı.a, to the already immense, and but half-tenanted territories of the United-States. As the warmth of the controversy . . . subsided, and party considerations gave place to more liberal views, the wisdom of the measure began to be generally conceded. . . . It gave us the sole command of the great thoroughfare of the interior, and placed the countless tribes of savages, who lay along our borders, entirely within our controul; it reconciled conflicting rights, and quieted national distrusts. (9)

Critics have chosen for the most part to ignore the specificity of Cooper's scene, reading the setting as a surreal tabula rasa on which the novelist engages in a dissection of society, a reading encouraged by Cooper's unconvincing and vague rendering of the landscape. But to the degree that such readings fail sufficiently to account for the reasons why Cooper sets such an experiment in the site of the Missouri Compromise and at the time of the nation's previous great factional battle, they fail to understand what was at stake for Cooper as he wrote what he thought would be the final Leatherstocking Tale. What is immediately striking about this tale is not its surreal landscape but its surreal history—its attempt to rewrite the history of the Purchase as a story of nonsettlement.

Cooper's understanding of the value of the region is much akin to that of the early colonizationist St. George Tucker who, writing during the heat of the debates surrounding the Purchase, saw the region as a vast barrier that would provide both an impermeable border to the nation and a place to which all those who were not Americans could be removed. With the purchase, Tucker argued in his 1804 pamphlet, the union was

Fig. 5. George Freeman, "Portrait of Elizabeth Cooper" (1816). (Courtesy of the New York State Historical Association, Cooperstown, New York.) Cooper's romancing of Caesar Thompson and the "race of blacks" to which he belonged might have its origins in Joseph Stewart, who served the family as slave and servant for over twenty years. Here he is portrayed in a portrait of the author's mother. For Cooper's father, the servant functioned in the painting, like the foliage in the background, to highlight the centrality of Mrs. Cooper and to symbolize his own "taming" of the environment. For the son, even the marginal presence of the African American in the portrait is potentially threatening.

preserved, its boundaries protected, and its foreign enemies expelled. But even more significantly, Tucker continued,

> we now shall have it in our power to propose to the Indian nations now settled within the United States an exchange of lands beyond the Mississippi, for those which they now hold; by this means we shall be able to dispose of all the lands on this side of the Mississippi to those who will cultivate them, who are already civilized, who speak the same language with us, and who will be ready and willing to harmonize and become one people with us, if they be not so already.[44]

Further, he proposed in relation to the new Purchase a "Utopian idea," one that would become increasingly engaging to Cooper and his generation: "The southern parts of Louisiana bordering upon the gulph of Mexico lie under a climate more favourable for the African constitution than any part of the United States. Thither, . . . we may colonize those unhappy people, whom our ancestors have brought in chains from their native country, and we continue to hold in bondage" (25).

As Cooper's novel also would seem to argue after the fact, Tucker preached against the settlement of Louisiana, seeing the territory as a barrier and a place of exile. That Tucker's pamphlet of 1804 mirrors in so many ways the logic of Cooper's novel set in 1804 is significant, for in their respective consideration of the territory—one as an early advocate for colonization, the other in the aftermath of the Missouri Crisis—both indulge in fantasies of the territory as a place to colonize those who are not and never will be Americans.

There are, of course, no African American characters in *The Prairie.* If it is Cooper's fantasy that blacks, like Indians, will vanish from the nation, he has certainly been careful to make them vanish from his novels in the later 1820s. Where *The Spy* figured a black character in a prominent role, and *The Pioneers* portrayed a slave for racist comic effect, in the novels to follow there is scarcely any representation of African American slavery (see fig. 5).[45] As Cooper wrote in 1821 of his slave character in *The Spy*:

> The race of blacks of which Caesar was a favorable specimen is becoming very rare. The old family servant, who, born and reared in the dwelling of his master, identified himself with the welfare of those whom it was his lot to serve, is giving place in every direction to that vagrant class which has sprung up within the last thirty years, and whose members roam through the country unfettered by principles, or uninfluenced by attachments.[46]

Cooper's romancing of this noble slave and his "vanishing" is, not coincidentally, similar to his romance of the noble savage, whom he evaporates in a similar inescapable logic: "The ordinary manner of the disappearance of the Indian is by a removal deeper into the forest. Still, many linger near the graves of their fathers. . . . The fate of the latter is inevitable; they become victims to the abuses of civilization without ever attaining to any of its moral elevation."[47] Indians and blacks either retain their nobility by vanishing or remain and degenerate. In the former case they are no longer present to be Americans, in the latter they are no longer qualified to be Americans.

Although no African American characters appear in *The Prairie,* slavery does, embodied in the person of Inez, a Spanish noblewomen kidnapped from her American husband, and slave traders are represented by her kidnappers, "dealer[s] in black flesh" who have now "drove the trade into white families" (92). Fantasies about the slave trade entering "white families" were familiar to the political rhetoric of the Missouri debates. The New York Federalist Rufus King, for example, in arguing before the Senate the case for the Missouri amendment, attempted to prove that "five free persons in Virginia, have as much power in the choice of representatives to congress . . . as seven free persons in any other states in which slavery does not exist"—arguing that the Compromise of 1787 instituted tyranny, not for defining an African American as three-fifths a human being, but for making northern whites five-sevenths of a man.[48] This calculation points out something easily missed in the history of the Missouri Crisis: the way in which many in the North sought to rewrite slavery as an injustice to whites.

Thus, that *The Prairie*'s "slave" turns out to be a Spanish noblewoman is crucial to Cooper's project of playing out another Missouri Crisis, in which various allegiances are made, battles fought, and debates over the meaning of the law and race are staged so that his notion of the American freed from race can finally be realized. *The Prairie,* chronologically the last of the tales, serves for Cooper as a starting over, an imagining of the crisis of American race in its barest elements. He brings four groups into the prairie: Middleton's party (the natural leaders of the nation), Ishmael Bush's clan (the slave traders, and the lawless underclass), the Sioux (the corrupt Indians), and the Pawnees (the noble savages). The drama that takes place on the neutral ground of the prairie is an experiment that works to reconstruct the unsettled national identity of post-Revolutionary America in order finally to answer the question: What is an American?

If *The Pioneers* served for Cooper as a critique of the failures of his father's generation to found a stable national identity, here Cooper's concern is to bring to rest finally the impulse unleashed in the person of Natty Bumppo. It is Natty, the idealized pioneer, who puts a halt to the coarser pioneers who would follow in his footsteps. Where he had been created in the first tale as a half-comic social crank, in this novel he becomes mythic, making his first appearance literally standing between Ishmael and the territory to which he would bring "slavery":

The sun had fallen below the crest of the nearest wave of the Prairie, leaving the usual rich and glowing train on its track. In the centre of this flood of fiery light a human form appeared, drawn against the gilded background, as distinctly, and seemingly as palpable, as though it would come within the grasp of any extended hand. The figure was colossal; the attitude musing and melancholy, and the situation directly in the route of the travellers. (14–15)

Like the opening scene in *The Pioneers*, this scene defines the action of the novel to follow, as Natty succeeds in getting Ishmael in the end to return to his rightful place on the lower rungs of society and to give up voluntarily his claims to his slave.

Much of the novel's action revolves around the various allegiances between the four main groups that converge on the prairie, and a series of debates about law, union, and race. The main point of contention between the contestants is whether Natty's party has the right forcibly to liberate Ishmael's captive, or whether the oaths that bind Inez to her servitude must be respected. After being robbed early in the novel by the rapacious Sioux, Ishmael takes his clan and his remaining property—Inez included—and establishes a rude "fortress." Those who would free the enslaved Inez must then decide on the best policy to achieve these aims. The problem proves no easy moral issue.

Ishmael has bound to him almost everyone concerned in a series of oaths and debts. In addition to the enslaved Inez, Ishmael also holds dominion over Ellen Wade, a distant cousin, whose suitor, Paul Hover, has followed from Kentucky. Ellen has served unwillingly as caretaker of Inez throughout the difficult voyage into the "desert," but as odious as she finds her connection to Ishmael's clan she will not renounce the oaths she made to defend his "property." Doctor Battius, a scientist who has come to the prairie in search of new discoveries, has himself "entered into a compactum or agreement" with Ishmael for safe passage. Even Inez is reluctant to accept freedom, being herself sworn not to escape.

These oaths make matters very difficult for the would-be liberators. The rash Paul advocates force and dismisses out of hand all agreements made with Ishmael, and his violence eventually persuades his more reasoning companions. Natty alone chooses to abstain from a forceful removal of Ishmael's "property." While Ishmael and his clan are hunting, the "fortress" is stormed, but here Paul and the others encounter unexpected resistance in Ellen who stands ready to defend it. "I have sworn a solemn oath," she insists. Although the doctor tries to nullify her oath with the claim that "a compactum which is entered into, through ignorance or in duress, is null in the sight of all good moralists," Ellen rejects his reasoning: "We are both solemnly, terribly sworn" (150–51).

As Cooper had said of the Missouri Crisis, the allegiances that bound the North to defend the South's rights as slave owners could not be taken back, for they were allegiances sealed by the most serious oath of all, the Constitution. Just as Ellen cannot "justify myself for even being neutral, while you attempt to invade the dwelling of my uncle, in this hostile manner," so too does Cooper in *Notions* describe the necessity of defending the rights of the South to make their own determinations regarding slavery. The question central to this novel is: When can unions be broken? Ellen has reluctantly but irrevocably entered into a union to defend slavery; can she morally be asked to break her oath? Natty—and the novel— says no: "A Promise is a promise, and not to be thrown aside and forgotten, like the hoofs and horns of a buffaloe" (151).

Shortly after Inez's violent liberation, a debate begins between Natty and the doctor over the meaning of race. The doctor, a disciple of Buffon, preaches the standard monogenist position that had remained the dominant line of racial science since Samuel Stanhope Smith's defense of 1787: "A homo, is certainly a homo . . . so far as the animal functions extend there are the connecting links of harmony, order, conformity, and design, between the whole genus; but there the resemblance ends. Man may be degraded to the very margin of the line which separates him from the brute, by ignorance; or he may be elevated to a communion with the Great Master Spirit of All by knowledge" (180). Like Buffon and Smith, Battius believes that all distinctions between races arise from cultural and environmental differences, and he imagines the possibility of a return to the ideal of the original parents from which modern man in all his varieties has degenerated. Natty terms the doctor's reasoning as "neither more nor less than mortal wickedness" (181), for arguing that man can change his inborn nature, even so far as "to become the Master of all learning, and consequently equal to the great moving principle." Natty proves to be a staunch believer in polygenism: the theory, hinted at by Jefferson in his *Notes*, that the races constitute separate species.

As a test of the doctor's system of classification, Natty sends him into a thicket to report what he finds. The doctor reappears with a startling discovery: "It is a basilisk! . . . An animal of the *order* serpens. . . . Never before have I witnessed such an utter confusion of [nature's] Laws, or a specimen that so completely bids defiance to the distinctions of *Class* and

Genera" (182). Natty has led the doctor to the "snake" in the garden who resists his methods of classification, a serpent who turns out to be an Indian in disguise. The debate between the doctor's reason and Natty's "instinct" is decided in favor of the latter. Natty knew he had sensed an Indian, and though the doctor defines instinct as "an inferior gradation of reason," Natty's racial instincts prove consistently able to tell white man from red, where the doctor cannot even tell the Indian from the snake.

This Indian, the Pawnee chief Hard-Heart, is the novel's noble savage, noble in large measure because he is continually trying to disappear into the landscape, in spite of the whites who keep interrupting his vanishing. His appearance throws the doctor's schema into disarray: "It is . . . a violent race; and one that it is difficult to define or class within the usual boundaries of definitions" (185). Hard-Heart provokes a debate over racial origins between Natty and the doctor, the doctor maintaining his belief "that colour is the fruit of climate and condition and not a regulation of nature" (191), but Natty dismissing such racial theory as "follies and idle conceits."

The doctor finally suggests that the question be settled by Hard-Heart himself: "he is of a reddish tint, himself, and his opinion may be said to make us masters of the two sides of the disputed point." Natty puts the question to the chief: "What does my brother think? all whom he sees here have white skins, but the Pawnee warriors are red, does he believe that man changes with the season, and that the son is not like his fathers?" (191), to which the chief responds imposingly: "The Wahcondah . . . fashioned his children with care and thought. What he has thus made never alters!" (191). Thus, Cooper's noble savage himself weighs in on the side of polygenism. The Vanishing American declares the races to be separate species after all and devotes the rest of the novel to defending the distinctions that justify his own extinction.

Cooper is here giving voice to a growing perception in European and American racial science; at the time he was writing, scientific racism was being born in the early work of racial theorists who would "prove" Hard-Heart correct. For example, Charles Caldwell, long an outspoken critic of Samuel Stanhope Smith and monogenism, was at this time studying the heads of contemporary Native Americans and comparing them to ancient Indian skulls, arriving at the conclusion that "when the wolf, the buffalo and the panther shall have been completely domesticated . . . then, and not before, may we expect to see the *full-blooded* Indian civilized, like the white man."[49] The results of his lifelong efforts on behalf of polygenism were published shortly thereafter in his *Thoughts on the Original Unity of the Human Race* (1830) in which he claimed to provide the proof, focusing on the history of African Americans in the United States, that the inherent nature (and worth) of a race is fixed, unaffected by environmental conditions: "It is nearly two centuries since the Africans were first introduced into our own country. The eighth generation from the original stock is now living, and the race is unchanged."[50]

If the races are indeed separate species, then the problem of reconciling racial hierarchy with republican principles is made moot. Indeed, the novel's remaining adventures serve to hammer home these answers to the debates surrounding race, union, and slavery that Cooper has staged in the desert. The succeeding drama focuses on the desire of the degenerate chief of the Sioux, Mahtoree, to make Inez his wife. To prevent such a fatal "admixture of the varieties of *species*" (221), Hard-Heart leagues with Natty and his party against the Sioux and Ishmael's "tribe." The noble chief battles the degenerate chief to preserve racial categories, and Hard-Heart's resistance to admixture even goes so far as to make him unable to accept Natty's offer of adoption when the Sioux are about to put him to death. At the novel's conclusion, when Inez is in Hard-Heart's power and Middleton fears the worst, the noble savage will not contemplate the sin of miscegenation for which Mahtoree had been condemned to death.

It is this issue of racial mixture that finally breaks down the alliance between the Sioux and Ishmael: Ishmael's claims to Inez are repulsed, and he is offered a Sioux woman in her place. Ishmael's wife does not take kindly to the compromise, chastising her husband for even listening to such an offer: "Would ye disgrace colour, and family, and nation, by mixing white blood with red, and would ye be the parent of a race of mules?" (298).

This harangue offers a potential missing link in Cooper's replaying of the Missouri Crisis and his reinvention of the disputed territory as a barren abyss into which the racial other can finally be made to disappear. For it is in the figure of the doctor's mule, Assinus, that we can perhaps locate Cooper's stand-in for the African American in this novel. Assinus occupies precisely the same place structurally as Agamemnon in *The Pioneers* or Caesar in *The Spy*: he is the devoted, cowardly, and comical servant. The identification of a mixed-race child with the mule points back toward Cooper's own racial theories about the infertility of blacks. Commonly used in the latter part of the nineteenth century to refer to the supposed infertility of mulattoes, Cooper would seem here to invoke the mule as a symbol of the vanishing black who will accompany the Indian into obscurity.[51]

With the destruction of the Sioux, the novel now must send back to the United States all who rightfully belong there, while leaving in the desert those who never will be Americans. But first there remains the settling of the "legal" issue that had turned the whites against one another in the first place. Ishmael brings Natty's party to "trial," charging them with the loss of his human "property" and charging Natty in particular with the death of his son. The defendants react to the charges with outrage, "unexpectedly required to answer for conduct, which, in their simplicity, they had deemed so meritorious" (346). But Ishmael undermines the moral high ground of the liberators by charging them with crimes against their oaths and compacts, only to absolve them voluntarily of their punishment. Cooper certainly does not harbor any respect for his character; Ishmael is everything his creator despised: crude, lawless, and swarthy. Nor does he approve of Ishmael's bringing "slavery" into the Missouri Territory. The point here, as it was explicitly spelled out in *Notions,* is to complicate the moralizing of northerners who believe they have the right to go back on their word and dissolve slavery. The novel serves as a reminder of the compacts that bind the whites together, and for Cooper even a compact so odious as slavery must be respected if its rejection will cause white to turn against white. As Cooper fantasized in *Notions,* here the slave owner, Ishmael, voluntarily divests himself of his captive and all the white Americans are able to return to the settlements.

Almost all: Abiram, the slave trader, is revealed at the end to be the murderer of Ishmael's son, and he falls victim to the stern justice that is spared Natty and his party. And Natty, who reappeared in this novel to rewrite American history by turning back Ishmael and bringing about the voluntary end of "slavery," must remain behind as well. If Natty was created in *The Pioneers* to give the lie to a national identity founded on race and to restore the nation to its proper relation to British culture, here he is put to rest in the prairie along with the pioneering impulse he represents. Natty's bones stand guard over those who would vanish once and for all so that America could at last be freed from the burden of race, and the novel concludes with the inscription on his grave: "*May no wanton hand ever disturb his remains*" (386). Thus, Natty turns back those who would follow in his footsteps, admonishing his would-be disciple, Paul, to "forget any thing you may have heard from me, which is nevertheless true, and strive to turn your mind on the ways of the inner country" (373). For the territory to remain an emptiness into which the nonwhite races can disappear, the white pioneer must cease to be because white society must now remain on the other side of the boundary. Natty dies without issue, "the last of his race," vanishing with the Pawnees and Sioux into the desert so that the rest of the characters can do their pioneering in society.

Indeed, this is what occurs in the novel's final pages: all the remaining Americans return and assume their proper roles. The problem of race is left behind in the desert; the nation finally becomes ordered. *The Prairie* leaves the Louisiana Purchase as empty as it was before the settlers arrived. Clearly the significance Cooper imagines in the prairie has little to do with its population, but with a fantasy of the Purchase in general, and the soon-to-be Missouri Territory in particular, as a place for vanishing. D. H. Lawrence set the tone for a generation of Cooper criticism when he defined the tales as writing a myth of American rebirth: "That is the true myth of America. She starts old, old, wrinkled and writhing in an old skin. And there is a gradual sloughing of the old skin, towards a new youth."[52] This is precisely how the prairie functions for Cooper in this novel: as a ground for starting the nation over again, stripped of its old skin, the skin of race.

Imagining this new land as a barrier to further westward expansion, the territory comes to have political significance for Cooper; as Natty says, "I often think the Lord has placed this barren belt of prairie behind the States to warn men to what their folly may yet bring the land!" In the Missouri Territory of 1804, Cooper stages a Missouri Crisis in miniature, in which Natty brings about a peaceful abolition of slavery, turns back the tide of immigration, and remains in the desert to watch over the vanishing of the Indians, the slave trader, and even the mule, left behind at the novel's end. Cooper brings the "types" of American society to the frontier not to settle it, but to return them to their proper order in the east, and he sets up his reenactment of the crisis not to analyze its elements, but to rewrite history so as to eliminate the source of the crisis itself.

Thus, Cooper's novels can be seen to be concerned with more than simply the creation of a unique set of American myths. The drive to reimagine national origins is also a desire to distance national identity from the increasingly problematic touchstone of race. If Brown could not imagine an American identity without racial difference, Cooper's historical tales rewrite the nation's early history so as to write race out of the crisis that was unleashed in the 1820s—a crisis that literally will divide the nation. He works to reimagine a national identity built not on racial metaphor and fantasy but restored to what he hopes will prove the more substantial foundation of a white European inheritance. Moving from *The Pioneers*—the site of his personal origins—to *The Prairie*—the contested site of the Missouri controversy—Cooper writes increasingly desperate compromises designed to free national identity from the narratives and facts of racial difference.

V

The logic I have described in these novels is not unique to Cooper, although his novels, in their popularity during his lifetime and their influential role in the establishment of a national literary culture, remain perhaps the most significant manifestation of this fantastical plot. As the following passage from a *North American Review* essay on the Missouri Crisis indicates, many who considered the issue of race after 1819 were drawn toward similar fantasies:

> Among the individuals of a society thus composed [of many races], no feeling of respect, no permanent union of strength for common defense and support can exist. Though necessarily brought continuously into contact, they cannot coalesce. . . . If harmony and strength are desirable objects in the formation of new and extensive states, reason and example concur in believing, that they must be formed by a free and unmingled race of men.[53]

In the 1820s the idea of reform and the imagination of utopian Americas took on many shapes and visions, a good number of them focusing on the problem of race. From Fanny Wright's utopian community at Nashoba, which practiced amalgamation through miscegenation, to the American Society for Colonizing the Free People of Color, which worked to purge the nation of free blacks, the impulse behind much of the reform of the period was anxiety about the rising population of blacks in the United States.[54] What is significant in Cooper's "solution" to the problem is the way it came to speak to those who would consider problems of race, nation, and writing in succeeding decades. The revisionist drive of the period—in its desire to recover the "original" purpose of the nation—collided with the rhetoric of race and the repressed facts of African American slavery.[55] As it is most powerfully described in the history of the Missouri Compromise, this collision led to impossible acts of repression or relentless acts of revision. If a "national literature" is truly born with the novels of Cooper, then this literature must be understood as one in some real measure indebted to this crisis in American race and to the fantastical flights it generated.

As a coda to this study of Cooper, and as a preface to the reading of Edgar Allan Poe's *Narrative of Arthur Gordon Pym,* I turn briefly to a consideration of two very different novels of the period, *Symzonia* (1820) and George Tucker's *A Voyage to the Moon* (1827), two works of early "science fiction" that similarly indulge in fantasies of an America without race.

Symzonia—which has survived in literary history largely as a footnote to the writings of Poe—provides a useful example of the way in which other utopian projects of the period imagined the erasing of racial difference. One of the novel's central concerns lies with proving John Cleves Symmes's "theory of concentric spheres." One of the period's more flamboyant visionaries, Symmes devoted his life to trying to convince the nation of the existence of an internal world—supposedly accessible through an opening in the Arctic Circle—inhabited by a race of pure beings. The evangelical fervor this theory generated is characterized by a review in the *American Quarterly Register* of 1827:

> For the last nine or ten years, [Symmes] has been using every exertion to convince the world of its past errors, and to inculcate his own new and true theory. The newspapers have teemed with essays; circulars have been addressed to all the learned societies of Europe and America; addresses and petitions have been presented to our national and state legislatures; certificates of conviction and "adhesion" have been produced from men in high literary and political stations; the master and his disciples have traversed the whole country . . . so that all men, in all places, might be enlightened as to the truth.[56]

This utopian novel, often attributed to Symmes or one of his followers, recounts a fictional voyage to this internal world, and in it we see how Symmes's theory offers recourse to a fantasy of a nation without racial difference as an advertisement for the real voyage this novel sought to inspire.[57]

Describing the adventures of "Captain Seaborn," *Symzonia: A Voyage of Discovery* is one part science fiction, one part Swiftian satire, and one part propaganda encouraging a national expedition to the internal world. On his way to the polar regions, Seaborn encounters a community of penguins on the Falkland Islands whose "polity and habits" serve as a promising type for the Symzonians themselves.[58] After admiring the organization of the "colony" and the "pure white" of the penguins' bodies, Seaborn determines to pursue his aim of following Symmes's theories, reasoning that "a world, in which the brute creatures were so neatly formed, so polished in their manners, so social in their habits, and so quiet and well behaved, must, if men existed in it, be the abode of a race perfect in their kind" (32, 34).

When Seaborn enters the internal world he immediately names the land he discovers after the visionary of his voyage: Symzonia. Here he meets with the perfect beings who inhabit the inner world, and he is suddenly made aware of his own inadequacies, his own impurity. His first encounter with a Symzonian brings Seaborn's racial identity to a crisis:

> He walked round, and surveyed my person with eager curiosity. I did the like by him, and had abundant cause; for the sootiest African does not differ more from us in darkness of skin and grossness of features, than this man did from me in fairness of complexion and delicacy of form. . . . I shoved up the sleeve of my coat, to show them, by the inside of my arm (which was always excluded from the sun,) that I was a white man. I am considered fair for an American, and my skin in my own country thought to be one of the finest and whitest. But when one of the internals placed his arm, always exposed to the weather, by the side of mine, the difference was truly mortifying. I was not a white man, compared with him. (108–9)

In this pure white country, in which no trace of blackness can be found, Seaborn learns he is "not a white man" after all. In the ensuing adventures during his attempts to immigrate to this "utopia," he comes to recognize more of his own and his people's inadequacies as he comes to admire the perfection of the people he has "discovered." Seaborn falls into Gulliver-like spasms of self-loathing: "I saw that the internals owed their happiness to their rationality, to a conformity with the laws of nature and religion; and that the externals were miserable, from the indulgence of inordinate passions, and subjection to vicious propensities" (130).

But Seaborn soon learns that, like the United States, Symzonia has had its own problems with degeneracy and contamination. Early in their recorded history, a portion of their population had been corrupted by contact with a neighboring inferior nation, afflicted with "intemperate indulgences" that brought disease, sloth, and crime for the first time to this internal utopia (131). These degenerates were eventually transported to a

land far at the northern limits of the internal world, where they degenerated further until "they became dark coloured, ill favoured, and mis-
shaped men, not much superior to the brute creation" (132). Quickly, the
leaders of Symzonia discovered that contact with inferior peoples brought
corruption to their country, and this lesson served as "the origins of the
system of casting out the corrupted members of society" (166).

The burden now falls on Seaborn to prove that he is not one of this
degenerate race as he vainly attempts to convince the internals of his
worthiness to remain among them. His books (Shakespeare and Milton
among them) only add to the evidence his complexion and manners have
already provided to lead the wise men to the conclusion that he is a
descendant of the exiled race and therefore merits, with his crew, the
punishment prescribed: a lifetime of hard labor and confinement "in the
hopes that, in process of time, their gross appetites might be scourged out
of them" (177–78). In his own and his nation's defense, Seaborn attempts
to prove that the true descendants of the degenerate Belzubians are the
English, not the Americans who share with the Symzonians a desire for
purity: "I admitted that there was a race on the external world, inhabitants
of some islands far to the north, who, from their vicinity to the place of
exile, might be the descendants of the outcasts." He argues that the
evidence that is being arraigned against himself and his crew is derived
primarily from books written by the descendants of this race (the English), books that "had no reference to my country" (179).

Seaborn begs the Symzonians to make themselves known to his countrymen so as to purify his own race from the corruption under which they
inevitably still suffer due to their long contact with contaminated Externals. If Americans could be allowed to emulate the purity of the Symzonians, Seaborn argues, they will achieve their true potential. But his arguments are punctuated everywhere by a desire for personal gain, and his
pleas are finally rejected. Upon his return, Seaborn quickly learns the
justness of the Symzonians' judgment against his people as he is first
betrayed by his own crew, and then by deceitful merchants and lawyers at
home who rob him of his fame and fortune.

Symmes's utopian fantasy was taken seriously enough by himself and
others to merit extended petitions to Congress for public financing of a
mission similar to that recounted in his novel. For the mission to be
successful, the novel had attempted to demonstrate, it must be a national
one. What Symmes promises is not simply a geological curiosity, but a
new New World; as one of his defenders wrote, "The first adventurer that
makes the wonderful discovery, will merit and acquire a more glorious

name than the great COLUMBUS!" Symmes's disciple concludes by insisting that public funding of Symmes's voyage "is . . . all-important to the interest and honor of the nation."[59] Symmes promised a land inhabited by beings who would teach Americans the real meaning of national and racial purity, and a world in which real purity can be practiced. In opposition to the colonization movement of the day, which sought to liberate the nation from the burden of race by exporting freed slaves to Liberia, *Symzonia* imagined that the United States could be purified by colonizing white Americans. In 1823, the year of the Monroe Doctrine and Cooper's first Leatherstocking Tale, Symmes's plan had achieved sufficient popular acceptance to demand its formal consideration in Congress in response to the many petitions legislators had received on behalf of the would-be explorer.[60]

Utopian science fiction—a genre in which *Symzonia* is arguably a pioneer—seems intriguingly interconnected with the project Cooper himself is engaged in in the Leatherstocking Tales.[61] It is interesting to observe that Symmes's theory found its origins in the Missouri Territory, from which he issued his broadside "Light Gives Light, To Light Discover—Ad Infinitum" in 1818 as the territory itself was preparing its petition for statehood. "I declare the earth is hollow," Symmes wrote in his inaugural publication. "I engage we find warm and rich land, stocked with thrifty vegetables and animals if not men."[62] Over the next year, as the Missouri debates exploded around his St. Louis trading post, Symmes sent out further circulars seeking patronage, testifying to his sanity, and offering further details of his theory of concentric spheres.

At the same time, James Fenimore Cooper was beginning his own career as a novelist, with what must be accounted an almost equally fantastic ambition: to become a professional novelist in the United States. Both of these young authors are writing under the shadow of extremely powerful pioneering father figures—for Cooper his father, and for Symmes his uncle, Judge John Cleves Symmes, owner of the Miami Purchase and a founder of Cincinnati—and both are engaged in writings that clearly seek to stake claims for their authors as pioneers in their own right, writings that strive to write the son in the place of the pioneering father. We see in *Symzonia*'s utopian science fiction a drive also found in Cooper: an attempt to reimagine a point of origin for the United States that will allow questions of proprietorship and identity (questions that we have seen had long been conceived in terms of race) to be refigured so as to remove the problems raised by racial difference from the equation. For *Symzonia*, the solution is to take the imagination of a pure "American race" to its ultimate conclusion with the ideal of the Symzonians. For Cooper, the solution is more conflicted and more complicated, as he seeks to rework the history of the United States itself in order to free it from racial difference.

In 1827, when Cooper was writing *Notions* and *The Prairie*, George Tucker, kinsman of St. George Tucker, wrote his own science fiction novel, *A Voyage to the Moon*. The first novel of interplanetary adventure, Tucker's novel is another important source for Poe. Tucker introduces the novel to the public as a national production, "a story of domestic origin," although no part of its story takes place on American soil.[63] Its hero, Atterly, is captured at sea and imprisoned in Burma where he meets a Brahmin who tells him the secret of interplanetary travel. Together they voyage to the moon, where they encounter a degenerate race of beings. For the most part the novel uses the inhabitants of the moon to satirize the customs and society of earth, especially those of the intellectual class.

Although the book ridicules almost all intellectual debate as empty and vain, it spares one set of concerns from this critique: the question of racial difference. On the way to the moon, the Brahmin calls Atterly's attention to the continent of Africa receding below their ship. The sight raises questions about racial hierarchies, and the Brahmin argues for an environmental explanation of such differences: "The climate, being hot and indolent, can only produce a race which is itself uninclined to discipline and ambition" (52). This claim prompts his disciple to ask, "Do you think then . . . that there is no such thing as natural inferiority and differences of races?" The Brahmin responds with a circular logic:

> "I have been much perplexed by the question," said he. "When I regard the great masses of mankind, I think there seems to be among them some characteristic differences. I see that the Europeans have every where obtained the ascendancy over those who inhabit the other quarters of the globe. But when I compare individuals, I see always the same passions, the same motives, the same mental operations; and my opinion is changed. The same seed becomes a very different plant when sowed in one soil or another, and put under this or that mode of cultivation." (52–53)

Atterly does not find this a satisfactory response and interrogates the Brahmin's metaphor to determine whether environment can change the nature of race itself after a long continuance in the same "soil," the question plaguing Americans since Raynal and Buffon made their pronouncements upon the fate of white Americans. The Brahmin offers as a response a reconciliation of Smith's environmentalism with Jefferson's nascent polygenism, as he suggests that if the "plant" "has generally degenerated, it may, by opposite treatment, be also gradually brought back to its original excellence" by a removal to its proper environment (53). Thus, environment can advance or impede the general state of the plant (race), but the plant itself has a certain unique potential that differentiates it from other plants. This metaphor is raised one last time as the two express their good wishes for the colonizationist project in Liberia, the Brahmin adding that "if they can get this grain of mustard-seed to grow, there is no saying how much it may multiply" (53).

Thus, the debate, which begins with the Brahmin arguing in terms Samuel Stanhope Smith and the monogenists would have gladly embraced, concludes by moving over toward a Jeffersonian position of inherent and irreversible racial difference. The Brahmin considers the lack of culture among African nations and decides finally that "we [cannot] justly ascribe the difference to the enervating influence of the climate, for the temperature of the most southern parts of Africa differs little from that of Greece," a reference to Jefferson's argument in defense of his theory of the inferiority of blacks.[64] "On the whole," the Brahmin concludes, "it does seem probable that some organic difference exists in the various races of mankind, to which their diversities of moral and intellectual characters may in part be referred."[65]

Like Updike Underhill thirty years before him, Atterly is converted to advocacy of America by his captivity abroad, and the debate over racial difference that begins his voyage to the moon provides an important framework for this transformation. When America comes into view as the earth recedes below them and Atterly expresses a desire to return to the United States, he is told that he will not be allowed to do so "until you will be enabled to make yourself welcome and useful there, by what you may see in the lunar world" (61). What he learns on the moon points toward the way America is to proceed if it is to truly reach "a higher point of excellence than has ever yet been attained" (63).

After visiting the inhabitants of the moon and exposing their foibles and conceits, the Brahmin takes Atterly to visit the Happy Valley, an allegorical space clearly representing the United States, or an ideal vision of what America itself could be. The history of this utopian community parallels that of the United States: in a time of religious fervor two centuries ago separatist colonists came to the Happy Valley and founded the Lunar Paradise, purchasing the land "of the hunting tribe to which it belonged" so as to govern themselves by their own laws and their own religion (185–86). At first the settlers attempted to found a government of perfect equality, but they soon found this plan impractical. Recognizing that the principles of natural inequality that operate between races operate within races as well, these enlightened people instead established a system of government based on natural inequality but equal political rights. Maintaining a policy of strict isolationism, they now devote their energies to each producing, according to their proper station, all their necessities within the valley.

Thus, *A Voyage to the Moon* offers a utopian vision remarkably similar to that presented in *Symzonia*, and a political vision remarkably close to that of Cooper, who himself turned to this genre in his novel *The Monikins* (1835), a bizarre Swiftian satire involving a polar exploration to a land inhabited by a race of sentient monkeys. Set, not coincidentally, in 1819, the novel describes the voyage of an English idealist, Goldencalf, and an American seaman, Noah Poke, to the land of the Monikins. The novel is punctuated by a series of debates about racial science as the Monikins and the humans argue over the hierarchies that define their relative positions in the chain of being. The first half of the novel is a satire directed against England (Leaphigh, in the novel); but the second half focuses on America (Leaplow). Here Goldencalf, Poke, and a cabin boy named Bob are each elected, before they have even touched Leaplow's shores, to congress as representatives of opposing parties: the Horizontals, the Verticals, and the Tangentials.

The three adventurers take on their new elected duties in the middle of a heated debate as to whether *white* should be changed to *black* and *black* to *white*. The resolution has produced great divisiveness, and when Goldencalf tries to determine what is at stake in the matter, he is informed that the parties "had long been at variance on *the mere coloring property of various important questions,* and the real matter involved in the resolution was not visible."[66] Goldencalf researches what Leaplow's constitution has to say on the matter and discovers a clause guaranteeing that "the Great National Council shall, in no case whatever, pass any law, or resolution, declaring white to be black" (267). But when Goldencalf attempts to bring this evidence up before the congress in opposition to the proposed amendment, he is told that the constitution is irrelevant and is shouted down from the floor. Instead, a "compromise" is passed whereby it is solemnly determined "that the color which has hitherto been deemed to be black, is really lead-color." In defending the compromise, Bob argues that "he did not believe that public opinion was satisfied with maintaining that black was black, but he thought it was not yet disposed to affirm that black was white. He did not say that such a day might not arrive; he only maintained that it had not yet arrived" (273).

Thus, a central scene in Cooper's 1835 satire of the United States—one that perhaps borrows from *Symzonia* and *A Voyage to the Moon*—turns out to be a thinly veiled parody of the Compromise of 1819–20. For Cooper, in the hammering out of the compromise, the Constitution had been ignored, and, in the name of partisan politics, black was changed, if not quite to white, to a neutral color in between. The inherent meaning of racial difference was thus elided and confused in legalistic banter; as Poke argues in *The Monikins* in favor of the proposed amendment, "There was pretty much no such thing as color at all" and "words had no just value" (268–69). Thus, to deny that black was black and white was white, for Cooper, now becomes tantamount to arguing that words themselves have no value—and no vision of the world could be more troubling to America's "first" national novelist. The future of such a state of affairs is not a pretty one, as the uneducated cabin boy's rise to prominence in Leaplow politics would certainly suggest for Cooper, and the day is not far off when the fundamental difference between black and white, a difference Cooper believed the Constitution had sworn to defend, would be overturned once and for all.

As Cooper contemplated the Missouri Compromise at the end of his life, he wrote,

> The "compromise" is a false principle. . . . If a compromise, it is a constitution within a constitution, and whence does Congress derive its power to make a new constitution? That which has been termed the Missouri Compromise is at the bottom of all this evil. The question must be met, face to face, sooner or later, and the sooner the better. . . .
>
> You know I have never been affected by a false philant[h]ropy. Property in man is no more opposed to Christianity than property in a horse. . . . But, this equilibrium doctrine can not be tolerated an hour. The country will split on it.[67]

By the time Cooper wrote this letter, in 1850, it was patently clear that the Union was in serious jeopardy and that the compromise—which sought to preserve the Union at all costs—was very much at the heart of the impending crisis. Cooper's vision of an America freed from racial difference—or different races—had failed to come about. The nightmare that Cooper and his contemporaries foresaw in the 1820s, in which the repressed fact of slavery would lead to the sundering of the nation, was now upon them. In the end, Cooper's vanishing act of the 1820s was not so very different from Symmes's voyage to the center of the earth or Tucker's voyage to the moon—bizarre flights of fancy that sought to imagine a national identity without racial difference, to rewrite a national identity American letters had helped script in the first place.

CHAPTER 5

Poe's "Incredible Adventures and Discoveries Still Farther South"

> And now we rushed into the embraces of the cataract, where a chasm threw itself open to receive us. But there arose in our pathway a shrouded human figure, very far larger in its proportions than any dweller among men. And the hue of the skin of the figure was of the perfect whiteness of the snow.
>
> Poe, *Narrative of Arthur Gordon Pym* (1838)

I

Like the novels of Cooper discussed in the previous chapter, Poe's *Narrative of Arthur Gordon Pym* (1838) is set in an earlier time, in this case in 1827, the year in which Cooper published *The Prairie* and was writing *Notions of the Americans*. In his work, as we have seen, Cooper directed attention to specific historical scenes of conflict in order to revise the racialized formulations of national identity that grew out of them. There is strong evidence that Poe's chronological positioning of Pym's tale, however, has more to do with a biographical crisis than a national one—or, more precisely, with a biographical crisis symptomatic of a national one. In March 1827, after the long-standing conflicts with his guardian, John Allan, had reached the breaking point, the eighteen-year-old Poe wrote to explain his reasons for leaving Allan's house:

> My determination is at length taken—to leave your house and indeavor to find some place in this wide world, where I will be treated—not as *you* have treated me. . . .
>
> You have . . . ordered me to quit your house, and are continually upbraiding me with eating the bread of Idleness, when you yourself . . . were the only person to remedy the evil by placing me to some busi-

ness—You take delight in exposing me before those whom you think
likely to advance my interest in this world—

You suffer me to be subjected to the whims & caprice, not only of
your white family, but the complete authority of the blacks—these
grievances I could not submit to; and I am gone.[1]

Two months later, Poe traveled from Richmond to Boston. There he
hoped to make his way in the "wide world" as a professional writer and to
discover a world where he would not be treated as Allan had treated him:
kept from his rightful place in the world, humiliated in front of his supe-
riors, and, worst of all, submitted to the "complete authority" of slaves.[2]

In June 1827 A. Gordon Pym also set out to seek his own way in the
"wide world," but instead of following Poe's unsuccessful voyage north,
Pym sails south—farther south, in fact, than any "civilized" man had ever
gone before. At the conclusion of his adventures, Pym discovers a contradictory "truth": to pursue the dream of ultimate whiteness is to cease to
exist, but to fail to pursue it is also to risk annihilation. It is this dilemma
that literally destroys Pym in his attempt to transcribe his journey's end.
This whiteness cannot be written—Pym's attempts to do so marks his end;
and yet, the logic of the story implies, if he had not pursued the perfect
whiteness of the farthest south, he would have been destroyed nonetheless—with the rest of his crew in the race war on Tsalal.

After his death, Pym's discovery is left in the hands of a fictional aca-
demic editor who attempts to make sense of the fragmented manuscript.
For this "editor," as for many editors and critics since, the novel's central
lessons lie in the concluding scenes on Tsalal. It is here that Pym and the
crew of the *Jane Guy* discover a land of utter blackness, it is here that an
apocalyptic race war ensues, which Pym survives only by being buried in
an underground cavern during the devastating landslide the Tsalalians
unleash on the whites. Like Huntly's awakening within his own cavern (a
scene Poe explicitly borrowed from later in "The Pit and the Pendulum"),
Pym's awakening leads to the discovery of the lessons that will transform
him into a pioneering hero. Like Huntly, he finds a weapon that indicates
a previous presence in the caverns, in this case a musket, and like Huntly
he finds himself gripped by a torturous hunger.[3] Most important, it is
here, in this cavern, that Pym discovers the lessons of race: not, as did
Huntly, in a band of savages, but in the writing on the wall: "The sides
were now entirely uniform in substance, in colour, and in lateral direction,
the material being a very black and shining granite. . . . The precise forma-

tion of the chasm will be best understood by means of a delineation taken upon the spot; for I had luckily with me a pocketbook and pencil" (193).

Pym carefully maps the black caverns he walks through without recognizing what he is transcribing as writing, allowing the "editor" to discover in the transcription a fundamental opposition that Pym himself could not read: the caverns spell out "To be shady," while the indentures on the wall read "To be white" (208). From this opposition of white and black, the editor can draw only one lesson, in the form of a pseudo-biblical prophecy: "*I have graven it within the hills, and my vengeance upon the dust within the rocks*" (208). The apocalypse approaches, Pym's editor tells us, born of what is for Poe and for many racial theorists of the 1830s and '40s the most primal opposition of all: the inescapable opposition of black and white, a primal opposition embodied in an act of writing—"graven . . . within the hills"—that "proves" what many American writers had long suspected: that writing and racial difference are inextricably related.

In *Pym,* Poe rewrites the "utopian" fantasies of the 1820s, inscribed by Cooper, Tucker, and Symmes, in a novel that explores the black and white of writing and the "black and white" of racial difference. Pym discovers a world in which the fact of racial difference is inescapably bound up in the material existence of writing itself—where to flee racial difference, as Pym does at the novel's end, for a fantasy of an original perfect whiteness, is to come to a place where writing cannot exist. "It is feared," the "editor" writes in the novel's "Note," "that the few remaining chapters which were to have completed his narrative . . . have been irrecoverably lost through the accident by which he perished himself" (207). In the tale that served as the precursor to *Pym,* "MS. Found in a Bottle" (1833), Poe's narrator offers a potential explanation of that loss: "It is evident that we are hurrying onwards to some exciting knowledge—some never-to-be-imparted secret, whose attainment is destruction."[4]

Pym is unique among Poe's writings for several reasons: its length, its scene of action, and its explicitly American characters. In the many fictions of his short career, Poe was relatively alone among American writers in setting few of his tales in the United States and rarely peopling them with recognizably American characters. "Of my country and of my family I have little to say," characteristically begins one of his narrators. "Ill usage and length of years have driven me from the one, and estranged me from the other."[5] The most familiar explanation of this is Poe's avowed contempt for much of what democracy entailed and his desire to fashion in his fictions a no-place and a nowhere that might be anywhere but here.

Thus, Poe's tales famously tend toward interiors—and interiors within interiors. A coffin is buried within a catacomb within a castle, within which lies the body of the narrator (or the beloved), within whom lies something still more interior, something that might live forever. Central to so many of these tales is the question of whether there is some ultimate interior thing that can survive the calamities that befall exteriors. Ships capsize, houses collapse, bodies decay, nations divide: does there remain something primal—something buried—that can survive these calamities? The soul, the race—the "whiteness"?

Indeed, these questions are central to Poe's early "marriage tales." In "Berenice" (1835), for example, one of the earliest tales Poe published in the *Southern Literary Messenger,* the narrator, a man entombed in his study and his books, tells of his beautiful cousin, his opposite in every way. Where he is solitary and philosophical, she is sensual and gregarious. Together they achieve a kind of perfect harmony, until a "fatal disease" descended on their house that so ravaged Berenice's frame as to "disturb[ ] even the identity of her person!" (226). Disfigured by her disease and now become utterly repugnant to the narrator, still one aspect of Berenice remains obsessively fascinating: "The white and ghastly *spectrum* of the teeth. . . . The teeth!—The teeth!—they were here, and there, and every where, and visible and palpably before me; long, narrow, and excessively white, with the pale lips writhing about them, as in the very moment of their first terrible development" (230–31). So all-consumed is the narrator with the excessive whiteness of these teeth, that, at the story's end, he breaks into her tomb and wrenches the teeth from her mouth to preserve their purity for himself. If everything else about Berenice has decayed and putrefied in the wake of the terrible disease, her teeth—in their perfect whiteness—offer a vision of the "first terrible development," an original whiteness that promises to live on after the disease, after the plague, after death itself.

As we will see, this ghoulish fascination with the grave robbing and the dismemberment of bodies in search of a primal whiteness was not unique to either Poe or his characters. At the same time, others were also searching deep within graves for buried bodies in hopes of finding the origins of races and their proper ordering in the world. With Samuel George Morton's analysis of his massive collection of skulls in the 1830s and '40s, the American school of racial anthropology came of age and the origins of race were at last "discovered"—not, as had been long believed, in an original perfect whiteness, but in an opposition between black and white as old as time itself.

II

There has been a resurgence of interest of late in Poe's thoughts on slavery—a somewhat curious resurgence in that Poe's opinions on the subject have long been quite visible: he supported slavery both as a southerner and as an individual.[6] Critics earlier in the century took for granted Poe's proslavery feelings, largely on the basis of an 1836 proslavery review in the *Southern Literary Messenger* that had been attributed to him. Thus, Ernest Marchand could cite, in 1934, this review as clear evidence of Poe's position on slavery and his belief in the inferiority of African Americans.[7] When, however, a letter from Poe to the southern jurist and novelist Beverley Tucker was found granting authorship of the notorious review to Tucker, after 1941 the Poe canon was amended accordingly.[8] Even without the evidence offered by the review, however, little serious doubt was cast on Poe's position on slavery.

But the letter and the review reemerged again in 1974, when Bernard Rosenthal offered an interesting argument in favor of Poe's authorship, suggesting that the letter from Poe to Tucker might refer to another essay on slavery published earlier in the *Messenger*.[9] For a long time Rosenthal's argument passed largely for what it was: an important and highly speculative argument on a fundamentally undecidable textual debate. In the last several years, ever since Toni Morrison's claim that "No early American writer is more important to the concept of American Africanism than Poe," critics have lined up to interpret every aspect of Poe's lights and darks, from *Pym* to the late poetry, in terms of his supposed polemic on behalf of slavery.[10]

What Morrison argues is a relatively straightforward but important point, one also found in the earlier criticism of Harry Levin, Sidney Kaplan, Leslie Fiedler, and Harold Beaver: that Poe, especially in *Pym,* was engaged in a troubling consideration of the African American presence in the United States, and that this presence had ramifications for the way Poe treated other questions of identity.[11] But what is important in Morrison's suggestion is largely lost in the "revisionary" criticism that followed. For many, the disputed review becomes the key to uncovering the central and supposedly repressed aspect of Poe's "politics." Dana D. Nelson deplores the "recent trend to sweep Poe's politics under the rug," especially on the part of those who would deny the "evidence" offered by Rosenthal.[12] Scott Bradfield identifies Poe as a "proslavery ideologue" on the basis of Poe's authorship of the disputed essay.[13] Most recently, Joan Dayan has painted a picture of outright conspiracy, in which "male mem-

bers of the Poe Society" have attempted to suppress her identification of
the review as Poe's "greatest love poem." At the heart of Dayan's tale is
the explicit argument that "some Poe critics—the founding fathers of the
Poe Society, for example—sound rather like . . . proslavery ideologues."[14]
Now, it seems, all moments of domination, subservience, blackness, and
whiteness in Poe are no longer obscure, troubled, or self-contradictory,
but can be instantly deciphered through the great decoder provided by
"Poe's" proslavery review.[15]

Whether or not Poe is the sole author of the review (and it remains
unlikely that he is), a close examination of the review reveals strong evidence of his hand in its rhetoric and vocabulary. There are passages in the
review that one would have difficulty believing are not owing to Poe's
editorial influence, while much of it sounds decidedly like the work of the
vitriolic southern romancer Beverley Tucker, author of *George Balcombe*
and *The Partisan Leader* (both 1836) and a frequent contributor to the
Messenger. The debate as it is framed by those who would insist on Poe's
authorship of the proslavery review is misconceived from the start; those
engaged in it are misled by their desire—symptomatic of the critical climate of the day—to uncover a clear statement of Poe's position on the
most important issue of his day: African American slavery. Instead, the
real significance of the disputed review for a reconsideration of Poe's
project lies not with what it reveals about Poe's attitudes toward the
institution of slavery, but with the insight it provides into his understanding of the discourse of race and its relationship to writing. I want to
reorient the debate over the review away from questions of biographical
evidence and toward the evidence the text provides as to the logic of race
for the southern institutions (and the *Messenger* in particular) within
which Poe came of age as a writer.

Poe very much curried Tucker's favor, as evidenced by an early letter in
which he commended Tucker's poetry ("I sincerely think your lines excellent") and a laudatory review of *Balcombe* in the *Messenger* ("*the best
American novel*").[16] The reasons why Poe would have wanted Tucker on
his side are clear. Tucker's early high opinion of Poe's talents helped
secure him a job on his return to Richmond with the *Messenger*'s proprie-
tor, Thomas W. White,[17] and Tucker was at the center of a group of
Virginia intellectuals and politicians with strong influence in the community of which Poe wanted to be a part. With Thomas R. Dew and Abel
Parker Upshur, Tucker was among the most powerful figures contributing
to the *Messenger*, during Poe's short tenure, some of the period's most

strident defenses of southern institutions, at the forefront of which was, of course, slavery.

Thomas Dew made his notorious fame as a racial theorist in the wake of the Virginia debates on emancipation of 1831–32, when he wrote, "The emancipated black carries a mark which no time can erase; he forever wears the indelible symbol of his inferior condition; the *Ethiopian cannot change his skin, nor the leopard his spots.*"[18] The mark of African Americans' inferiority was etched in their skin, Dew's new version of the old tautological argument went, and only by literally stripping their blackness could you hope to make a black man equal to a white. This being the case, Dew concluded, slavery became the most humanitarian solution. "Domestic slavery, such as ours," wrote Dew in the March 1836 *Messenger,* "is the only institution which I know of, that can secure that spirit of equality among freemen, so necessary to the true and genuine feeling of republicanism."[19] Dew was a leading propagandist for the idea of "natural" racial hierarchies that redefined slavery as a benevolent system to be defended by all lovers of democracy. He continued: "The slave is happy and contented with his lot, unless indeed the very demons of Pandemonium shall be suffered to come among us and destroy his happiness by their calumnious falsehoods and hypocritical promises. He compares himself with his own race and his own color alone, and he sees that all are alike—he does not covet the wealth of the rich man . . . but he identifies all his interests with those of his master."[20]

For the southern theorists on race in the mid-1830s (when, according to Tise, proslavery finally developed a unified ideological front) slavery was not only justifiable, but an important keystone of American democracy.[21] The original natures of whites and blacks made the master-slave relationship a natural and mutually beneficial system. As William Gilmore Simms wrote in 1837, "The truth is that our rights depend entirely upon the degree of obedience which we pay to the laws of *our creation.*"[22] The northern attack on slavery, far from the humanitarian cause it pretended to be, was here defined as nothing more than an attempt to destroy this "central institution" and so to bring the South to its knees. Overturning slavery, the argument went, was tantamount to overturning all of southern society. No text of the period made this argument more strongly than Tucker's novel *The Partisan Leader,* which told a tale of the not-so-distant future in which the abolitionist North has subjected the South to its rule through the dismantling of the slave system. As Upshur wrote in his review of the novel in the *Messenger* in 1837, "The reader rises from the perusal of the book with the solemn impressions of the probable truth of all the writer's speculations; and he naturally asks himself, by what means the evils he has seen depicted may be prevented."[23] The answer is clear: through the defense of "the institution of domestic slavery."

Poe came into his own as a professional writer and editor in this circle. His job at the *Messenger* was to compose and edit the "Critical Notices" section, a series of unsigned reviews at the end of each issue, and the disputed review, entitled "Slavery," is found among these notices. The review says little about the two proslavery books at hand, serving instead as a polemic on the institution in general. It begins with an account of reform movements of all kinds, which are divided into two groups, the fanatic and the irreligious. And at the root of all these movements, the author insists, is property: "Under such excitement, the many who want, band together against the few that possess; and the lawless appetite of the multitude for the property of others calls itself the spirit of liberty."[24] The author then goes on to make the by-now familiar connection between the threat of racial upheaval and the excesses of the French Revolution:

> It should be remembered now, that in that war against property, the first object of attack was property in slaves; that in that war on behalf of the alleged right of man to be discharged from all control of law, the first triumph achieved was in the emancipation of slaves.
>
> The recent events in the West Indies, and the parallel movement here, give an awful importance to these thoughts in our minds. They superinduce a something like despair of success in any attempt that may be made to resist the attack on all our rights, of which that on Domestic Slavery (the basis of all our institutions) is but the precursor. It is a sort of boding that may belong to the family of superstitions. All vague and undefined fears, from causes the nature of which we know not, the operations of which we cannot stay, are of that character. Such apprehensions are alarming in proportion to our estimate of the value of the interest endangered; and are excited by every thing which enhances that estimate. Such apprehensions have been awakened in our minds by the books before us. (337)

In these paragraphs we see signs of Poe's editorial hand. For, however we might attribute authorship of the surrounding text, the second paragraph strongly evidences both Poe's style and concerns. Words like "vague," "undefined," and "boding" were favorites of Poe in tales and sketches published in the *Messenger* during this period.[25] There are several reasons why Poe might have inserted the rhetorical markers of his style in Tucker's essay. He offers one in the disputed letter he wrote Tucker after the essay's publication, apologizing for "making a few immaterial alterations in your article on Slavery, with a view of so condensing it as to get it in the space remaining at the end of the number."[26] This letter, the sole evidence of Tucker's authorship of the proslavery review, also provides important evidence of Poe's hand in editing Tucker's review.[27]

More important, Poe's editorial "alterations" suggest that he wanted readers to believe the anonymous essay was by him. Far from disowning the review in any way, Poe carefully positions it at the end of the April issue where it is followed by a series of puffs from other periodicals in which Poe is lauded as the sole author of all the reviews in the Critical Notices section of the *Messenger*.[28] By inserting the markers of his own style into Tucker's polemic on behalf of slavery, Poe indicates his desire to be mistaken as the author of these views and as a member of the inner circle of proslavery intellectuals whose favor he courted.[29]

Central to the discussion at hand, this paragraph (possibly inserted by way of "condensing" a longer diagesis on the connections between revolution and abolition) shows that for Poe the issue of race and slavery had less to do with the institution of slavery itself—in which he had little personal interest—than with the gothic effects of race. The concerns exposed here are common to much of his work: the effects of terrors that cannot be defined and the search for an origin by which to define and know them. "Vague and undefined fears" plague Poe when considering racial upheaval, "from causes the nature of which we know not." To know the "causes" of the fear race inspires—to possess, that is, the true origins of race—would free the individual from the terror it inspires. The race wars of the West Indies bring about "despair" and "superstition" regarding the inevitable consequences of the overthrow of slavery. In imagining the scene, Poe is transformed into a character out of his early tales: the narrator of "Berenice," for example, or, even more strongly, Usher, a man who lives in fear of fear itself: "I dread the events of the future, not in themselves, but in their results. . . . I have, indeed, no abhorrence of danger, except in its absolute effect—in terror."[30] As the tale's narrator recognizes in the skull-like house "a barely perceptible fissure" that portends the final destruction of the House of Usher, so Poe here sees in Tucker's prophecies the fissure that will tear a still larger house in two.[31]

Although Poe was undoubtedly proslavery insofar as he supported the rights of southerners to their "property" and believed blacks fitted for little else but slavery, his interest in race has more to do with his search,

like the narrators of his tales, for an origin and a vocabulary by which to
define "the vague and undefined fears" that surround race. These fears
inspire the search for something definite, something immortal, some original condition that could resist the coming "shadow"—the "pestilence" in
the wind, the "fissure" in the very foundations of the nation. In this desire
Poe was not alone, and as American science sought to make a name for
itself on the international stage, it returned to the materials upon which it
had, at the turn of the previous century, already laid its own foundations:
race. The rest of the essay, which reads more like Tucker, emphasizes "the
moral influences flowing from the relation of master and slave" with
melodramatic sickbed scenes portraying the "natural" sympathies between the two.[32] Such scenes are used to evidence the unalterable difference between the races, a difference increasingly being put forward as
scientific and divine "fact." "Our theory is a short one," the review argues.
"It was the will of God it should be so."[33] Here a polygenist argument is
understood as fully reconcilable with God's will. God made blacks to be
slaves and whites to be masters, and the "devotion" of the one and the
"parental attachment" of the other proves it to be so.

Poe was necessarily ambivalent about the polygenism implicit in the
"Slavery" review and explicit in the arguments put forth by the American
School of racial science: not because he shared the religious scruples of
the clerical community, but because polygenism denied once and for all
the fantasy that had been kept alive from Smith to Symmes—the fantasy
of an original whiteness, a world without racial difference, to which the
nation might somehow return. It is this ambivalence that underwrites the
impossible conclusion of *Pym*.

III

Like many of his fellow armchair scientists in the 1830s, Poe was drawn
toward phrenology, the avatar of mid-century racial anthropology.[34] As
Reginald Horsman writes, "In the 1820s and 1830s the phrenologists
were in the vanguard of those who perceived innate differences between
races, and although their specific analysis of the brain was eventually
rejected by American scientists, they at first exerted considerable influence by their supposed empirical comparison of physical structure."[35]
The study of heads and skulls, Poe wrote in the *Messenger* in 1836, "as a
science, ranks among the most important which can engage the attention
of thinking beings."[36] He wrote Frederick W. Thomas in 1841 regarding

Upshur: "He is not only the most graceful speaker I ever heard, but one of the most graceful & luminous writers. His head is a model for statuary— Speaking of heads—my own *has been* examined by several phrenologists—all of whom spoke of me in a species of extravaganza which I should be ashamed to repeat."[37] That great men such as Upshur (and of course Poe himself) had magnificent skulls proved a most essential point—that hierarchies were scripted by nature on the very bodies of men, and it was a script that could not be rewritten. As Poe wrote, "Individuals may obtain, through the science, a perfectly accurate estimate of their own moral capabilities—and, thus instructed, will be the better fitted for decision in regard to a choice of offices and duties in life."[38] Based on such logic, the incorporation of phrenology in racial science was inevitable. Founded in large measure on phrenological principles as to how heads were measured and interpreted, a long line of argument in American racial science arrived at its fullest articulation in 1839 with the work of Samuel George Morton.

Looking at the pages of Morton's *Crania Americana* (1839), one begins to realize that Poe's obsession with skulls, the dead, and the secrets they withhold was not so unique as might first appear. For this influential book contains pages of graphic illustrations of skulls, some with mummified flesh still attached, accompanied by explanations of what they "mean." What they mean is nothing less than the final solution to the problem that had been plaguing racial theorists in the United States since 1787. Through the careful measuring of the skulls in his monumental collection, Morton was able to state positively what many white Americans had suspected all along: that races had separate origins. Morton sought to lay to rest the monogenist-polygenist debate: scanning the skulls meticulously laid out before them, readers could no longer doubt the truth of polygenism.

The famed Swiss naturalist Louis Agassiz wrote to his mother after emigrating to the United States to study and practice racial science: "Imagine a series of 600 skulls, most of Indians from all tribes who inhabit or once inhabited America. Nothing like it exists anywhere else. This collection, by itself, is worth a trip to America."[39] Morton's collection of skulls, which he began amassing in the 1820s, "provided the 'facts' that won worldwide respect for the 'American school' of polygeny."[40] Morton has a simple goal for his collection: to use phrenological techniques to determine once and for all how the races measured up. In his "Introductory Essay on the Variety of the Human Species," he reviews the familiar arguments that had dominated racial science since Samuel Stanhope

Smith won the day in 1787. "The prevalent belief is derived from the sacred writings, which, in their literal and obvious interpretation, teach us that all men have originated from a single pair," he writes; thus, "it has been hastily and unnecessarily inferred" that all racial differences are the result of environmental circumstances. But this is not necessarily the case: "We may inquire, whether it is not more consistent with the known government of the universe to suppose, that the same Omnipotence that created man, would adapt him at once to the physical, as well as to the moral circumstances in which he was to dwell upon the earth?"[41] In other words, as Morton goes on to argue, since we see the existence of distinct and immutable racial categories in the oldest skulls in the deepest graves, is it not more reasonable to assume that the races were created separate from the start—that racial differences are God-given and to a purpose—rather than to suppose that all the vast differences we see before us are the result of a short millennium of environmental effects?

One of the main reasons many people were ready for such an argument in 1839 (but had not been fifty years earlier) is that it was becoming increasingly clear that Buffon's prophecies for the fate of the future American were not going to be realized. White Americans were not being turned into "savages" by their continued contact with a savage environment—far from it, they were actively demonstrating their mastery over that environment (and the "savages" it once contained) by a rapidly accelerating westward expansion. Thus, Morton's work only "proved" what Manifest Destiny assumed: that the Native American was of a completely other race, a race completely other as far back as one could go. Indians had always been Indians and always would be—they were so not because of the American environment but because they were created to be different.

More encouraging news for white Americans was to be found in Morton's tabulations. Following his account of the seventy skulls studied (and reproduced in ghoulish detail at the book's end), he provides a long note "On the Internal Capacity of the Cranium in the Different Races of Men," extending further the consequences of his conclusions. Caucasians, it turns out, possess the biggest skulls, averaging 87 cubic inches. The other races fall short, but they do so in a very carefully hierarchical manner: the Mongolian measures in at 83 cubic inches, the Indian at 82, the Malay at 81, and the Ethiopian at 78.[42]

In the appendix, George Combe, Poe's favorite father of phrenology, offers "Phrenological Remarks" on the data gathered by Morton to substantiate further the hierarchies explicitly laid out by Morton's conclusions. Combe argues that not only brain size (which for Morton was directly related to intelligence) but also other qualities such as "self-esteem" and "benevolence" can be measured in this collection of skulls. Combe compares Morton's data with a Swiss skull to demonstrate how, for example, where the Indians average 4.42 in "firmness," the Swiss specimen, "a standard by which to compare the skulls of the other tribes," scores a impressive 5.5.[43] Morton's conclusions are richly echoed by the English Combe: "In America . . . Europeans and native Indians have lived for centuries under the influence of the same physical causes; the former have kept pace in their advances with their brethren in the old continent, while the latter, as we have seen, remain stationary in savage ignorance and indolence" (273).

Yet, if Morton assuaged one long-standing anxiety of white Americans with his first book, in his second he set out to solve once and for all the crisis that loomed most large behind all racial debates in the 1830s and '40s: African American slavery. In *Crania Aegyptiaca* (1844), expanded from a lecture delivered before the American Philosophical Society two years earlier, Morton gives himself a twofold project: first, to determine which race had originally inhabited ancient Egypt, "the parent of civilization"; and, second, to figure out what role blacks played in that ancient civilization.[44] He again presents the skulls with great care, but here the immediate problems of racial classification become even more dizzying. Stripped of their flesh, the mummified skulls offer few signs by which race is traditionally determined; thus Morton must turn to the tool racial theorists had long relied on: intuition. Those skulls that seem to Morton to be Caucasian in feature are placed in one group; those that appear "Negroid" are placed in another. Not surprisingly, when he then measures the skulls he has so divided, Caucasians once again come out on top.[45] Morton's fantastically tautological argument—whereby those skulls "which present the finest conformation" are classified as the type that then proves the supremacy of the Caucasian race—is based on his own presuppositions as to what Caucasian and Negroid skulls should look like when placed side by side. As he comments on some of the "Negroid" skulls in his collection, "There is much of the Negro *expression* in the bony structure of this head. . . . A small head, with a low receding forehead, and strong, small nose, projecting mazillae, and obvious Negro expression."[46]

Not only do Morton's measurements "prove" yet again the inferiority of blacks; his findings more strikingly claim to demonstrate that blacks existed in ancient Egypt in precisely the same capacity in which they exist in the modern-day United States: as slaves. "We have the most unequivocal evidence," he argues in summation, making explicit the historical precedent of slavery, "that slavery was among the earliest of the social institutions of Egypt. . . . Of Negro slavery, in particular, the paintings and sculptures give abundant illustration" (59). And if blacks were slaves to the ancient Egyptians—who were, after all, Caucasians—then surely environmental arguments are disproved once and for all. Moreover, Morton finds in ancient Egyptian monuments evidence that the Caucasians of the earliest recorded time were as concerned with race and the precise ordering of racial differences as are Morton and his contemporaries: "Negroes are abundantly represented on the pictorial delineations of the Egyptian monuments of every epoch. Complexion, features and expression, these and every other attribute of the race, are depicted precisely as we are accustomed to see them in our daily walks . . . and, moreover, as if to enforce the distinction of race by direct contrast, they are placed side by side with people of the purest Caucasian features" (60–61).

Out of these fleshless skulls, Morton reads many blessings for those who possessed white skin. His conclusions provided many white Americans with the answers they had been looking for; the white American was shown to be naturally and inevitably superior, giving scientific credibility to the racist presuppositions that had long underwritten racial theory. As Morton promised, and as this promise was disseminated by the popular press and lecturers, the speculations of average white Americans about the racial others they encountered in their daily walks were now endowed with the authority of both modern science and ancient history. Finally, in their descent from the Egyptians, white Americans were invited to see in the triumphs of that ancient civilization the full promise of their own.

For the proslavery South, Morton brought a mixed blessing—the blasphemy of polygenism with the scientific "proof" to justify slavery as an institution. But, as we have seen in the 1836 Tucker-Poe review, God's word was already proving less of an obstacle to proslavery claims about the divine origins of racial difference. Indeed, by 1839, the *Messenger* along with many other publications of the period (northern and southern) had fully adopted polygenist assumptions: "We can see at a glance, that the civilized and polished European, is in many respects *an essentially different* being, from the savage red man of America, the wandering and ignorant Tartar, or the degraded and brutish Hottentot."[47] The "proof" that the races are "different beings" lies now in the kind of observations that even "the most casual observer" could make: whites look superior, therefore they are.[48]

Poe's engagement with phrenology and proslavery no doubt fueled his interest in the origins of racial differences, but he shared, as well, the more general enthusiasm of his age with the search for origins. As John T. Irwin has shown, Poe shared the widespread interest in Champollion and the deciphering of the Rosetta Stone—a fantasy of recovering the origins of language.[49] His fascination with the plans under way to fulfill, at long last, Symmes's fantasy of a national polar exploration reveals a related interest in finding a point of origin for the earth itself at the South Pole. But Symmes's fantasy of an escape to an original whiteness at the earth's core was being undermined by polygenism. What Pym discovers in his search for origins (of the earth, of race, and of language) is that all derive not from a point of perfect whiteness from which the modern has degenerated, but from the very fact of racial difference itself. As polygenism complicated the ideal of an original whiteness, Poe in his novel *Pym* explores why the myth of "pure" origins must be finally, if reluctantly, laid to rest—both in fiction and in life.

IV

"In fiction and in life," I write, but it is precisely such a distinction that Poe consistently challenges throughout his career. *Pym,* centrally concerned with questions of race, surprisingly begins with questions of genre. In writing the preface to his own adventures, our narrator, Pym, goes to great lengths to clarify the confusion that surrounds the origins of his text. Explaining why he had initially turned his story over to "Poe," a writer of fiction, Pym writes, "having kept no journal during a greater portion of the time in which I was absent, I feared I should not be able to write, from mere memory, a statement so minute and connected as to have the *appearance* of that truth it would really possess" (55). Unable to give the facts of his voyage the "appearance" of truth, Pym saw that his story would be read as a work of fancy and so allowed Poe, "lately editor of the Southern Literary Messenger" (55), to publish it *under the garb of fiction*" on the condition that his "real name should be retained" (56). Unable to write himself as a real-life adventurer, Pym at first was content to be written as a hero of a fiction.

Of greater importance than whether Pym will be understood as a hero of fiction or a historical explorer is the strict maintenance of his tale's generic category. Pym is determined that his story be read one way or the other. But now, he goes on to inform the reader, the public has begun to question the status of the "pretended fiction" that Poe had originally published in the *Messenger.* His readers have seen through Poe's hoax and recognized the story for what it was, and Pym now reemerges as the teller of his own tale, reclaiming his fiction as fact. As if to educate his readers in determining fact from fiction, Pym chooses to leave Poe's contributions in place as they were published originally in the *Messenger,* concluding: "It will be unnecessary to point out where his portion ends and my own commences; the difference in point of style will be readily perceived" (56).

This elaborate preface has encouraged many readers from Poe's day to our own to see Poe's novel as a "hoax," or, at the very least, as a satire on the public's penchant for sensational stories. Poe borrows heavily from both factual and fictional exploration narratives, and he calls attention to the realistic detail with which Pym observes his surroundings on one hand even as he underscores the contradictions and improbabilities that expose his "facts" as "fiction" on the other. As a result, it is difficult indeed to determine whether he is trying to hoax his readers, whether he is simply writing carelessly, or whether he is writing, quite deliberately, about writing itself. Several Poe scholars have pointed to the novel's willful play on generic conventions as being the focus of its project, one that challenges the reader's assumptions about fact and fiction and the ability to discern between them.[50] Indeed, in addition to the recent criticism that has focused on the novel in relation to racial issues, there is a strong tradition of scholarship that has examined the novel as a "fundamental investigation of the problematics of writing."[51] As J. Gerald Kennedy writes, "*Pym* has become focal for theoretical critics because it calls attention to its own insufficiency as a written text, [and] raises the question of how writing can . . . represent truth."[52] Thus, for many readers of the novel, the central concern is language itself: its doubleness, its duplicity, and its strategies of evasion. The adventure is being played out on a landscape literally made up of writing.[53]

John Carlos Rowe, writing in *Through the Custom-House,* articulates the position that emerged out of this poststructuralist interrogation of Poe: "This text enacts the deconstruction of representation as the illusion of the truth and prefigures the contemporary conception of writing as the endless production of differences."[54] Rowe's more recent historicist inquiries into *Pym* can be used to summarize the other important issue around which critics focus their reading of *Pym*: "Poe was a proslavery Southerner and should be reassessed as such in whatever approach we take to his life and writings."[55] Both of these claims are right in an important sense, but only insofar as a reading of the novel's textual and theoretical questions is brought together with a reading of its consideration of racial issues; in this way we see that it is Poe's project to show that the crises in writing and in race are necessarily related. In other words, Poe's concern in *Pym* is not with slavery in itself, nor is it precisely with "the contemporary conception of writing as the endless production of differences"; rather, it is in racial difference as the condition—the ground—for an American writing.

Pym is one of Poe's rare early fictions with an explicitly American narrator, and it presents a hero who is stupefied by distinctions—racial and textual —he is unable to read. Two of Poe's only other early tales narrated by "Americans" similarly focus on the conjunction of textual and racial interpretations. In "The Psyche Zenobia" (1838), the narrator is a Philadelphia bluestocking who goes to Britain to learn how to write an article for *Blackwood's,* only to be decapitated by an Edinburgh church clock while her black servant—upon whose shoulders she stands—sullenly refuses her command to help her down. In "The Man That Was Used Up" (1839), the narrator searches for the "true story" of a famed Indian fighter, only to discover him to be a dismembered victim of the Indians' savagery—a composite of prosthetics reassembled each day by a mocking slave. In their attempts to get at the meaning of texts, these American narrators instead encounter scenes where bodies are literally torn apart by racial difference.

Pym carries himself toward a similar landscape, beginning with his first disastrous adventure with his friend, Augustus, in which his small boat is torn in two by a whaling ship, significantly named *The Penguin.* As we know from *Symzonia,* one of Poe's several sources for the composition of *Pym,* the penguin had a specific meaning for those who theorized, as Poe did, about the possibility of a hollow earth. For Seaborn, penguins—in their perfect whiteness—promised the purity of the inhabitants within the earth's interior. For Poe, as well, the penguin is marked by the "purest white imaginable" (151) but is always also bound to the fierce blackness of its cohabitant, the albatross. In Pym's narration, late in his long adventure south, the penguins serve a similar function as they do in *Symzonia,* only here it is not their purity that urges the explorer on, as it did for Captain Seaborn, but the perfect harmony of their system of cohabitation with the albatross. Their "city" is laid out with perfect rationality "upon a plan concerted between the two species—that of the albatross being placed in the centre of a little square formed by the nests of four penguins" (151–52). "In short," Pym continues, "nothing can be more astonishing than the spirit of reflection evinced by these feathered beings, and nothing surely can be better calculated to elicit reflection in every well-regulated human intellect" (153).

This vision is the South as romantically pictured by Tucker and Poe in the "Slavery" review—a world where black and white exist together in perfect balance—each always in his place, a state of "perfection" the South had supposedly achieved in the full flowering of the slave state, the fall from which it is the novel's task to describe. Indeed, in contradistinction to this vision of the perfect ordering of black and white, the novel presents us with a series of diastrophisms on the national-racial landscape that lead progressively toward the apocalypse of the conclusion.

His small vessel torn apart, in the novel's opening pages, by the whaling ship, Pym has his first of many bizarre experiences with death, burial, and dismemberment. Aboard *The Penguin*, Pym witnesses his first foreboding of revolution, as the crew threatens mutiny against their heartless captain. From these early experiences Pym discovers in himself a love of "shipwreck and famine; of death or captivity among barbarian hordes." And so he stows away aboard Augustus's father's ship, *The Grampus*, the killer whale—a name signifying, like *The Penguin*, the joining of blackness and whiteness into one body, but here an image not of peace and "reflection" but of violence and destruction.[56]

Buried within the hold of *The Grampus*, Pym waits for Augustus's signal to come on deck and make himself known. After days without word or provisions, Pym finally receives, attached to his dog, Tiger, a note of warning. Buried in the hold of yet another mutinous ship, cut off from the revolution above him, Pym's only hope of comprehending his fate lies in the page he cannot read. Deprived of light, Pym illuminates the paper by placing it on a book (*Lewis and Clark*) and showering it with phosphorous, only to discover in the "clear light" that the page tells of "nothing but the dreary and unsatisfactory blank" (78).[57] All he sees is a sheet of white, and, in a fury, Pym tears the page to pieces.

When it finally occurs to him that the message might have lain on the other side of the page, he reassembles, with Tiger's help, the scattered page. Reproducing the experiment, he is finally able to make out only one line: *"blood—your life depends upon lying close"* (80). All he can see is this fragment, or, more properly, a fragment of that fragment: "'*Blood*' . . . that word of all words—so rife at all times with mystery, and suffering, and terror—how trebly full of import did it now appear—how chillily and heavily (disjointed, as it thus was, from any foregoing words to qualify or render it distinct) did its vague syllables fall, amid the deep gloom of my prison, into the innermost recesses of my soul!" (80). The isolated word—here strangely echoing with multiple "syllables"—is horrifying to Pym precisely because it is disjointed from any others that might provide context; it strikes terror into his soul both by its synecdochal relation to his own isolation and its seemingly metaphoric relation to his own danger. Like the "vague and undefined fears" described in the "Slavery" review the previous year, the "vague syllables" of the disassociated word "blood" here produce a nameless terror—in the words of the review, "alarming in proportion to the value of the interest endangered."

The word, however, turns out to be not figurative at all, but quite literal. Once he is released from his dungeon, Pym is able to see it in its proper context: "*I have scrawled this with blood*," Augustus wrote, wasting valuable time (and blood) upon a seemingly irrelevant piece of information. Blood, it turns out, is not what the writing is trying to describe—it is what the writing literally is; as Michael J. S. Williams writes, "It names only its own materiality."[58] The novel's lesson in language's "materiality," however, is in the service of the still-larger lesson of the novel's conclusion in which writing becomes materially equivalent to racial difference.[59] Augustus's note proves that to write revolutionary stories is to write not about blood, but to write blood itself. Similarly, in the concluding lessons on Tsalal, the novel will argue, to write American stories is necessarily to write not about racial difference, but to write racial difference—the thing itself. Here, without blood, there is only the blinding white page. On Tsalal, without racial difference, there is only the blinding white of the abyss. Thus, this preliminary lesson in writing and reading in the hold of the *Grampus* comes full circle at the novel's end, when Pym encounters in the cavern on Tsalal the fragments that inscribe the origins of black and white.

The tale Augustus tells Pym is of a horrible revolution in the order of things, in which the ship was captured by a mutinous crew led by the black cook who butchered the whites systematically, striking them on the forehead with his ax and then throwing them overboard one by one (86). The installments originally published in the *Messenger* end here. As had Brown with his scenes of Indian atrocities, so Poe clearly saw in the scene of a black-led uprising his best advertisement for the novel to follow.[60]

We learn that Augustus alone had been spared from the cook's ax, rescued by the intervention of one of the mutineers, Dirk Peters, who is revealed to be a bizarre amalgam of racial types:

Peters himself was one of the most purely ferocious-looking men I ever beheld. He was short in stature—not more than four feet eight inches high—but his limbs were of Herculean mould. His hands, especially, were so enormously thick and broad as hardly to retain human shape. His arms, as well as legs, were *bowed* in the most singular manner. . . . His head was equally deformed, being of immense size, with an indentation of the crown (like that on the head of most negroes), and entirely bald. To conceal this latter deficiency . . . he usually wore a wig formed of any hair-like material which presented itself. (87)

Peters is Poe's grotesque Natty Bumppo. He is a "half-breed"—Indian and white man—but also clearly marked (by the "bowed" legs and the crown of his head) in terms of the stereotypical descriptions of African Americans found in writings by Poe and others of the period.[61] Throughout the novel Peters is referred to as "the hybrid," and his resemblance to the simian culprit of "Murders in the Rue Morgue" is striking.[62] Pym will explore the ultimate frontier of race with this bizarre guide.

The revolution is far from over even after the captain has been thrown overboard. No sooner has the mutinous crew gained control of the ship than it divides up into two "parties": one, led by the mate, determined to turn pirate, and the other, led by Peters, determined to continue on the voyage south. The standoff turns bloody as the mate succeeds in killing off his opponents one by one, until finally all the survivors but Peters have gone over to his side. Knowing his life is in danger, Peters enlists Augustus and Pym to help overthrow the ship once again. Pym comes up with a plan to dress himself up as one of the recent victims of the violence, in order to play "upon the superstitious terrors and guilty conscience of the mate" (107).

Pym had already proved himself a master of disguise by dressing as a drunken sailor to thwart his grandfather's attempts to prevent him from going to sea. Now, as Peters applies Pym's war paint, he puts on a more complex mask in a more deadly game: "Peters then arranged my face, first rubbing it well over with white chalk, and afterward splotching it with blood, which he took from a cut in his finger. The streak across the eye was not forgotten, and presented a most shocking appearance" (109). This act of racial cross-dressing—painting Pym white and red—is familiar to the fiction we have examined, but unique in one sense at least. Here the act of racial cross-dressing is being equated to, significantly, an act of writing—the fiction that Pym's party is trying to pass off as reality on the gullible mate and his crew depends on Pym himself being written upon with the signs of racial difference. Painted white and red with chalk and blood—

two implements of writing in this novel—Pym leads his companions against the mate and the cook.

The war is won: instead of turning pirate (equivalent to turning "savage"), the crew of four—Pym, Augustus, Peters, and Parker, the lone survivor of the mate's crew—continue on their original southern course. But the mutiny, the subsequent violence, and a series of devastating storms have left the ship a "mere log, rolling about at the mercy of every wave" (117). Floating aimlessly for weeks, with few provisions, the desperate refugees of the *Grampus* at last spy a ship in the distance headed their way: "The vessel in sight was a large hermaphrodite brig, of a Dutch build, and painted black, with a tawdry gilt figurehead" (123). As the ship erratically approaches the hulk of the *Grampus,* Pym spies, leaning over the bow, "a stout and tall man, with a very dark skin. He seemed by his manner to be encouraging us to have patience, nodding to us in a cheerful although rather odd way, and smiling so constantly as to display a set of the most brilliantly white teeth" (123).

These hopes are dashed, however, as the ship runs alongside the *Grampus,* and the four discover that the entire crew has been destroyed by a mysterious plague and is now food for seabirds. The "hermaphrodite brig" offers a horrifying forewarning of the dangers that await the beleaguered crew of the *Grampus* as they travel "still farther south." The white European crew has turned black, cannibalized by white birds. This fate seems promised to Pym and his companions as well when a feasting gull drops "a portion of clotted and liver-like substance" (125) on the deck of the *Grampus.* It is fulfilled shortly thereafter, when the crew is forced to draw cannibal lots and devour Parker. Worse still, a wound Augustus has sustained rapidly turns gangrenous, and he dies a shriveled "mass of putrefaction"—like the crew of the Dutch brig, a blackened shadow of his former self. "His arm was completely black from the wrist to the shoulder" (142), Pym tells us, a grotesque detail made even more striking by the fact that Augustus's wound was in his leg. Poe continues a long tradition of playing on fears of a blackness that could devour white Americans, a tradition that had grown out of environmental theories of racial difference: if blackness or "savagery" were the result of environmental conditions, could not these same effects be worked on whites as well?

Beyond the obvious shock value of these gruesome passages at the center of the novel, Poe is also further laying the ground for the landscape of writing and race he will discover at the novel's end. The ghost ship's hermaphrodite pairing of black and gilt can be read as an unnatural imitation of the union of dark and light found in the *Penguin,* the *Grampus,* and Peters himself. Studying the approaching ship closely for some sign of their salvation, Pym and his companions can see only the darks and lights—first the "brilliant white" teeth and the "very dark skin" and then the "white plumage" of the bird "spattered all over with blood" (125). Yet in his scrutiny of the ship's stern, one so intense that the teeth of the dead man seemingly beckoning to them could be noted, Pym failed to read its name: "We might have easily seen the name upon her stern, and, indeed, taken other observations which would have guided us in making out her character; but the intense excitement of the moment blinded us to everything of that nature" (126).[63] As in the scene in the hold of the *Grampus,* Pym is again blind to writing, laying further groundwork for his final inability to recognize the writing in the caverns on Tsalal. Whatever the name written on the stern might have told him, we are right to speculate that, like the *Penguin* and *Grampus* and like the writings on Tsalal, it would have signified black and white. Yet Pym, who can see blacks and whites with a remarkable keenness of sight, cannot read the writing that both signifies and is signified by the troubled interdependence of these colors.

Pym and Peters are rescued from a seemingly inevitable doom by a British exploring and whaling ship, the *Jane Guy,* whose weak-willed captain grants Pym authority to direct the ship on a course of polar expedition. As it approaches the Antarctic Circle, the *Jane Guy* makes two important discoveries. First, far from being ice-locked, as previous explorers had warned, they find the Antarctic waters open and surprisingly temperate. Second, everything they discover in this most southern region is either black or white, and, indeed, once they have traveled south of the "city" of the penguins and the albatross, the two are never be found juxtaposed again.

That this south is meant to allegorize an American South is underscored, as many readers have noticed, by the discovery of an island "bearing a strong resemblance to corded bales of cotton" (165). This is the border that separates the ideal South of Poe's imagination from Poe's apocalyptic vision of the future South—a vision he shared with Tucker's *Partisan Leader.* For south of these "corded bales of cotton," through a sea of "an extraordinarily dark colour" (167), the crew discovers a people so entirely defined by darkness that even their teeth are black. The island of Tsalal—on the brink of the polar abyss—is the opposite in every way of that internal world imagined in *Symzonia*: here everything is perfect black, and everything white is shunned with horror. There is no possibility of whiteness and blackness mixing here—as they did in the colony of the penguins and albatross—and even the water that flows through the island obeys strict segregationist principles: "Upon collecting a basinful, and allowing it to settle thoroughly, we perceived that the whole mass of liquid was made up of a number of distinct veins, each of a distinct hue; that these veins did not co-mingle; and that their cohesion was perfect in regard to their own particles among themselves, and imperfect in regard to neighbouring veins" (172). Pym discovers in the principles that govern this water "the first definite link in that vast chain of apparent miracles with which I was destined to be at length encircled" (172).

The second of these links is the series of awful consequences that follow the crew's attempt to ignore this natural principle of segregation. At first they take the people of Tsalal for ignorant but cooperative savages, and they begin to establish a colonial system of harvesting the *bêches-de-mere* in abundance on the island. The blacks fulfill all of the whites' expectations: displaying cartoon-like gestures of delight and superstition, eager to please and easy to master. But behind this facade, the inhabitants of Tsalal plot the massacre of all the whites on the island. What follows is a race war of apocalyptic proportions, as first a mountain of earth is hurled upon the unsuspecting whites, and then a cargo of powder aboard the *Jane Guy* wreaks havoc among the equally unsuspecting blacks.

Pym and Peters (whom Pym has now conveniently redefined as a "white man") alone escape the ambush of the "most barbarous, subtle, and bloodthirsty wretches that ever contaminated the face of the globe" (180). With a black captive, Nu-Nu, they make their escape from Tsalal in search of a land "still farther south" where they might escape the vengeance of the race war that has been unleashed. But to escape this "most wicked, hypocritical, vindictive, bloodthirsty, and altogether fiendish race of men upon the face of the globe" (201), Pym discovers—repeating the qualifying phrase—is, in fact, to leave "the face of the globe." To pursue the fantasy of a world without racial difference—the internal world imagined by Symmes—is to leave the world altogether.

As they approach the polar abyss long promised by Symmes, suddenly everything turns from black to white. Even the sea turns white, and the explorers find themselves enveloped in white ashes that fall from an unknown source. So abrupt is the change that their Tsalalian captive dies of fright, as if one so black could not survive in a world so white; and Peters, the hybrid, drifts into a comatose state. As Daniel Hoffman writes, "It is Pym and Pym alone who witnesses the revelation of the white superhuman figure at the brink of the chasm."[64] Pym alone is conscious as they approach the "limitless cataract"—and he alone is received by the giant form that reaches through the "white curtain" (205) at the novel's end, one "very far larger in its proportions than any dweller among men. And the hue of the skin of the figure was of the perfect whiteness of the snow" (206). Thus, Peters, who we are told in the "Note" survives Pym, has no tale to tell, nothing to offer to clarify the meaning of this awesome encounter—because it was one he has not, and could not, experience. It is left to the editor at the end to clarify the meaning of the whiteness of the conclusion.

The polygenism of the day helps us make sense of the end to this novel, as a fantasy of a point of reunion with an original parent—with the white "Adam," or the white god—a reunion neither Peters nor the Tsalalian could witness. But, notably, it is a reunion that the (presumed white) reader is barred from as well. W. G. Ramsay, writing in the *Southern Agriculturalist* in 1839, spelled out the heretical assumption implicit in the new polygenism: "We are almost tempted to believe that there must have been more Adams' [sic] than one, each variety of colour having its own original parent."[65] What had formerly been a monogenist belief in the possibility of a return to a unifying whiteness is now imaginable for Poe only as a fantasy of a return to a womblike state before civilization, before society, before writing. Here, with the witnessing of "pure whiteness," the story necessarily ends, and we are told by the anonymous editor that Pym has suddenly died—not, as one would expect, in the encounter at the abyss, but in the writing of the experience ten years later.

This editor, who picks up his manuscript after Pym's untimely end, cannot describe the encounter at the abyss, but he can translate the writing in the caverns. With Pym dead and Peters vanished into the American West, it is left to the editor to translate the text of Pym's landscape; and this translation provides the conclusion that Pym could not and "Poe," we are told, would not write. For his translation uncovers the original act of divine writing that collapses the distinction between the writing and the thing itself. As Sidney Kaplan writes in his pioneering study of *Pym* and race, "In Tsalal, the word is the thing—both were created together; and the word is in the language of the creation itself."[66] Tsalal serves as the boundary between here and oblivion, the point at which the primal "thing" (racial difference) and the primal "words" (black and white) are discovered to be one and the same.

This point of origins spells out literally and representatively the distinction between black and white in the caverns on Tsalal. The two cannot be separated: the distinction between black and white is the occasion for this act of divine writing. "To be shady" (207), the caverns spell out, "whence all the inflections of shadow or darkness," our editor translates; "To be white," reads the writing on the caverns, "whence all the inflections of brilliancy and whiteness" (208). But this writing not only spells out the distinction between black and white, it literally is what it represents: the walls of the cavern are "very black" (193), the writing on the caverns is made of "white arrowhead flints" (194).

Language critics have long seen the story of writing told in *Pym* as one that reveals language's struggle to posit its own original, stable truth; race critics have largely read the story as one about imperialism and slavery. Read in conjunction, we might now see the novel confronting what Poe imagines as an inextricable relationship between writing and racial difference. The search for origins (of language, of the earth, of the nation) leads to the discovery of the origin of racial difference itself. The editor scrambles in his closing comments to make sense of this discovery in the caverns on Tsalal, explaining what critics have repeated for generations afterwards: that "nothing *white* was to be found at Tsalal, and nothing otherwise in the subsequent voyage to the region beyond" (208). Beyond this obvious lesson, however, the editor has only one, a "scriptural" quotation that signifies at once the divine origin of racial difference—"*graven . . . within the hills*"—and a promise of an approaching apocalypse. Like the explanation of the origins of racial hierarchy offered in the "Slavery" review—"*It was the will of God it should be so*"—racial difference finds its origins here in a act of divine writing, which is at once a point of origins and an apocalyptic conclusion.

Pym's narrative abruptly ends at the point at which he prepared to narrate his union with the desired figure of pure whiteness. To attempt to escape a world of racial difference—to find a world where all is perfect whiteness—is, in the logic of this novel, to arrive at a point at which writing can no longer exist. Like the writing of the caverns ("to be white" inscribed on "to be shady") or like the printed page (black printed on white), the very fact of writing this American fiction for Poe depends necessarily on racial difference—as Brown had suggested in *Huntly* forty years earlier. But unlike Brown, Poe sees no happy future for either the nation or its literature, for the formula upon which both are founded proves an unstable equation. Only with everything perfectly in its place can this dynamic keep from destroying itself; and the United States, Poe well knows, is not a nation adept at keeping things in their places. This perfect stability is represented in the novel by the island "city" of penguin and albatross, who form together, as Irwin has demonstrated, a quincunx—"a

God-given design that orders the universe."[67] As Poe and his fellow south-ern romancers believed, such a harmony was achieved in the South under slavery. But once the order of things is overturned—and we know from the black cook's rebellion that all is overturned from the very start of Poe's American tale—black and white will inevitably destroy each other, as they do on Tsalal. Once the perfect balance is destroyed, there is only a flight toward fantasies of perfect whiteness "whose attainment is destruction."

V

As Morton "proved," the search for the origins of racial difference led not, as monogenists had long supposed, to an original, edenic whiteness, but to a racial landscape that looked very much like the nineteenth-century United States. *Symzonia*'s fantasy of a world of perfect whiteness, a world before racial difference, racial anthropology now proclaimed, was pure fantasy. In the beginning, there was black and white. It is in such terms that *Pym*'s final projection of an indescribable perfect whiteness is de-fined, articulated one last time even as Poe acknowledges it as one that can no longer be written. In this light we can begin to make sense of Poe's ongoing obsession with Jeremiah N. Reynolds, the man who perpetuated Symmes's theory long after it had been rejected as pure fantasy by the nation at large.

Toward the end of the narrative, Pym offers a long digression on the history of exploration of the Antarctic south, a history that culminates in the work of "Mr. J. N. Reynolds, whose great exertions and perseverance have at length succeeded in getting set on foot a national expedition" (159). It was an expedition very much on Poe's mind as he was writing his novel. Beginning in August 1836, he wrote a series of articles detailing the plans for the Great United States Exploring Expedition—the fulfillment of Symmes's dream and Reynolds's tireless efforts on its behalf as suc-cessor and promoter. Poe's first essay, which celebrated those who had devoted their lives to its cause, especially Reynolds, focused its elaborate defense of the expedition on the expansion of national empire and on "national honor and glory" that would result.[68]

The following January, in the same issue of the *Messenger* that con-tained the first installment of *Pym*, Poe reviewed Reynolds's *Address* on the necessity of the polar expedition. Poe's praise for Reynolds and his vision is uncharacteristically gushing: "We must necessarily begin with Mr. Reynolds. He is the originator, the preserving and indomitable advocate, the life, the soul of the design. Whatever, of glory at least, accrue therefor from the expedition, this gentleman, whatever post he may occupy in it, or whether none, will be fairly entitled to the lion's share, and will certainly receive it" (1235). As he is composing his own fictional adventure to parallel that of Reynolds, Poe anticipates, "with an intensity of eager expectation, which we cannot think we have ever experienced before," the "published record of the expedition" that Reynolds would compose (1240).

But as Poe surely suspected, Reynolds would gain no role in, nor credit for, the expedition. Although Reynolds had done his best to distance himself publicly from the more visionary claims of his mentor, Symmes, nevertheless once the expedition began seriously to be considered by Congress moves were underway to remove Reynolds from any position of responsibility. There were strong reservations about bringing Symmes's "proselyte" along as a "diplomatic agent to Symmesonia."[69] As Poe sympathized with Reynolds in the *Messenger,* such attacks are "perfectly in unison with the history of all similar enterprizes, and of the vigorous minds which have conceived . . . them."[70] But the cause was already lost. Reynolds's original vision of the mission was transformed by the administrations that sponsored it, so that by the time the mission was ready to sail, it was little surprise to anyone that Reynolds himself had been excluded. But if Reynolds was to be excluded from the actual voyage, he was not to be excluded from Poe's fictional one. Pym's long nautical digressions make for some of the more tedious reading in the novel, but the role they accord to Reynolds is significant. Alongside the written accounts of actual explorers are placed Reynolds's writings, and that Reynolds was only a theorist does not make his explorations of the Pole any less valid for Poe.

Poe was by no means alone in his interest in the polar expedition. Samuel George Morton also had strong personal and professional interest in the mission.[71] Among the crew that sailed with Wilkes was Morton's friend and associate Charles Pickering, chief naturalist for the United States Exploring Expedition. One of Pickering's main responsibilities at the completion of the voyages was the compiling of a treatise on the races of man in light of what he had experienced in the South Pacific. Pickering corresponded with Morton during the voyage, claiming to have discovered three new races to supplement the five cataloged by Morton. Not surprisingly, he also found in the peoples of the South Pacific evidence to support what Morton had discovered by measuring skulls with mustard seeds and buckshot: that the races had been created separately to meet the peculiar needs of their natural environments. Attempts were made to suppress Pickering's work by the defenders of monogenism, and indeed the government for a time delayed its publication. But the results were finally published, providing what William Stanton identifies as "the most comprehensive survey of the races of men that . . . had ever been published" (348).

Pickering's book was published, however, with some clear concessions to the defenders of monogenism, most manifest in the preface by a British physician in the 1850 London edition of *The Races of Man*, which proclaims, "We are fully satisfied, that all the races of man are, as the Gospel clearly expresses it, 'of one blood'—THAT THE BLACK MAN, RED MAN, AND THE WHITE MAN, ARE LINKS IN ONE GREAT CHAIN OF RELATION-SHIP, AND ALIKE CHILDREN WHICH HAVE DESCENDED FROM ONE COMMON PARENT."[72] Although it is not clear how the doctor derived this monogenist conclusion from the book that follows, whether by way of compromise or because it no longer seemed a question worthy of debate, Pickering throughout offers little didactic argument in favor of polygenism. The races were different—more different, and more varied, it turned out, than had been previously supposed. They had been different for as long as history can record, so there was little evidence save Scripture left to argue for the "COMMON PARENT." The strategy on the part of Pickering and other racial scientists in the antebellum period was to let Scripture have its say and then proceed with the "evidence." Pickering himself makes little reference to the debate, merely pointing out in his opening "Enumeration of the Races" that "the existence of races . . . is a phenomenon independent of climate."[73]

Pickering's study of race, like Morton's, offers as its conclusion the promise of white supremacy on the world theater. In his chapter "Numerical Proportions" whites are said to constitute the numerical majority at 350,000,000, followed by Mongolians and Malaysians, with Negroes far behind at 55,000,000. Pickering's work on race, however, is at least on the surface less polemical than Morton's, presented as a collection of impressions and data gathered from his travels and research. Nevertheless, one driving concern does present itself against the deliberately dispassionate tone Pickering assumes throughout: the belief that each race has a preordained destiny to fulfill within its specific boundaries:

> While admitting the general truth, that mankind are essentially alike, no one doubts the existence of character, distinguishing not only individuals, but communities and nations. I am persuaded that there is, besides a *character of race*. . . .

In the organic world, each new field requires *a new creation*; each change in circumstances going beyond the constitution of a plant or animal, is met by a new adaptation, until the universe is full; while among the immense variety of created beings, two kinds are hardly found fulfilling the same purpose. Some analogy may possibly exist in the human family; and it may even be questioned whether any one of the races existing singly would, up to the present day, have extended itself over the whole surface of the globe. (289; emphasis added)

Pickering's rhetoric is characteristically elusive, but what is being argued here, just below the surface, is significant. First, contained in this paragraph is an assertion of polygenism, as Pickering uses the analogy of the "organic world" to suggest a theory of multiple creations and the resulting "immense variety of created beings." Here, as elsewhere, Pickering refuses the explanation of environmental adaptation, insisting on "creation" as the root of all racial difference. But he goes further in suggesting that the races were created each for a distinct destiny uniquely imprinted on their racial character, one that can only be fulfilled within their proper place on the globe. This veteran of the United States Exploring Expedition concludes with what amounts to an argument against the kind of imperialist expansion the expedition had been sponsored to foment, suggesting that it might be not only wrong, but even dangerous, to believe that one's racial destiny extends "over the whole surface of the globe."

That Pickering concludes his treatise on the races of man with an isolationist argument makes sense only in reading backwards to his earlier discussion of the "Negro Race." After describing the physical characteristics of that race, Pickering maps its original geographic boundaries in Africa, concluding: "These limits, to all appearance, would not have been exceeded to this day, aside from foreign interference; but, as one consequence of the events of the last two centuries, the Negro race seems destined to fill hereafter an important place in general history" (188). Racial geography, for Pickering, identifies natural borders that must be maintained. The slave trade brought about an unnatural migration of blacks into a "naturally" white America, creating a situation that Pickering is not alone in foreseeing in terms of a historical crisis. Thus, for Pickering, crossing of racial boundaries—whether through importing slaves or exporting white Americans—is a risky business. One's racial destiny lies in one's own backyard, a logic that potentially gives new meaning to what has long been considered one of the central lessons of *Pym*: "*blood! your life depends upon lying close.*"

Reynolds's dream of the exploring expedition had its roots both in *Symzonia*'s fantasy of the Internal World of perfect whiteness and in the logic of Manifest Destiny. The racial scientist who actually completed the expedition, on the other hand, implicitly questioned the validity of both projects. *Symzonia*'s monogenist fantasy that the nation could return to a world before racial difference is denied by Pickering's polygenism. The myth of imperial destiny—which was rapidly becoming, in the wake of the drive to annex Texas, explicit national ideology—is challenged as well by Pickering's argument on behalf of a divinely ordained geographic segregation, one remarkably similar to that which Pym found in the waters and inhabitants of Tsalal. Without the possibility of a return to an original whiteness through the effects of American environment or institutions, those who continued to work on behalf of an "American" (that is, white) race would be forced in the second half of the century increasingly toward positions similar to that advocated at the end of Pickering's study: isolationism, colonization, and, later, restrictions on immigration, social Darwinism, and the defense of an increasingly reified notion of American "blood." Thus, we see the shift to a logic of racism that will dominate the second half of the century and beyond, just as Poe's novel portrays the end of the fantasy that had dominated American racial theory and literature since the earliest days of the Republic.

VI

With *Pym* Poe had sought out the meaning and the origin of the "vague and nameless terror" inspired by the contemplation of race in the "Slavery" review of 1836. This is an impulse common to much of his fiction: to comprehend the underlying meaning of terror—"to reduce the horror to rules," as Larzer Ziff describes it.[74] After *Pym* Poe considered how these rules could be applied to the creation, criticism, and marketing of literature in the United States. He was not alone in imagining a connection between the discoveries of racial science and the prospects of literary nationalism. In the *Gentleman's Magazine* in 1839, while Poe was serving as assistant editor, John Beauchamp Jones offered his "Thoughts on the Literary Prospects of America": "If the distinct races are differently gifted, and various climates peculiarly characterized in a mental point of view, the Americans may claim all the advantages resulting from either, inasmuch as they derive their origin from the most cultivated nations, and the extent of their territory embraces every variety of climate."[75] If the study of races and the study of literature were so intimately connected, then the task for Poe was to understand how the lessons of one could be applied effectively and systematically to the other.

As Edward Hungerford has shown, Poe had already translated his interest in phrenology into literary-critical terms.[76] As early as 1836, he began using the terms found in phrenological studies as critical terms to judge and measure the value of literary texts: "veneration," "causality," and so on. "Mr. Dickens' head must puzzle the phrenologists," he wrote in 1844. "The organs of ideality are small; and [yet] the conclusion of the 'Curiosity-Shop' is more truly ideal (in both phrenological senses) than any composition of equal length in the English language."[77] At the same time that Poe was working on *Pym,* his interests in phrenology also brought him to a new subject of inquiry: autography, the theory, in his words, "that the mental features are indicated . . . by the handwriting."[78] Here was a real test for the equivalencies between phrenological and literary-critical principles he had been experimenting with in some of his more infamous critical reviews.

Poe's first notes on "Autography" appeared in the *Messenger* in 1836 and were reprised and expanded in *Graham's* in 1841. They were immensely popular, both for the "savagery" of their critical and personal assessments and for their author's display of wizardry as a reader of hidden signs.[79] "A Chapter on Autography" published in *Graham's* fully developed the principles more playfully applied in the earlier *Messenger* installments. Here Poe seriously attempts to translate phrenological techniques to the study of handwriting, and his "results," to say the least, are astounding. As one reviewer commented on the popular series, "Mr. Poe is a wonderful man. He can read the hieroglyphics of the Pharaohs, tell you what you are thinking about while he walks beside you, and criticise you into shape without giving offense."[80] No assessment would have pleased Poe more, for this is precisely the image he had been trying to cultivate since beginning with the *Messenger* in 1835: a reader of secret writings, a diviner of secret thoughts, and a critic to chasten the literary nation toward true greatness.

If *Pym* taught Poe that there was no escape from American writing's dependence on racial difference, he sought in his "Autography" series to put the lessons to good use. If American writing is dependent on—indeed, as the conclusion to *Pym* would have it, all but equivalent to—racial difference, then the task for Poe is to apply the techniques of racial science to the study of American writing itself. To do so—to be a Morton or a Pickering of American letters—would be the greatest critical achieve-

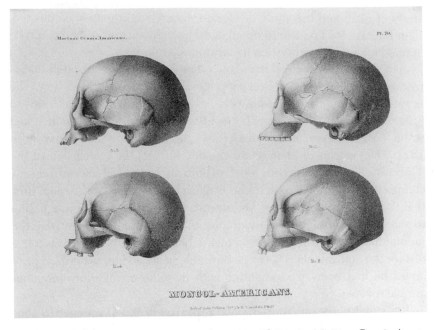

Fig. 6. Plate 70, "Mongol-Americans," from Samuel George Morton, *Crania Americana* (1839). (Courtesy of the Milton S. Eisenhower Library of the Johns Hopkins University, Baltimore, Maryland.)

ment, one that would allow the critic to guide the destiny of American writing by unearthing the hierarchies inherent in handwriting itself.

Poe sets out in 1841 to gather signatures together in a collection much like Morton's collection of skulls. Like *Crania Americana*, Poe's "Chapter on Autography" reproduces the objects of its study—the autographs—meticulously, in fine woodblocks, while below each specimen, Poe, the diviner of chirography, unearths the hidden meaning of the handwriting as if it were, in fact, a skull (see figs. 6 and 7). Poe's collection of the signatures of American writers constitutes one of the earliest concerted efforts to offer, in the words of one reviewer, a "general sketch of American literary character."[81] In his collection of signatures, like Morton's collection of skulls, Poe seeks out the truth of the "character" not only of the individual authors, but of the national culture as well.[82]

Thus, "Autography" is an attempt to rationalize the study of American literature, to define it in terms of the "objective" principles of analysis and hierarchization Poe admired in phrenology. What he finds in the collection before him is a truth less optimistic than that offered by Combe's

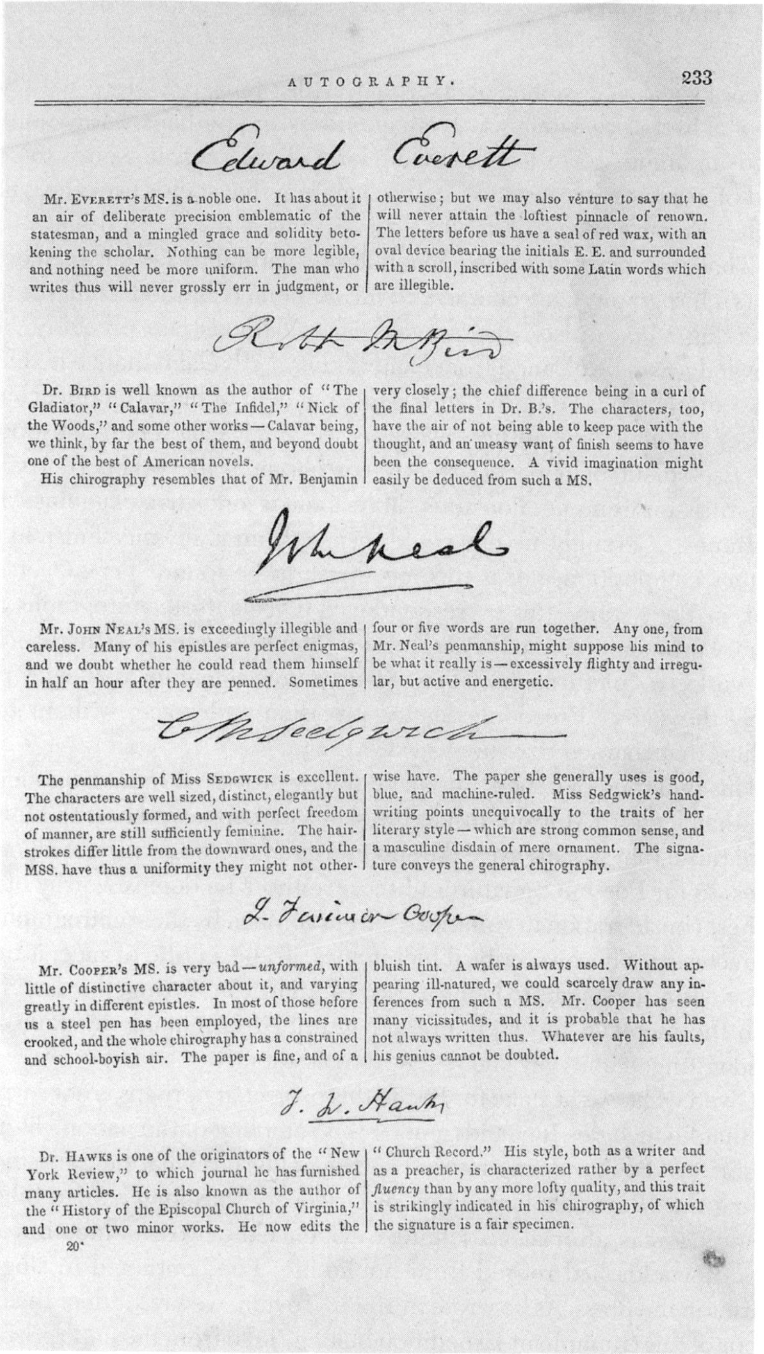

Edward Everett

Mr. EVERETT's MS. is a noble one. It has about it an air of deliberate precision emblematic of the statesman, and a mingled grace and solidity betokening the scholar. Nothing can be more legible, and nothing need be more uniform. The man who writes thus will never grossly err in judgment, or otherwise; but we may also venture to say that he will never attain the loftiest pinnacle of renown. The letters before us have a seal of red wax, with an oval device bearing the initials E. E. and surrounded with a scroll, inscribed with some Latin words which are illegible.

Robt M Bird

Dr. BIRD is well known as the author of "The Gladiator," "Calavar," "The Infidel," "Nick of the Woods," and some other works — Calavar being, we think, by far the best of them, and beyond doubt one of the best of American novels.

His chirography resembles that of Mr. Benjamin very closely; the chief difference being in a curl of the final letters in Dr. B.'s. The characters, too, have the air of not being able to keep pace with the thought, and an uneasy want of finish seems to have been the consequence. A vivid imagination might easily be deduced from such a MS.

John Neal

Mr. JOHN NEAL's MS. is exceedingly illegible and careless. Many of his epistles are perfect enigmas, and we doubt whether he could read them himself in half an hour after they are penned. Sometimes four or five words are run together. Any one, from Mr. Neal's penmanship, might suppose his mind to be what it really is — excessively flighty and irregular, but active and energetic.

C M Sedgwick

The penmanship of Miss SEDGWICK is excellent. The characters are well sized, distinct, elegantly but not ostentatiously formed, and with perfect freedom of manner, are still sufficiently feminine. The hair-strokes differ little from the downward ones, and the MSS. have thus a uniformity they might not otherwise have. The paper she generally uses is good, blue, and machine-ruled. Miss Sedgwick's handwriting points unequivocally to the traits of her literary style — which are strong common sense, and a masculine disdain of mere ornament. The signature conveys the general chirography.

J. Fenimore Cooper

Mr. COOPER's MS. is very bad — *unformed*, with little of distinctive character about it, and varying greatly in different epistles. In most of those before us a steel pen has been employed, the lines are crooked, and the whole chirography has a constrained and school-boyish air. The paper is fine, and of a bluish tint. A wafer is always used. Without appearing ill-natured, we could scarcely draw any inferences from such a MS. Mr. Cooper has seen many vicissitudes, and it is probable that he has not always written thus. Whatever are his faults, his genius cannot be doubted.

F. L. Hawks

Dr. HAWKS is one of the originators of the "New York Review," to which journal he has furnished many articles. He is also known as the author of the "History of the Episcopal Church of Virginia," and one or two minor works. He now edits the "Church Record." His style, both as a writer and as a preacher, is characterized rather by a perfect *fluency* than by any more lofty quality, and this trait is strikingly indicated in his chirography, of which the signature is a fair specimen.

20*

Fig. 7. Page from Edgar Allan Poe's "A Chapter on Autography," in *Graham's Magazine* 19 (1841). (Courtesy of the Milton S. Eisenhower Library of the Johns Hopkins University, Baltimore, Maryland.)

phrenological assessment of Morton's skulls, however. Here we see a national literature a long way from greatness and perhaps, "Autography" seems to argue, never to achieve the kind of greatness it aspires to—the kind of greatness represented in the signature that stands over the whole study: "Edgar A. Poe."

"That a strong analogy *does* generally and naturally exist between every man's chirography and character, will be denied by none but the unreflecting," Poe insists, and he goes on to demonstrate precisely what knowledge can be gleaned from handwriting.[83] His claim that he is able to make autographical determinations independent of his own critical opinions of the individual authors' works is seemingly called into question as the assessment of one consistently corroborates the other. In Irving's signature, for example, Poe finds "little about it indicative of genius." Poe continues: "Certainly, no one could suspect from it any nice finish in the writer's composition, nor is this nice finish to be found" (17). Over and over, in Poe's study, this correspondence reveals itself. Autographs and literary productions confirm each other: John P. Kennedy's signature, like his works, is "picturesque"; Mrs. Sigourgney's signature possesses precisely the same "Freedom, dignity, precision and grace, without originality" that characterizes her works (21, 23).

This founding of a theory upon tautology proves no more troubling to Poe than it did to Morton. Just as the skulls that appeared best to Morton were those that would prove the superiority of the white race to all other races, so for Poe the signatures of those authors he deems worthy of the highest consideration in American letters confirm by their chirographical characteristics his own critical hierarchies. To be a critic of race, it turns out, is easily analogous to being a critic of American writing: the destiny of both the race and the literature are inscribed immutably in skulls and handwriting, if one only knows how to read them.

Given what was at stake for Poe in this project, it perhaps is not surprising that he includes Reynolds among this sampling of the nation's literary celebrities. Poe's ongoing interest in Reynolds and what he persisted in calling the "Reynolds Expedition of Discovery" has long baffled biographers. There is, after all, no definitive evidence the two ever met. But long after Reynolds had retired from public life, Poe continued to sing his praises in the press. As he wrote in 1843, "To him, we say . . . does the high honor of this triumphant Expedition belong. Take from the enterprise the original impulse *he* gave . . . and what would the world have had of it but *the shadow of a shade?*"[84] Without Reynolds's genius, the Wilkes's Expedition—including Pickering's writing of the racial map—would have existed in the same imaginary no-place as do Pym's final missing pages.

In the "Chapter on Autography," Poe continued to celebrate the man whom the nation had forgotten: "Mr. Reynolds occupied, at one time, a distinguished position in the eye of the public, on account of his great and laudable exertions to get up the American South Polar expedition."[85] "He had written much," Poe concludes, "and well." But Reynolds's is a strange signature to include in the study for reasons beyond his dubious claims to inclusion among the literati, for his is the one signature that proves truly baffling to Poe's powers of interpretation: "His MS. is an ordinary clerk's hand, giving no indication of character." Reynolds's character remains hidden behind his signature, preserving his anonymity despite all of Poe's valiant attempts to expose him to the world. Thus, it is perhaps not surprising that this signature most closely resembles, in size and style, the signature that opens the "Chapter on Autography"—that of Poe himself.

In *Pym* the landscape of American writing is shown to be fundamentally bound up with the landscape of racial difference, even as the latter threatens to consume the nation in an apocalyptic race war. This is the crossroads to which Pym's adventures bring him: to pursue the fantasy of a world without racial difference is to cease to exist, to disappear like Pym behind the white curtain at the edge of the world, or like Reynolds behind the blank at the edge of the page. For Poe to remain and claim a "name" in American letters, he must expose and organize the inherent hierarchy in writing. Only by training the nation to apply to American letters the same reading skills and principles used to unearth inherent racial hierarchy could an American literature finally and fully come into its own.[86]

CHAPTER 6

Douglass and the Rewriting of American Race

Fashion is not confined to dress; but extends to philosophy as well—and it is fashionable now, in our land, to exaggerate the differences between the negro and the European. If, for instance, a phrenologist or naturalist undertakes to represent in portraits, the difference between the two races . . . he will invariably present the *highest* type of the European, and the *lowest* type of the negro.

Frederick Douglass (1854)

I

At roughly the same time that Poe was wrestling with the problems of authorship and the seemingly inextricable relationship of race and writing in antebellum America, another man was facing similar issues, although from a very different place in the literary and political scene. For as he set out to write his *Narrative* in 1845, Frederick Douglass had to confront unique challenges to his narrative authority and authenticity, challenges Poe only played at. Was he really the author of his own text? Had he really been a slave? Was he in fact really who he claimed to be at all?[1] An audience trained in writings like *Pym* had ready ammunition to doubt Douglass's credibility when he sat down to write his story. And they had good reason to want to doubt it: for many, the mere possibility that the slave could write his own story constituted a fundamental challenge to the very basis of the slave system itself. Thus, for Douglass the problems of anonymity carried with them a catch-22 more deadly and dangerous than those facing the author of *Pym*. For Douglass, to be anonymous was to not be heard, and therefore implicitly to perpetuate the system of slavery that he had vowed to defeat. On the other hand, to be recognized as the author of his text was to risk, as Douglass indeed did, a return to the slavery that he had only recently escaped.

Writing was for Douglass, as he records in his *Narrative,* a means to freedom. But writing, as he recognized even when still in slavery, was in the United States also intimately bound up in the technologies of race that had determined that he be a "slave" while his own father was a "master." Douglass's troubled relationship to writing and literacy has been noted by many scholars, most notably by Robert B. Stepto, who identifies in Douglass a simultaneous "exaltation of literacy and the written word" and an increasing "distrust of the American reader."[2] This distrust encouraged Douglass to take to writing largely as a way of educating his audience into being better readers. I argue that his increasing recognition of the consequences of bad reading on the part of white America led to Douglass's split with William Lloyd Garrison and the abolitionists under whose auspices he had written his first great work. In the fight against slavery, Douglass recognized that not merely the overturning of the institution was at stake, but also the still more challenging task of overturning an American way of writing and reading, one that made it impossible for him to pick up his own pen and write his own story without the risk of reinscribing the very slavery he was trying to write out of existence. To defeat the forces that made slavery itself possible as an institution in the democratic United States, Douglass soon realized, one had to separate once and for all what Poe had found apocalyptically inseparable: race and writing.

Douglass's slave narrative was by no means the first to recognize the ways in which race and writing were uniquely bound together in the United States. For many slaves, indeed, bore the marks of this "writing" of race upon their very bodies; the earlier narratives of William Grimes and Moses Roper, like Douglass's narrative written without editorial mediation, focus on writing as a vital technology in the manufacture of racial meaning. In both of these narratives we see early formulations of the idea central to Douglass's challenge to the literature of American race in the 1840s and '50s: that the conception of racial difference upon which Americans founded the institution of slavery is not written by God, but by man—written, in fact, on the bodies of those whom white Americans would define as "slaves."

The most common symbol of this grotesque "writing," one found throughout the writings and speeches of fugitive and former slaves in the 1830s and '40s, is the scarred back. By displaying these scars, the slave testifies to the cruelty of slavery and, at the same time, to his or her own status as a slave, thereby securing what is for the slave narrator always the most tenuous commodity: the (white) reader's faith. "My back is scarred by the lash—that I could show you," Douglass told a Boston audience in 1842; "I would, I could make visible the wounds of this system upon my soul."[3] Slave narratives were commonly framed by letters of testimonial, letters from white men and women guaranteeing for the white reading public that the author of the narrative was indeed African American, was indeed a slave, was indeed the author of what they were about to read. In addition, however, the narrator often felt compelled (and in some cases, no doubt, was compelled by his patrons) to go through a second act of testimonial, exposing (rhetorically or literally) the lash marks on his back as another sign of writing that guaranteed his status as black, as slave, and as author of what the audience was about to read (or hear). "The marks which they left," Roper writes, "at present remain on my body, a standing testimony to the truth of this statement of his severity."[4] These two acts of writing—the narrative and the "marks" on the ex-slave's body that vouch for the narrative's "truth"—are in some real way collapsed by these generic demands. Together they place the author in a dizzying, and seemingly inescapable, chain of dependence on the very kind of "writing," by white Americans, that had defined him as a "slave" in the first place.

Thus, the writer of antebellum slave narratives is bound not only to the framing writing of white northerners that vouches for his or her status as ex-slave and author, but also to the "writing" of white southerners—the whip scars and the printed advertisements for the former slave's recapture—that vouches for the narrator's status as slave and subject.[5] The slave narrator is placed in a position where he is allowed access to writing only through the written mediation of whites, and even then only insofar as he reinscribes the signs of his identity inscribed by other whites. For this reason, Douglass, for example, was repeatedly counseled by the white abolitionists to avoid editorializing about race and politics, and to remain within the boundaries of his own story as a slave.

We thus find in these narratives a measure of the consequences of this authorial model and an attempt to expose what may be the most important discovery that those who escaped from slavery had to offer to their readers: the fact that whites cannot read racial difference without first inscribing it. If racial difference is immutable and divinely authored, these narratives ask, why do whites need to manufacture so many manmade signs to mark the bodies of slaves as racially other? And if whites are such good readers of racial difference, the narratives even take some pleasure in suggesting, why are they so easily duped into reading wrongly? Grimes and Roper each recount scenes of passing in which the slave appropriates writing and uses it to fool the slave owners themselves into believing the narrator is white. It is not surprising that white America has such a vested interest in limiting access to writing for African Americans, as these narratives argue implicitly (and Douglass will argue explicitly), for unless white Americans control the technology whereby racial identities are manufactured, racial categories will have no fixed meaning at all.

This is precisely what we see enacted, if only temporarily, in the narratives. "I have frequently walked the streets of Savannah in the evening, and being pretty well dressed . . . and having a light complexion, (being at least three parts white,) on meeting a guard, I would walk as bold as knew how, and as much like a gentleman; they would always give me the wall."[6] So writes Grimes, describing the moment at which he recognizes how easily manipulated are the signs whereby Americans differentiate between racial "types," and the pleasure Grimes takes in recounting the scenes whereby he fooled those who would police the boundaries of slavery—a rare pleasure he affords himself in his bitter narrative—is unmistakable.

We find a similar scene repeated several times in *A Narrative of the Escape of Moses Roper* (1838), in which Roper uses his light complexion and writing to convince those who would have returned him to slavery that he is in fact a white man, an Indian, anything but a black man. As Roper insists, being part Indian, part black and part white, he has an equal "right" to claim his identity from among his various inheritances. As he recounts his scene of birth: "As soon as my father's wife heard of my birth, she sent one of my mother's sisters to see whether I was white or black, and when my aunt had seen me, she . . . told her mistress that I was white, and resembled Mr. Roper very much."[7] Roper's story spends much time describing the consequences of being born a "very white" slave, as he is repeatedly punished for the transgression of his birth first by his father's wife and then by a series of owners (2). "My resembling my father so very much, and being whiter than the other slaves, caused me to be sold to what they called a negro trader," he reports, but the trader finds it impossible to sell him because of his color, finally disposing of him to a planter who "soon sent me to his Cotton plantation, that I might be burnt darker by the sun" (3, 5).

But what the sun will not perform, his next owner soon determines, the whip will, and Roper is beaten daily, as if the marks of the lash would provide a more than adequate substitute for black skin: "When I failed in my task he commenced flogging me, and set me to work without any shirt, in the cotton field, in a very hot sun, in the month of July" (8). It is here that Roper's many attempts at escape begin, and the subsequent contest is fiercely fought between the master who would brand him as slave and Roper who would manipulate the slave owners' difficulty in telling black from white. Time and again he is defeated by his master's wide array of allies, the white southerners who were legally bound to turn him over to the law. It is not, in fact, until he begins to manipulate language—first through storytelling, then through writing—that Roper truly begins to discover his route to freedom.

During one of his many escape attempts, Roper comes to the farm of a Mr. Crawford and tells him "the following story": "I said, that I had been bound to a very cruel master when I was a little boy, and that having been treated very badly, I wanted to get home to see my mother. This statement, may appear to be untrue, but as I understood the word *bound*, I considered it to apply to my case" (26). In telling this story, based on his understanding of the ways in which words might be given more than one meaning, Roper soon discovers that the very whites who would eagerly defeat his attempts to escape servitude as a black "slave" would willingly aid and abet his freedom as a white "servant." This early escape plan fails, as do many others before he finally achieves freedom, but in it he learns a valuable lesson. His master, meanwhile, redoubles his attempts to blacken him—whipping him, loading him with chains, and attempting literally to burn him dark: "The first thing he did was to pour some tar on my head, then rubbed it all over my face, took a torch, with pitch on it, and set it on fire." "The marks of this treatment," Roper tells the reader, "still remain upon me" (55).

To justify and defend slavery, the slave must be blackened, marked, scarred, and in other ways inscribed with the marks of his racial difference. At one point in his story, Roper describes his experiences serving a slave trader in which it was one of his duties to apply the blackface to those who were about to ascend the auction block: "I had to grease the faces of the black every morning with sweet oil, to make them shine before they are put up to sell" (62). These manufactured marks, then, provide the very grounds upon which racial difference is defined and defended by proslavery theorists like Tucker or Dew as if its meanings were natural and inviolable. Here Roper makes explicit the tautology of racial meaning by exposing the human hand behind the "divine" marks of slavery. But at the same time as he exposes the fallacy of these signs, he is forced himself to rely on them as the testimonial to his experiences and his authorial status.

Roper finally achieves his freedom by tricking a series of people into writing passes for him that attest to the fact that "he is free, and though dark, is not an African" (87). Once he arrives in the North he is able to avoid recapture by his possession of another document: "I have a document in my possession to call me to military duty. The law is, that no slaves or coloured person performs this, but that every other person, in America, of the age of twenty-one, is called upon to perform military duty" (99). Roper reproduces, in full, a "COPY OF THE DOCUMENT"—both as a way of laughing, like Grimes, at the inability of the whites to tell black from white without an act of writing to show the difference, and at the same time as a testimony to a fact that he is, as he has been arguing throughout, in fact entitled to define himself as "white." With this "official" document, he believes, there is none to prove him wrong. But agents from his former master follow him north and eventually, like Douglass after him, Roper is forced to flee to Britain, whence he concludes: "May the period come, when God shall wipe off this deep stain from her constitution, and may America soon be *indeed* the land of the free" (108).

Pointing to the Constitution as the document that glaringly exposes the hypocrisies of the slave system was a familiar rhetorical move in the narratives of the period. More than simply a mirror of white American hypocrisy, these narrators recognize, the Constitution serves as a site of origins for the definition of national identity that made them slaves in the first place. *The Life of William Grimes, the Runaway Slave* (1824) contains one of literature's most powerful images of the ways in which marking the body of the slave was an act of writing equivalent to the writing that marked the founding of the nation's identity. At the end of his bitter account of his experiences at the hands of southern slavery and northern prejudice (he importantly refuses to differentiate clearly between the two scenes of suffering), Grimes concludes:

> I hope some will buy my books from charity; but I am no beggar. I am now entirely destitute of property. . . . If it were not for the stripes on my back which were made while I was a slave, I would in my will leave my skin as a legacy to the government, desiring that it might be taken off and made into parchment, and then bind the constitution of glorious, happy, and *free* America. Let the skin of an American slave bind the charter of American liberty![8]

Grimes's narrative is relatively unique in that it was written for profit, as a means of supporting the author and his family. It is also rare in that it is written without the support and authorization of abolitionist organizations, not surprising given that Grimes spends so much energy in describing his miserable treatment in the North after he escaped slavery. Thus, his narrative is not surrounded by the usual letters of testimony from white abolitionists, and he studiously avoids until the very end the gesture of exposing the wounds on his back as testimony.

The scene at first appears to be a gesture similar to that by Roper, gesturing toward the Constitution as a way of pointing to the gross inconsistency between slavery and the avowed principles of that founding document. As William L. Andrews writes,

> Grimes knows that to enclose and entitle the Constitution with a slave's skin . . . would demonstrate major contradictions in the myth of America. . . . Grimes also knows, however, that his skin will never make good parchment since it has already been marred by the whips of his former owners. Yet if these stripes signify his former binding in slavery, they also delineate him as a text inscribed by the whip (slavery's perverse pen) and thus empowered to bleed meaning once the wounds are opened.[9]

Andrews's account helps us begin to make sense of the scene, for surely he is right in articulating Grimes's own recognition of the marks on his back as a kind of writing, and of his body as a kind of text. But Grimes also recognizes that the meaning this text has to offer is one entirely authored by the slave owner; far from seeing the exposing of this "perverse" writing as a kind of empowerment, Grimes is taking note of precisely what is lost in making meaning of these wounds. For what he surrenders here is the power to trump the Constitution with his own writing. Although a slave's writing could potentially bind the Constitution—proving by the act of writing itself the equality between black and white that the Constitution should have been sworn to defend—Grimes's writing cannot because his writing, at least in this final act of exposing the wounds on his back, necessarily transcribes the "writing" of the slave owners, a "writing" that defines and defends the fundamental inequality of the races his own text (and life) would disprove.

The narratives of Roper and Grimes thus recognize the ways in which writing gave the slave narrator a path to freedom, to recognition, and even potentially to profit. But they also simultaneously articulate the recognition of the limitations of this writing, of the ways writing in the United States—metaphorized in its own founding document, the Constitution—

Narrative contains some of American literature's most powerful and moving celebrations of the powers of literacy, most notably its account of the series of transformations that takes place after his former mistress tries to teach him to read. Upon going to Baltimore to serve Hugh and Sophia Auld, the young Douglass finds in Sophia something he had never before experienced in his years of slavery: "a white face beaming with the most kindly emotions" (74). Motivated by her kindness, Mrs. Auld—who had never before owned a slave—sets out to teach the young Douglass how to read. But when she proudly displays for her husband her new pupil's achievements, he angrily forbids her to continue, giving her her first lessons in slave owning: "To use his own words . . . , he said, 'If you give a nigger an inch, he will take an ell. A nigger should know nothing but to obey his master—to do as he is told to do. Learning would *spoil* the best nigger in the world. Now,' said he, 'if you teach that nigger (speaking of myself) how to read, there would be no keeping him. It would forever unfit him to be a slave'" (78). "These words sank deep into my heart," Douglass writes; and in them he learns the secret that had long eluded him: "to wit, the white man's power to enslave the black man. It was a grand achievement, and I prized it highly" (78).

This passage, which occurs centrally in the narrative, marks a turning point for the young Douglass in his transformation from slave to man. Out of this discovery of the intimate relation between writing and independence, Douglass discovers the "pathway from slavery to freedom" (78). At the same time, however, as Auld had predicted, he discovers for the first time the true bitterness of his situation as a slave. There was indeed no "keeping him" once he had learned to read. But Douglass is equally concerned here with charting the transformation of his would-be teacher as a result of this episode as he is with marking the change it wrought in himself. After Mrs. Auld has been forbidden to teach him to read, "the tender heart became stone, the lamblike disposition gave way to one of tiger-like fierceness" (82), and "the angelic face gave place to that of a demon" (78). Instead of teaching him his ABC's, Mrs. Auld now devotes all of her energies to keeping him from taking the "ell" her husband had warned Douglass would soon be claiming. Douglass, who throughout his narrative reveals a keen pleasure in playing with words (for example, "I began to want to live *upon free land* as well as *with Freeland*"), relishes the pun implicit in this scene. "Mistress," he writes, "in teaching me the alphabet, had given me the *inch,* and no precaution could prevent me from taking the *ell*" (82); and he goes on to explain, in meticulous detail, how he secured that "ell" by watching the white carpenters working in a shipyard: "When a piece of timber was intended for the larboard side, it would be marked thus—'L'" (86).

Thus begins Douglass's active resistance to those who would enslave him, a resistance frequently staged over and through the written word. But it is important to recognize in this central passage that even as Douglass records stealing letters as if they were commodities or keys to freedom, he specifically marks these letters as the property of his masters. "I wished to learn how to write, as I might have occasion to write my own pass," he writes, describing the surreptitious hours spent writing in the blank spaces of his master's son's copybook, "until I could write a hand very similar to that of Master Thomas" (87). And indeed, in an aborted escape plan that he organizes for himself and several of his fellow slaves, Douglass appropriates the writing of his masters so successfully as to write forged passes that testify to the "liberty" of himself and his co-conspirators. Douglass reproduces the document, in which the forged signature of a slave owner provides the subscription to a pass, as Roper had in his narrative. "Written with mine own hand" (125), the forged letter is subscribed, emphasizing the ways in which Douglass's first act of authorship, to be successful, must necessarily be ascribed to the master's hand. In celebrating the power writing grants him, Douglass also recognizes that writing plays a central role in "the white man's power to enslave the black man." In laying his own claim to writing, Douglass shows how fragile and arbitrary are the powers that depend so strongly on a careful distinction between who writes and who is written upon.[15]

In one of his earliest recorded speeches, Douglass celebrates writing as a revolutionary force in slaves' drive toward freedom: "The slaves are learning to read and to write, and the time is fast coming, when they will act in concert, and effect their own emancipation."[16] This is precisely why Auld would have kept the young Douglass from writing. "To use his own words," Douglass writes in recounting Auld's diatribe on the dangers of African American literacy, "said he, 'if you teach that nigger (speaking of myself) how to read, there would be no keeping him.'" As Houston A. Baker Jr. writes of this scene:

> Mr. Auld is a representation of those whites who felt that by superimposing the cultural sign *nigger* on vibrant human beings like Douglass, they would be able to control the meanings and possibilities of life in America. One marker for the term *nigger* in Auld's semantic field is «subhuman agency of labor». What terrifies and angers the master, however, is that Douglass's capacities . . . are not accurately defined by

this marker. . . . Hence, the markers in Auld's mapping of *nigger* must include «agent capable of education». The semantic complexity, indeed the wrenching irony, of Auld's "nigger" is forcefully illustrated by the fact that the representation of Auld and *his* point of view enters the world of the learned by way of a narrative written by a "nigger."[17]

Thus, as Baker describes it, the act of writing turns the master who would call Douglass "nigger" himself into the "other," made visible and controllable by Douglass's act of autobiography. Here we see what might be described as a subversion of the very technologies of difference we have traced from 1787 on, in which Douglass recognizes that he who writes determines who is, in fact, the "other." Such an account is important insofar as it registers what is for Douglass a way of "using" the master's words against him, turning the same technologies of writing the subhuman other against those who profited daily from such acts of violence. But what Baker's account does not register is the fact of which Douglass here and elsewhere in his *Narrative* is pointedly conscious: if in this act of writing he is able to appropriate the writing and the words of the master and turn them against him, he is still necessarily using the writing and the words that "belong" to the master. "To use his own words," writes Douglass, keenly aware, like Grimes before him, of the ways in which his narrative necessarily reinscribes those same signs that are used to define him as racial other.

We see a similar recognition earlier in the *Narrative*, where, describing his suffering on Colonel Lloyd's plantation, Douglass writes, "My feet have been so cracked with the frost, that the pen with which I am writing might be laid in the gashes" (72). This image is resonant and difficult in much the same way as is Grimes's image of the binding of the Constitution. As Robert Stepto glosses the passage, "The pen, symbolizing the quest for literacy fulfilled, actually measures the wounds from the past, and the measuring process becomes a metaphor in and of itself for the artful composition of travail transcended."[18] Stepto rightly reads the difficult image as celebratory, but such claims are complicated by the ways in which the passage simultaneously registers writing as a source of enslavement.

For far from unambiguously celebrating this act of writing as a transcending of the wounds of the past, Douglass, with this rare gesture toward the testimonial of the exposed scar, describes the recording of the wound in the present as in some real way an act of reinscription. Douglass is not simply here, as in the words of one critic, "dramatiz[ing] how far removed he is from the boy once called Fred";[19] he is also showing how near he is to him still, how close the writing of this narrative has brought him to being that person again. Writing about how Lloyd had marked his body—scarring his feet with frost—in the past, Douglass poetically acknowledges the ways in which the writing in the present rewrites those wounds, so that he could now lay the pen "with which I am writing" in those earlier "gashes."

Wilson J. Moses usefully describes Douglass's double bind: "Douglass found that he had to confine himself within a literary box. The slave narrative was a means to freedom, but it also represented a tactical confinement and imposed what might be called a generic servitude that deprived its author of literary and intellectual elbow room."[20] Douglass's *Narrative* registers the double bind of writing the autobiography of an American slave, and he devotes his subsequent career to seeking a way out of this bind. But even here, before he had achieved the international fame that would foreground his split with the Garrisonians, we see Douglass attempting to imagine a way of undermining the dependence of his writing upon the racial codes of white America.

Perhaps nowhere is this resistance more clearly registered than in Douglass's subversion of the conventions of the testimonial letters that introduce his narrative. He tests these letters and the terms they employ periodically throughout his text. For instance, Garrison's preface, in recalling the moment in which he first "discovered" Douglass in an abolitionist meeting in 1841, records his own eloquence on behalf of his new protégé: "As soon as he had taken his seat . . . I rose, and declared that PATRICK HENRY, of revolutionary fame, never made a speech more eloquent in the cause of liberty" (35). Douglass clearly encourages the analogies between himself and the Founding Fathers that both Garrison and Phillips deploy, but he takes this conceit one step further, arguing of himself and his fellow slaves, "we did more than Patrick Henry, when he resolved upon liberty or death" (124). He similarly plays with the language of his mediators when he inverts the terms of Phillips's introductory applause for his book—"I am glad the time has come 'when the lions wrote history'" (43)—by describing one of his own first acts of writing upon reaching freedom in the North: "In writing to a dear friend, immediately after my arrival at New York, I said I felt like one who had escaped a den of hungry lions" (143).

Perhaps the *Narrative*'s most deliberate act of authorial resistance is in its concluding pages. For here, instead of relying on a white abolitionist to provide his conclusion, Douglass provides his own "Appendix," in which he defends himself against charges of heresy that had been leveled

against him as a result of his severe criticism of the church for its complicity in slavery. Within this appendix, Douglass includes a poem by a
Methodist preacher that parodies the hypocrisies of Southern churches.
"I soberly affirm," Douglass testifies, that this account "is 'true to life,' and
without caricature or the slightest exaggeration" (157). Borrowing from
the language of the testimonial letters that affirmed his own story as being
"entirely his own production" and "essentially true in all its statements"
(38), Douglass grants himself authority to endorse the account of black
slavery written by a white preacher. He claims authority over a story that
he, and not his white abolitionist colleagues, has experienced; and for
similar claims Douglass would come to be severely criticized by his colleagues for arrogance and ingratitude. But what is at stake here for Douglass is an attempt to learn if the tables can be turned, to see if he can claim
the power to authorize the writing of whites just as they claim the power
to authorize his own. If so, then Douglass has indeed written himself into
a place where he can begin to plot an escape from the servitude of writing
he records throughout the *Narrative*. Then he can truly claim the authority, as he does in the book's final line, to "subscribe myself, FREDERICK
DOUGLASS" (159).[21]

But if not—if his role as writer is not allowed to be equivalent to that of
the white abolitionists who endorse him—then writing itself becomes, not
a path to freedom and power, but another link by which the black man is
bound to a position of servitude and inequality. As Douglass tested this
principle in his dealings with the Garrisonians following the publication of
his *Narrative*, he found out how far there was to go before the logic of
American race might be rewritten.

III

Shortly after publishing his *Narrative* in 1845, Douglass sailed for England to begin a remarkable speaking tour. Not long after his arrival in
Britain, he found himself again under attack for fraud in the United
States, this time on the basis of the *Narrative* itself, the very document he
had written to convince his critics that he had indeed experienced slavery.
A.C.C. Thompson published a denunciation of the *Narrative*, claiming
firsthand knowledge of the Auldses and of Douglass himself when he was
a slave. Douglass, Thompson asserted, was utterly incapable of writing
such a narrative, even of writing at all. In a letter in 1846 written for
publication in the *Liberator*, Douglass responded to his accuser: "You

must not judge me now by what I then was—a change of circumstances has made a surprising change in me. Frederick Douglass, the *freeman*, is a very different person from Frederick Bailey, (my former name), the *slave*. I feel myself almost a new man—freedom has given me new life. I fancy you would scarcely know me. I think I have altered very much in my general appearance, and know I have in my manners."[22] Douglass's account of how his experiences in freedom had transformed him into a "new man," one new even in his appearance, may well have been directed equally to his detractor Thompson and to the recipient of this letter, William Lloyd Garrison. For in the months following the publication of the *Narrative*, Douglass had indeed become something of a new man, increasingly uncomfortable within the parameters of action and interpretation prescribed by the Garrisonians. And it was issues of writing, not surprisingly, that finally divided Douglass and Garrison at the end of the 1840s.

Both the abolitionist movement and its proslavery opponents were deeply concerned about writing and its powers. The third of Garrison's American Anti-Slavery Society's Declaration of Sentiments reads: "We shall circulate unsparingly and extensively anti-slavery tracts and periodicals."[23] The proslavery forces for their part sought legislation that would prohibit the circulation of such writing via the U.S. Post Office. Yet for all their differences, there was one issue relating to writing and interpretation on which the Garrisonians and their proslavery opponents did in fact agree: that the Constitution was written as a proslavery document.

As a result of this interpretation the Garrisonians staunchly rejected all political action, focusing their efforts instead on moral persuasion—on lecturing and writing to convince Americans of the immorality of slavery. Since the Constitution itself defended slavery, they reasoned, any political action under that Constitution was illegitimate. The Garrisonian reading of the Constitution as a proslavery document justified an antipolitical approach to abolitionism. Douglass, a staunch Garrisonian throughout the early 1840s, began his career in firm agreement with this interpretation and its consequences, and throughout his early speeches we find Douglass simultaneously rejecting political action and denouncing in fiery language the Constitution as a covenant with death. "The language of the Constitution is you shall be a slave or die. . . . For my part I had rather that my right hand should wither by my side than cast a ballot under the Constitution of the United States."[24]

Douglass left the Garrisonians in late 1847 to move to Rochester and establish his own newspaper, the *North Star,* against Garrison's own wishes and counsel. Although Garrison argued strongly for Douglass's responsibilities to the Anti-Slavery Society, Douglass had increasingly come to believe that his work lay in writing as much as, if not more than, in oration. The founding of a black-run paper, he felt, would do much work to repudiate the artificial hierarchies between blacks and whites. As white abolitionists had long argued, black literacy was one of the strongest weapons against arguments of inferiority, but it was a very limited model of black writing that the Garrisonians were willing to endorse. Douglass would later bitterly describe the Garrisonians' attempts to sabotage his paper: "They wrote in various directions predicting the failure of the paper, complimenting me as a speaker, and decrying me as a writer."[25] However, much of Douglass's original prospectus for the *North Star* was dedicated to assuring the white abolitionists that the founding of the paper was in no way a slight on their efforts, insisting instead that it was "essential that there should arise in our ranks authors and editors . . . for it is in these capacities that the most permanent good can be rendered to our cause."[26] Douglass's decision to strike out on his own as a writer and editor was not publicly condemned at the time by Garrison and his associates, but the origins of the break were clearly laid with Douglass's decision to start the paper.

It was with a piece of writing—or more accurately, an act of reading—published in the *North Star* that the final split occurred. Responding to an anti-Garrisonian abolitionist who had challenged him to a debate on the proslavery nature of the Constitution, Douglass wrote, "On close examination of the Constitution, I am satisfied that if strictly 'construed according to its reading,' it is not a pro-slavery instrument."[27] A short time later, Douglass was willing to go even further, describing in the *North Star* a "Change of Opinion" that served as the scene of his break with the Garrisonians. After long disapproving of his paper, the American Anti-Slavery Society had determined at last to endorse it, and a meeting had been called publicly to voice the society's new support for the *North Star.*

But Douglass took the occasion of this meeting to announce that he would have to excuse his paper from the society's endorsement on the grounds that he had reversed his position on the interpretation of the Constitution. Now, he argued, he believed the Constitution to be an antislavery document, and with this reversal he opened up the possibility of political action (legislation, electioneering, and lobbying)—and even military action—as a means of ridding the nation of slavery:

> We felt in honor bound to announce at once to our old anti-slavery companions that we no longer possessed the requisite qualification for

their official approval and commendation; and to assure them that we had arrived at the firm conviction that the Constitution, construed in the light of well established rules of legal interpretation, might be made consistent in its details with the noble purposes avowed in its preamble; and that hereafter we should insist upon the application of such rules to that instrument, and demand that it be wielded in behalf of emancipation.[28]

Douglass's public announcement of his new interpretation of the Constitution led to the violent split between Douglass and Garrison, for in the confusion that followed Garrison rose and exclaimed, "There is roguery somewhere!" (156)—by which he meant, as he made clear in the series of charges and countercharges that followed in the abolitionist press, that someone had led Douglass astray. Denouncing Douglass as an apostate and an enemy to antislavery, Garrison at the same time refused to allow that Douglass could have arrived at his own interpretation as an independent reader. His refusal to allow Douglass to be first an independent writer and then an independent reader led to ugly exchanges between the two former friends that lasted many months.

Douglass was careful to explain to his readers what had led to his change of opinion, describing how he had been misled at the start into a false way of reading, in which the text was interpreted not by its own terms but according to the actions of its authors. Douglass now proposes a new theory of reading in which all texts, like all men, must be judged by their own words and not by any false interpretations that have been derived from them. "We found, in our former position, that, when debating the question, we were compelled to go behind the letter of the Constitution, and to seek its meaning in the history and practice of the nation under it," he writes in announcing his "Change of Opinion" (156). Now the Constitution must be studied *"in the Constitution itself"* and not in terms of "the intentions of the framers of the Constitution" (157). Read in this way, the document becomes an antislavery document, and read in this way Douglass can at last advocate the use of the political institutions of the United States to take back the interpretation of the "more perfect union" from those who had willfully misread it in the service of disunion, inequality, and slavery.

In arriving at the conclusion that the Garrisonians had allowed themselves to be the dupes of the proslavery forces in accepting the proslavery interpretation of the Constitution, Douglass could now argue explicitly the crucial fact that white Americans were bad readers. And with this discovery came the recognition that more was needed than simply his own writing to prove the equality of blacks; white Americans had to be reeducated as readers as well. The root of the present crisis lay not with the writing of seventy-five years ago, but with the active misreading of the present day: a conscious act of misreading on the part of the slave owners and a potentially more troubling misreading on the part of the Garrisonians. This is not to say that Douglass now believed that the Founding Fathers were uniformly antislavery or that the Constitution did not include contradictory provisions for the maintenance of slavery. Rather, by shifting the emphasis from the biographies of the authors of the text to the spirit of the text itself as it is interpreted in the present, Douglass insists that the documents that would enslave him are not truly fixed, but are rewritten generation after generation so as to appear immutable.

Douglass declares his independence as writer and reader as the precondition for declaring himself an American—for making the nation's founding document his own. "Fellow citizens!" Douglass proclaimed in his famous address, "What to the Slave Is the Fourth of July?" (1852), "there is no matter in respect to which, the people of the North have allowed themselves to be so ruinously imposed upon, as that of the pro-slavery character of the Constitution. In *that* instrument I hold there is neither warrant, license, nor sanction of the hateful thing; but interpreted as it *ought* to be interpreted, the Constitution is a GLORIOUS LIBERTY DOCUMENT."[29]

IV

As Douglass began to conceptualize that the problem lay not in the document itself but in the fact that Americans did not understand how this document "*ought* to be interpreted," he set out to educate a nation of better readers. And one of his main object lessons after his break with the Garrisonians was the growing body of literature dedicated to proving the inherent inequality of the races, the work of the American School of racial science. He had early on taken up, against the advice of his fellow Garrisonians, the issue of racial science, the belief in "the inferiority of the slave."[30] His lectures and writing on the subject increased in intensity throughout the late 1840s, as he sought not only to disprove the idea of racial hierarchy itself, but also, perhaps even more important, to teach those who accepted its premises the fallacy of their way of reading.

"I will grant frankly, I must grant, that the Negroes in America are inferior to the Whites. But why are they so? is another question," Douglass said early in his career. "The people of America deprive us of every privilege—[then] they turn round and taunt us with our inferiority" (60–61). Definitions of "inferiority," Douglass explains in what will be a continuing refrain, are of human and not divine origins. The hierarchies imposed on the fact of racial difference are born of tautological definitions: marking the African American, through slavery itself, as inferior and therefore fit only for slavery. It is in the writings of men like Samuel George Morton—who first defines African Americans as ugly and then condemns them to slavery because of this "ugliness"—that these tautologies are validated as "fact." The logic of racial writing in the United States, whether written with the slaveholder's whip or the writer's pen, could only be defeated by teaching Americans how to be good enough readers to recognize the fallacies that underlie such logic.[31]

Douglass launched what was perhaps his most concerted effort to teach white Americans to read the literature of racial science in his published address "The Claims of the Negro Ethnologically Considered" (1854). After spending weeks researching the works of contemporary racial scientists, Douglass set out to overturn their principles, to prove them to be, at best, foolish readers (like the Garrisonians) and, at worst, willfully misleading writers (like the proslavery ideologues they abetted).[32] Douglass finds a historical ally in his study of racial science by returning to 1787, to the year in which the Constitution, American racial science, and an American literature were "born." Recovering the argument of Samuel Stanhope Smith and the principles of monogenism, Douglass works to prove that racial difference is, after all, a difference that has no innate, "natural" meaning.

Smith, Douglass writes, "says that 'man is distinguished from all other animals, in that he resists as well as adapts to his circumstances.' He does not take things as he finds them, but goes to work to improve them. Tried by this test . . . the negro is a man."[33] But as Douglass goes on to consider the problem, he realizes that Smith's answer is no longer sufficient for his own day and age:

> There was a time when, if you established the point that a particular being is a man, it was considered that such a being, of course, had a common ancestry with the rest of mankind. But it is not so now. This is, you know, an age of science, and science is favorable to division. There is, therefore, another proposition to be stated and maintained, separately, which, in other days, (the days before the Notts, the Gliddens,

the Agassiz[es], and Mortons, made their profound discoveries in eth-nological science), might have been included in the first. (504)

Douglass castigates this "phalanx of learned men—speaking in the name of *science*" who "forbid the magnificent reunion of mankind in one brotherhood." But he recognizes that their interpretations are no longer easily dismissed. He goes on carefully to dissect their way of reading racial difference in order to expose its fundamental tautologies, fallacies, and lies. With this lesson in bad reading (and dangerous writing), he hopes that he can cure Americans of a way of reading difference that has been cultivated since the earliest days of the Republic.

He begins with a history of the debate over racial science that pro-ceeded from 1787 to the present day: "The question had been raised, and pressed with increasing ardor and pertinacity, (especially in modern times), can all these various tribes, nations, tongues, kindred, so widely separated, and so strangely dissimilar, have descended from a common ancestry?" (504). Douglass first attempts to answer this central question, as Smith did before him, by recourse to the old argument of biblical mandate ("The credit of the Bible is at stake"), but he quickly shifts his argument to historical contingencies, considering the question in "rela-tion to the situation of things in our country, at this moment": "*One seventh* part of the population of this country is of negro descent. The land is peopled by what may be called the most dissimilar races on the globe. The black and the white—the negro and the European—these constitute the American people—and, in all likelihoods of the case, they will ever remain the principal inhabitants of the United States, in some form or other" (505–6).

This being the case, Americans must be especially careful in how they choose to read the facts of racial difference. The fate of the nation quite literally depends on the choices made in answering the central question of racial science. To pursue the course originally outlined by Smith in which racial difference is the temporary result of environmental conditions is to write a future for the nation in which the races might find "magnificent reunion" in "one brotherhood." But to follow the interpretive model dictated by polygenists from Jefferson to Morton by which racial differ-ence is understood as an irreconcilable and fundamental difference is to doom the nation to a future of slavery and race war: "Let it once be granted that the human race are of multitudinous origin . . . and at once you make plausible a demand for classes, grades and conditions, for dif-

ferent methods of culture, different moral, political, and religious institutions, and a chance is left for slavery, as a necessary institution. . . . There is
no doubt that Messrs. Nott, Glidden, Morton, Smith and Agassiz were
duly consulted by our slavery propagating statesmen" (507). In other
words, Douglass argues, the fate of the nation depends not on the racial
composition of the nation (which is fixed in black and white), but on the
way Americans choose to read the facts of racial difference.

Douglass then performs a close reading of Morton's work, demonstrating how this "author" had disqualified himself by displaying "ignorance,
malice [and] prejudice." He shows how the fact that Morton deliberately
"separate[d] the negro race from every intelligent nation and tribe in
Africa" is evidence of the fact that he "aimed to construct a theory in
support of a foregone conclusion" (507). Douglass identifies the motiva-
tion for this "foregone conclusion" in the fact that "Egypt is in Africa. Pity
that it had not been in Europe, or in Asia, or better still in America!" and
he exposes the deceits whereby Morton attempts to juggle his evidence so
as "to prove that the ancient Egyptians were totally distinct from the
negroes, and to deny all relationship between" (508). In this way, Douglass shows, Morton is able to fulfill his fantasy of uniting the achievements
of ancient Egypt with those of white America. This debunking is concluded with a tongue-in-cheek congratulation of Morton "for claiming
affinity with Egyptians. All that goes in that direction belongs to my side
of the question" (510).

This is Douglass's refrain: the meaning of race is never "a foregone
conclusion," but it is constructed as if it were. Those who wrote and
revised this literature of American race whose history we have traced
argued that the fate of the nation depended on the careful delineation of
racial difference and the defense of its borders. Douglass's project is to
return to the "founding" moment of the story—to the Constitution, to the
origins of racial science, to the meaning of American writing—to prove
that the fate of the nation depends instead on allowing those boundaries
to dissolve. Thus, he concludes his pamphlet by constructing his own narration of racial anthropology, excavating, like Morton, a series of American skulls—in this case the heads of the Founding Fathers themselves.
Studying these heads, Douglass writes, leads him to the conclusion that
one could "as well deny the affinity of the Americans to the Englishman,
as to deny the affinity between the negro and the Egyptian": "One may
trace the progress of this difference in the common portraits of the American Presidents. Just study those faces, beginning with WASHINGTON; and
as you come thro' the JEFFERSONS, the ADAMSES, and the MADISONS, you

will find an increasing bony and wiry appearance about those portraits, & a greater remove from the serene amplitude which characterises the countenances of earlier Presidents" (515).

What is at stake for Douglass's own "Crania Americana" is an attempt not simply to reclaim the environmentalist theory of racial difference, but, more important, to prove that all such theories, his own included, are necessarily fictions. His account is a valid as any other, not because it is based on facts but because all such accounts are necessarily inventions. It is therefore not to science that we must turn for the "meaning" of racial difference, but to ourselves—deciding whether we choose to embrace a fiction (as Poe did) that leads inexorably toward racial apocalypse and the end of writing itself, or a fiction such as Douglass proposes here, in which all nations and races are transformed "into Americans . . . causing them to lose, in a common American character, all traces of their former distinctive national peculiarities" (515). America, "our own great nation," Douglass insists, "is largely indebted to its composite character" (522). As earlier writers had discovered, however much some white Americans may fantasize to the contrary, without racial difference there is no United States. But it is not "a foregone conclusion" what this national "indebtedness" to racial difference must signify. Beginning with the *Narrative*, Douglass's writing was devoted to proving that the signs of racial difference were derived of man, not of God or even Nature, despite all the arguments of racial science and American racism. The future of this composite nation is scripted not by divine mandate but by the choices Americans make as writers and readers.

Douglass's "Melting Pot" image seems to look at once back toward the environmentalism of Crèvecoeur and Samuel Stanhope Smith and forward toward the assimilationist ideology of the Progressive Era. But Douglass's understanding of the "composite character" of the United States is not precisely equivalent to the theories of "Americanness" of either the monogenists or the Progressives. Instead, I would argue, Douglass is primarily interested in offering with his theory of American race an alternative fiction, in exposing how and why these fictions are made, and in laying the responsibility for scripting racial fictions in the hands of his contemporaries. How they choose to read and write racial difference determines if slavery will continue, if disunion is inevitable, and if "American" is to be a term of inclusion or exclusion. Gates's summation of the lessons Douglass learned in writing the *Narrative* serves as well as an excellent description of the lesson he is trying to teach his readers in his subsequent work: "Not only is meaning culture-bound and the referents

of all signs an assigned relation, Douglass tells us, but *how* we read determines *what* we read, in the truest sense of the hermeneutical circle."[34]
For here Douglass works to prove that it is not the demigods of the
Revolutionary generation, nor the divine hand of God, nor the mysterious
powers of a new environment, nor the uncontrollable effects of a national
identity—but Americans themselves who script the meaning and fate of
"America."

As Douglass set out in 1855 to rewrite his own narrative in *My Bondage
and My Freedom,* he rewrote himself out of the authorial dependencies of
the *Narrative.* In Eric J. Sundquist's useful description, he now writes "as
an *American* who happens to have been a slave of African descent."[35]
Douglass's new reading of the Constitution allows him to see himself as
one who writes the future for the nation rather than as a passive victim of
a prescripted fate, so that he can fully rewrite himself as a representative
American and a founding father. As Sundquist suggests, he is in *My
Bondage and My Freedom* able to look back not only on his experiences in
slavery but also on his early experiences in freedom, to reflect on the
writing of his *Narrative,* what it cost and what it taught him, and how
those lessons might best be applied. Incorporating African American and
white American history and heroes into his representative biography,
Douglass shows how our definitions not only of ourselves, but also of our
national and racial identities, are open to revision, emendation, and ex-
purgation. To write the story of the representative American, of race and
its effects, and of national identity and its limitations and potential, is to
write another fiction. In openly claiming responsibility for his version of
this fiction, Douglass's career marks an important step toward rewriting
the founding fictions of American race.

V

We can perhaps get a sense of how far from complete remains Douglass's
rewriting of the logic of American race in the copy of "The Claims of the
Negro, Ethnologically Considered" that lies before me. An original edition of the 1854 pamphlet obtained from the Burling Library at Grinnell
College, this copy has been appendixed with newspaper clippings that the
anonymous original owner pasted inside the covers in 1858. Inserted
directly below the last lines of Douglass's denunciation of racial anthropology is an article that brings full circle the favorite hobbyhorse of the
late-eighteenth-century magazines. The article, entitled "A White Man

Turned Black—A Problem for Physicians," tells of a man "who once was white, but is now black all over." The article suggests that the change may have occurred as a result of medication that the man had been taking, and it concludes with a call for the medical community to do more research into "this discoloration of the skin." "If any process of medication will make blackamoors of us, it is proper that we should know it," the article concludes.

Another article, entitled "Curious Facts," recounts the story of a girl "supposed to be a negro" who was purchased as a slave but was recently discovered to have "been stolen from a roving band of Cherokees." The courts released the girl to the Cherokees on the testimony of Dr. R. D. Gibbs, "a celebrated anatomist," who offered extensive testimony about the difference between Negro, Caucasian, and Indian hair. "He stated a very curious fact, as resulting from microscopical observation, that in the mulatto cross the hair of one or the other parent was present, and some-times hairs of both, but never a mongrel hair; that no amalgamated hair existed." The reason is that although the Indian and Caucasian have "true hair," "that of the Negro was not hair, but wool, and capable of being felted."[36] How exactly these facts were used to determine the racial iden-tity of the disputed girl is not stated, but the significance of the anato-mist's testimony for the writer of "Curious Facts" (and presumably for the owner of Douglass's pamphlet) lay in the new ammunition these "curious facts" provided in defining "the distinction of races."

In these articles we see that the rising science of race in the United States is given the last word over Douglass's attempts to rewrite it. In the 1780s and '90s, accounts of black men turning white, such as the famous story of Henry Moss, were used to provide evidence for monogenism, the environmental theory of racial difference, and the transformative effects of the American environment. At last, Moss's story seemed to say to many interpreters, here was evidence that all in the new United States would indeed be rejoined into one (white) race. But of course, as we have seen, such stories also contained within them what was for many white Amer-icans the dark potential of environmentalism—the possibility that the American environment could as easily turn a white man black or Indian. As this story is told in the 1850s, the environmentalist "happy ending" is no longer available. Rather, it is to men like the "celebrated anatomist" Dr. Gibbs that those white Americans who continued to believe in the need for an "American race" would turn in the second half of the nine-teenth and into the twentieth centuries. From digging up skulls to un-cover the hidden meaning of race, scientists would increasingly turn to the microscope to uncover the hidden signs of racial difference, making recourse to increasingly invisible and abstract notions of the meaning of race—to ideas of blood, spirit, and "culture."

Thus, even as these clippings show how much remained unfinished when Douglass was writing in the 1840s and '50s, they also show quite clearly why the logic of American race we have been tracing does significantly come to a kind of end at this time. When the question of race took its prominent place in the discourse and literature of national identity in 1787, it was widely considered and debated as an abstract metaphor with which conceptions of national identity could be hammered out and defended. Those who suffered the effects of white nationalist definitions of race—the displaced Native American and the enslaved African American—did not serve as the focus of these debates but as a mask by which the abstract concerns of nation-building could be given a visible face. Thus, racial difference was not a threat to the national identity of white Americans but a necessary precondition for it; as *Edgar Huntly* showed, it was by killing off the racial other that Americans proved they were fundamentally different from "aliens"—that is, white Europeans—and thus able to claim a unique national identity.

But, as we have seen, as the nineteenth century progressed, the pressures of African American slavery and the growing presence of freed African Americans made it increasingly impossible for those committed to a fantasy of a "white America" to celebrate racial difference as the foundation of a national identity. With each generation, those committed to the fantasy of a white nation found it more difficult to write that fantasy into fact. Thus, Cooper can successfully fantasize what Poe, who has a more complex and conflicted relationship to the issues raised, cannot: the return to a world of perfect whiteness, a nation without racial difference at all. As Poe discovered, to imagine such a nation was to do away with the foundation of American writing itself. And what in part forced him to articulate this conclusion was racial science, which "discovered" and read the racial "writing" that proved the inevitability of racial difference and the inequality of the races.

Douglass, in attempting to overthrow the discoveries of racial science, seeks to return the nation to its origins, asking it to celebrate, as did the first generation of writers and theorists, the nation's dependence on racial difference. But he does so from a radically new standpoint, describing the fantasy of the merging of these different races and nations into a composite whole—into "new men." Thus, Douglass resurrects and redirects the fantasy of an "American Race"—a race of citizens transformed from the white Europeans and black Africans of the Old World. But even as he writes, this model of "American race" has run its course, and those who would devote their lives to scripting hierarchies will turn increasingly to the invisible realm for their meanings, defining an American "blood" that must be protected and the invisible signs of the American "soul" that cannot be corrupted. The racialized literature of the second half of the nineteenth century—a literature that has been recently excavated by, among many others, Walter Benn Michaels, Kenneth Warren, and Eric Sundquist—is often defined by a scene of competition and cooperation by writers of diverse backgrounds for the contested soil of an "American literature."

This scene of struggle continues today in our literature, our classrooms, and our legislatures, as Americans continue to read and write increasingly invisible and elaborate definitions of all that divides them. It might be understood as a telling irony that it is this literature of identity that most persuasively defines an American literature as unique and "exceptional." In other words, we might allow for a moment that it is finally as a site for the struggle over identity that an American literature is most clearly defined as distinct from others. As it was difference—from white European models and, of course, from African Americans and Native Americans as well—that was the goal of the white nationalists who set out to found an American literature two hundred years ago, we might then suppose their project to have been successful, albeit in terms they never could recognize. We might also wonder whether this unwitting "triumph" of the "Founding Fathers" is not itself a story that remains to be rewritten. We have the opportunity to reconsider the meaning we ascribe to racial and ethnic difference in our definitions of national identity and our national literature. The power to be better readers remains, as Douglass tells us, in our hands.

NOTES

PREFACE

1. The debate over American English and its role in the development of literary and national culture has been the subject of several recent studies, including Gustafson, *Representative Words*; David Simpson, *Politics of American English*; Kramer, *Imagining Language*.

2. Berlant, *Anatomy of National Fantasy,* 29.

3. Lipsitz, "Possessive Investment," 369.

4. For an excellent survey of this important body of work, see Fishkin, "Interrogating 'Whiteness.'"

5. Castronovo's *Fathering the Nation* provides an example of such a literary history, albeit one focused primarily on later, midcentury texts and encounters. His work locates the mid-nineteenth-century voices that articulated the ambiguity and ambivalence that national narrative sought to erase; *Master Plots* focuses on the technologies by which this narrative came into being in the first place.

CHAPTER I: The History of White Negroes

1. Quoted in Tompkins, *Sensational Designs,* 109.

2. See Bercovitch, *American Jeremiad.* For a discussion of the centrality of the metaphor of slavery to the Revolutionary discourse see Bailyn, *Ideological Origins,* 232–35. For a discussion of Puritan anxieties about Indians, see Pearce, *Savagism and Civilization*; and Sanders, *Lost Tribes and Promised Lands.*

3. Crèvecoeur, *Letters,* 200–227; Bartram, *Travels,* 373.

4. Fields, "Slavery, Race and Ideology."

5. See Saxton, *Rise and Fall of the White Republic,* 1; Roediger, *Wages of Whiteness,* 21, 27.

6. Gellner, *Nations and Nationalism,* 48.

7. Bhabha, Introduction to *Nation and Narration,* 1.

8. Brennan, "National Longing for Form," in Bhabha, 48.

9. Lipsitz, "Possessive Investment in Whiteness," 369.

10. Sommer similarly speculates about the late emergence of the novel in Latin America, and she suggests that, in addition to the important fact of Spanish colonial proscription of fictional materials, we need to see the nineteenth-century rise of the novel in the context of the postindependence pressures of national "consolidation" (*Foundational Fictions,* 12).

11. Anderson, *Imagined Communities,* 26.

12. For a related argument in an English context, and one that helped me formulate my own, see Schmitt, *Alien Nation,* 12–13, 123.

13. Hudson, "From 'Nation' to 'Race,'" 247.

14. See Michaels, *Our America*; Michaels, "Slavery and the New Historicism."

15. Balibar, "Culture and Identity," 177.

16. Quoted in Jordan, *White over Black,* 544.

17. Wood, *Creation of the American Republic,* 495.

18. Belknap, *The Foresters,* 185.

19. See Arner, "Connecticut Wits."

20. Of course, what was actually being excavated from the Ohio territory at the time was evidence of an Indian civilization older and more advanced than previously believed; but most scientists refused to grant a connection between the civilizations responsible for the earthworks in Ohio and the present-day Indians. Instead, it was argued that these artifacts were the products of an older civilization that had since become extinct, possibly at the hands of the present-day savages. See Greene, *American Science,* 346–56, for an account of theories regarding Indian antiquities at this time.

21. Humphreys et al., *The Anarchiad,* 57.

22. "Speech of an Indian," 256–57.

23. Lycurgus, "History of White Negroes," 65. For identification of "Lycurgus" as the editor, Josiah Meigs, see Richardson, *Early American Magazines,* 251.

24. For accounts of "white negroes" in magazines, see Peale, "Account of a Negro"; "Account of a Remarkable Alteration"; "Some Account of a Motley Coloured Girl"; and Rush, "Observations," 292. The most famous such case of the day was that of Henry Moss: born a slave and serving as a soldier in the Revolution, in 1792 Moss began to develop white spots on his body and by 1795 was almost entirely white. Smith and Rush both found proof for their theories in Moss's case, and Moss used his newfound celebrity to raise money to purchase his own freedom. As one early critic of Smith and defender of polygeny, Charles Caldwell, wrote years later, the name of Henry Moss was "almost as familiar to the readers of newspapers and other periodicals" as that of "John Adams, Thomas Jefferson, or James Madison" (quoted in Stanton, *Leopard's Spots,* 6).

25. Lycurgus, "History of White Negroes," 65.

26. The *New-Haven Gazette*'s interest in slave rebellion was not unique, as reports of the horrors of the conflict on Santo Domingo were a regular staple of the magazines. But Meigs's paper was especially vigilant in its response, as early reports of violent uprisings on the island reveal. See, for example, volume 1 (1786) for an account "of the outrageous proceedings of the run-away negroes there, which may be relied on" (14), listing tortures and destruction of property, and a couple of issues later, another account of runaways laying fire to a wealthy estate, arming themselves, and giving "themselves to every excess of riot and drunkenness" (39). For an early magazine account of the revolt on Santo Do-

mingo, described as "an alarming insurrection of the negroes and mullatoes," see the *Universal Asylum* 7 (1791): 213; interestingly, this is followed by an account of Indian wars in the States. The response to the facts and fantasies of black revolution are addressed in chapter 3.

27. Lycurgus, "History of White Negroes," 65.

28. Quoted in Szatmary, *Shays's Rebellion,* 73. Tyler's commander, General Lincoln, wrote to Washington in 1786 that the Regulators were seeking to do away with private property and level society into "agrarian law" (72), language tellingly similar to the terms used to describe the Indians. As Henry Knox, secretary of war, wrote in 1789, the Indians needed to discover "a love for exclusive property" to become civilized; and as Lincoln himself wrote on his way to an Indian treaty in 1793, if the Indians did not embrace private property, "they will, in consequence of their stubbornness, dwindle and moulder away" (quoted in Pearce, *Savagism and Civilization,* 68–69).

29. Abraham Yates's "History of the Movement for the United States Constitution" (1789), an Antifederalist tract that claimed to illuminate the Federalist conspiracy, offers one contemporary response to the use of federal troops under the guise of Indian war: "That we were on the Eve of Hostilities, threatened by the Shawanese, Puteotamie, Chippawas, Tawas, and Twightwas (savage Nation, that live toward the Mississippi, Behind and to the southward of Virginia); [and] the Necessity of reinforcing the continental army with 1340 Non-Commissioned officers and privates. This delusion or if you please this Resolution carried with it a suspicious appearance. The ordering 1220 men of the Number to be raised in the four New England states—It was said near 200 miles from the Country where they were said to be wanted—showed that it was a Contrivance; intended at the same time to get the Continental Establishment augmented, and to terrify the Insurgents in the state of Massachusetts, who were greatly Reprobating the conduct of their Rulers and had attempted to obstruct the Courts of Justice" (244–45).

30. See Hamilton, Jay, and Madison, *The Federalist Papers,* for the use of the anxieties raised by Shays in support of the Constitution, especially by Hamilton. See especially nos. 6, 16, 25, and 28 for examples of Hamilton's recurring recourse to the specter of revolt; and his conclusion to the series, in no. 85, for a final paranoid landscape of what the United States will look like without the guarantees of a strong federal government: "It may be in me a defect of political fortitude but I acknowledge that I cannot entertain an equal tranquillity with those who affect to treat the dangers of a longer continuance in our present situation as imaginary. A NATION, without a NATIONAL GOVERNMENT, is, in my view, an awful spectacle" (527).

31. Letter to Joseph Willard, 24 March 1789, in Jefferson, *Writings,* 949.

32. Sheehan, *Seeds of Extinction,* 44.

33. Jordan, *White over Black,* 429.

34. Jefferson, *Writings,* 270.

35. Gossett, *Race,* 36.

36. Jefferson, *Writings*, 270.

37. Samuel Stanhope Smith, *Essay*, 4. His appendix, "Stricture on Lord Kaims's Discourse on the Original Diversity of Mankind," remains in place in the revised edition of 1810, in which Smith works directly to refute Jefferson's arguments.

38. Gould, *Mismeasure of Man*, 39–72, offers a useful overview of the monogenism-polygenism debate.

39. Jefferson, *Writings*, 211.

40. On one level, the issue at stake is often explicit opposition to the slave trade, an issue on which some magazines took strong positions—notably Matthew Carey's *American Museum*, the leading antislavery magazine of the period (Richardson, *Early American Magazines*, 323). But for the majority, the interest was grounded in the question of racial origins. Thus, for example, Thomas Clarkson's *Essay on the Impolicy of the African Slave Trade* (1788) was condensed in the *Massachusetts Magazine* (1 [1789]) to focus on the debate over the origins of skin color for those "who cannot attend to the perusal of a large voluminous dissertation" (672). For a similar series of essays, arguing on behalf of the slave trade, see "Observations on the Gradation in the Scale of Being," which argues in favor of a fixed "scale." These are simply two in a wide range of published essays of the period, including excerpts from Jefferson, Buffon, Kames, Smith, Peale, and Rush.

41. Smith, *Essay*, 109–10.

42. Davidson, *Revolution and the Word*, 41.

43. Ziff, *Writing in the New Nation*, x.

44. Davidson, *Revolution and the Word*, 45.

45. William Hill Brown, *Power of Sympathy*, 29; Rowson, *Charlotte Temple*, 35; *History of Constantius and Pulchera*, 3.

46. *Arabian Nights Entertainment*, 2:282.

47. William Hill Brown, *Power of Sympathy*, 99.

CHAPTER 2: The Prodigal in Chains

1. Smollett, *Roderick Random*, 21.

2. Similarly, in *Robinson Crusoe* (1719; first American ed., 1774), which we are told influences Updike's career (46), the prodigal is also provided for on his return from his pilgrimage by the profits reaped from his slave-run plantation in Brazil. Although Crusoe, like Updike, will serve several years as "a miserable Slave" to Africans, for the British prodigal this is but a minor digression on his path to spiritual and economic prosperity. For Crusoe's experiences as a slave to the Moors, see Defoe, *Robinson Crusoe*, 18–23.

3. Tyler, *Algerine Captive*, 43. All subsequent references will be cited parenthetically in the text.

4. The anonymous *Adventures of Jonathan Corncob* (1787), another pica-

resque clearly influenced by Smollett, contains a similar dream sequence in which Jonathan's mother dreams she will give birth to a "screech owl" (5), and a witch tells her the dream means her son is doomed. Like Roderick and Updike, Jonathan has an encounter with the slave system in Barbados, but its lessons, like Jonathan's national identity, are entirely ambiguous.

5. See Jordan, *White over Black*; Robinson, *Slavery in American Politics*; Diggins, "Slavery, Race, and Equality"; Morrow, "Problem of Slavery"; Freehling, "Founding Fathers and Slavery"; and Morgan's seminal essay, "Slavery and Freedom."

6. For biographical information concerning Tyler's early life I am indebted to Tanselle, *Royall Tyler*; Carson and Carson, *Royall Tyler*; and, for the Tyler-Adams romance, Gelles, "Gossip."

7. Gelles, "Gossip," 669–70.

8. For the family legend regarding Tyler's exploits during the rebellion, see the autobiography of his wife, Mary Palmer Tyler, *Grandmother Tyler's Book*, 105.

9. Tyler, *Prose*, 195. All "Colon and Spondee" essays discussed are drawn from this collection, following Peladeau's attributions. See Tanselle, "Editing of Royall Tyler," for a critical review of Peladeau's editing and for the problems of attributing authorship in these essays. For my purposes, however, the precise identification of Tyler or Dennie as author of particular entries is not pressing.

10. Tyler, *Prose*, 214.

11. For Rush's theory, see his "Observations." The paper, presented to the society in 1792, argued that blackness is a disease (and a potentially infectious one) that demanded cure, compassion, and quarantine.

12. Tise, *Proslavery*, 194, 196–97.

13. Buel, *Securing the Revolution*, 35. I am indebted to Buel's account of the political climate of the 1790s.

14. Bloch, *Visionary Republic*, 150–231.

15. Howe, "Republican Thought and Political Violence," 77.

16. Slaughter, *Whiskey Rebellion*, 115. Learning from the mishandling of Shays's Rebellion, Washington made a spectacle of federal strength in putting down this rebellion and the sympathetic democratic societies.

17. U.S. 3d Congress, 1st session, 1793–94, House of Representatives, Committee on the Naval Force (Philadelphia, 1794), 1.

18. My discussion of the Algerian Crisis owes much to Barnby, *Prisoners of Algiers* and Ray W. Irwin, *Diplomatic Relations*, as well as to contemporary accounts, especially Foss (discussed below), Cathcart, *The Captives*, and "Diplomatic Journal."

19. Madison, *Papers*, 15:220, 222, from a speech before Congress on 30 January 1794, in which Madison argued for retaliatory commercial policies against Britain. Madison played the twinned themes of Indians and Algerians repeatedly throughout the debates of the period, as in the debate of 6 February 1794 on the Naval Force appropriation bill in which Madison argued "that Britain could

render very essential service to the Algerines, without embarking in a war. She had not embarked in a war to the northwest of the Ohio; but she has done the same thing in substance by supplying the Indians with arms, ammunition and perhaps subsistence. . . . In the same way that they give under-hand assistance to the Indians, they would give it to the Algerines, rather than hazard an open war" (15:250).

20. Franklin, *Writings*, 1072.

21. Carey, *Short Account of Algiers*, 45.

22. Quoted in Ray W. Irwin, *Diplomatic Relations*, 64.

23. See, for example, Captain Richard O'Brien's letter in *Worchester Magazine* 1 (1786): 102–3; lists of captives and demanded ransoms in the *Universal Asylum and Columbian Magazine* 4 (1790): 285; "Curses of Slavery," 118–22.

24. For a description of "the Manheim anthology" as "the first collection of captivity horrors issued . . . purely for commercial gain," see Berkhofer, *White Man's Indian*, 85. See the title narrative in *Affecting History* (also portrayed on the frontispiece [fig. 1]) for an example of the extreme gothicism in the genre, in the gruesome account of the mutilation of two twin sisters (6). For Bleecker's as the first captivity novel, see VanDerBeets, *Indian Captivity Narrative*, 35. Although written some years earlier and published posthumously in 1797, Bleecker's gruesome and gothic novel is timely in its blame of Britain and France for the horrors of Indians war: "Would to Heaven!" said Madame De R., "that the brutal nations were extinct, for never—never can the united humanity of *France* and *Britain* compensate for the horrid cruelties of their savage allies" (Bleecker, *History of Maria Kittle*, 20:63).

25. Sieminski, "Captivity Narrative and the Revolution."

26. Ethan Allen, *Narrative*, 34, 37, 44.

27. For an overview of the literature of Barbary Captivity, see Baepler, "Barbary Captivity Narrative," 95–120.

28. Markoe, *Algerine Spy*, 67, 104–5. The novel ends with news from Algiers that the spy is now considered a double agent by his own government, at which point he embraces the United States: "I am free to delight in the freedom of others, and am no longer either a slave or a tyrant. At once Christian and a Pennsylvanian, I am doubly an advocate for the rights of mankind" (126).

29. In Rowson's play, the American slaves revolt, and the Dey is forced to plead for his life. The Americans convert him to democratic principles, commanding him to "Open your prison doors; give freedom to your people; sink the name of subject in the endearing epithet of fellow-citizen" (*Slaves in Algiers*, 71).

30. "Sidi Mehemet Ibrahim on the Slave Trade," in Franklin, *Writings*, 1157–60; also see the anonymous *American in Algiers*, which tells the parallel stories of an American captive in Algiers and an African slave in America to demonstrate the "Inconsistency of African slavery."

31. In his preface to the second, expanded edition of his work, Foss writes, "The success which my former narrative met with, which was merely an extract

from a Journal kept for my own amusement, has induced me to lay before the public a more copious detail of that work. . . . The importance as well as utility of having a work of this kind generally disseminated through the United States, must be apparent to every thinking person" (*Journal*, 3).

32. Butler, *Fortune's Foot-ball*, 1:64–70; 2:8–46.

33. For example, see the *History of Maria Martin* (1806), which combines history borrowed from Carey with a grisly account of suffering at the hands of the Algerines. The frontispiece, like that appended to the Manheim anthology, offers a highly sexualized image of female suffering with Maria weighed down with chains, her blouse torn open, in a "dark and dismal dungeon."

34. Tyler, *Prose*, 45–46.

35. For a useful summary of the critical reception of the novel, which from the nineteenth century on was admiring of the first volume and disappointed in the second, see Carson and Carson, *Royall Tyler*, 67. See Petter, *Early American Novel*, 295, for a contemporary version of this complaint.

36. Tanselle, *Royall Tyler*, 153.

37. Spengemann, *Adventurous Muse*, 120, 138.

38. Engell, "Narrative Irony in *Algerine Captive*."

39. Dennis, "Legitimizing the Novel."

40. See Engell, "Narrative Irony in *Algerine Captive*," 21–22, and Davidson, *Revolution and the Word*, 203, for readings of this Puritan "history" as the key to the novel's subversive project.

41. Adams, *Political Writings*, 7.

42. Warner, *Letters of the Republic*, 2.

43. For a counterpoint to Underhill's narrative, see Philip Vincent's *True Relation* (1638), which offers the "official" version of the conflict with the Pequots. As Slotkin reads the two narratives, they each utilized the war "to demonstrate the validity of their divergent religious and social philosophies and their different visions of the New World. Underhill's vision of a Calvinist Garden of Eden was pitted against Vincent's picture of orderly Boston, like an enclosed island awash in a sea of Indian and heretical chaos" (*Regeneration through Violence*, 69). For a history of the Pequot War and its legacy, see Drinnon, *Facing West*, 37–56; and Sanders, *Lost Tribes and Promised Lands*, 326–40, in which he argues that one of the legacies of the war was the origins of chattel slavery in the colony, as the surviving Pequots were sold into slavery in the West Indies, traded for cotton, tobacco, and black slaves (340).

44. Wayne Franklin reads this moment in Underhill's narrative: "This impacted, sometimes confused history simply breaks off at its midpoint (the action in suspense) as he surveys a group of wonderful sites for the peaceful expansion of English order. Like the wedge of force sent against the Indians, . . . this section of his book is a means of laying bare a further range of inviting American land" (*Discoverers, Explorers, Settlers*, 43).

45. Underhill, *Newes From America*, 30–31.

46. Slotkin, *Regeneration through Violence*, 78.

47. Tyler, *Prose*, 219. This is the punch line to a series of definitions, written concurrently with the publication of *Algerine Captive*, in which Tyler shows that "aristocracy" was ultimately less to be feared than "hogocracy" (rule by "an ignorant booby"), "pigocracy" (rule by an effeminate dandy), "ribocracy" (rule by a woman), and worst of all, "mobocracy"—"But I beg pardon, this is only a species of Democracy."

48. As he begins his apprenticeship, Updike meets one of the doctor's patients, a blind man with a remarkable ability to perceive human difference, who claims, "there is not a greater difference between the African and the European than what I could discover between the finger nails of all the men of this world" (60). These skills of observation are in the blind man so refined that difference has come to dominate and system is impossible to discern. As Updike laments for this extraordinary man, "Notwithstanding his accuracy and veracity upon subjects he could comprehend, there were many on which he was miserably confused," and the chief among these deficiencies is that "he had no adequate idea of colors" (61). Updike's teacher uses his gifts to give the blind man sight, to teach him colors, just as he will teach Updike to refine his new skills of observation.

49. There was another John Hunter who, in 1775, published an important paper on race, cited by Smith in his *Essay*, and it is entirely possible that Tyler, like Smith, is conflating the two. For the John Hunters, and their influence on both Stanhope Smith and the formulations of early polygenists Charles White and John Augustine Smith, see Stanton, *Leopard's Spots*, 16–17; Gossett (who seems to repeat Smith's elision of the two Hunters), *Race*, 36–37; and Jordan, "Introduction," xxxiv–xxxv, xxxviii.

50. Indeed, in the most important case of his career on the Supreme Court of Vermont, Tyler demonstrated this antipathy by deciding against the recognition of slavery in any form in the state. For Tyler's report on "Selectmen of Windsor vs. Stephen Jacob" (1802), see *Prose*, 388–94.

51. Quoted in Barnby, *Prisoners of Algiers*, 305.

52. Davidson, *Revolution and the Word*, 209.

53. Mary Palmer Tyler, *Grandmother Tyler's Book*, 258.

54. Spengemann, *Adventurous Muse*, 138.

55. Bercovitch writes, "The motive of these Federalist Jeremiahs is transparent in the momentous choice they posed: on one side, apocalyptic disaster; on the other side, millennial glory earned through a process of *taming, binding, curbing, restraint*" (*American Jeremiad*, 135–36; emphasis in original).

CHAPTER 3: Edgar Huntly's Savage Awakening

1. Fiedler, *Love and Death*, 157. Fiedler's Brown derives its inspiration from R. W. B. Lewis's suggestion that the Brownian hero is the prototype for the "American Adam," albeit one "not . . . entirely naturalized" to Lewis's machinery

of citizenship (*The American Adam*, 98). See also Chase's important early appreciation of *Huntly* in *The American Novel*, 35–37.

2. For the best version of this influential reading of the Indians in *Huntly*, see Slotkin, *Regeneration through Violence*, 369–93. For different approaches that valorize the psychological, see, for example, Schulz, "*Huntly* as Quest Romance"; Hughes, "Archetypal Patterns in *Huntly*"; Stineback, "Introduction." Slotkin's consideration of Huntly's identification with the Indian in the second half of the novel is ultimately mapped back onto the familiar Oedipal drama: Huntly's hunt for Clithero and the Indian is really a hunt for himself, the true murderer of his parents. As Slotkin concludes, "We are both blood-guilty Indians and helpless captives of Indians" (390). Other important readings have similarly failed to challenge the original paradigms. Grabo's new critical reading of the novel, while raising many issues in excess of the mytho-psychological model, finally sees the novel as yet another version of "the perpetual opposition of fathers and sons . . . a very sophisticated fable of adolescent self-assertion and resentment against parental prerogative, along with the guilt that inevitable accompanies those gestures toward complete adulthood" (*Coincidental Art*, 83–84). And Axelrod's historicist account falls back on an analysis of Brown's appropriation of *Oedipus* (*An American Tale*, 161–71).

3. *Edgar Huntly* is a rewriting of Brown's unpublished first novel, "The Sky-Walk, or the Man Unknown to Himself," the published extract of which—all that remains today—contains many of the elements of *Huntly*: somnambulism, a mysterious Irish immigrant, and the remote frontier landscape. What is notably absent from the original conception of the story is the Indian. Yet, when Brown returns to the story it is the Indian that serves as his best summary of the novel's concerns. See "An Extract from 'Sky Walk,'" in Charles Brockden Brown, *Rhapsodist*, 136–44.

4. Charles Brockden Brown, "Fragment": "The following narrative is extracted from the memoirs of a young man who resided some years since on the upper branches of the Delaware. . . . Similar events have frequently happened on the Indian borders; but, perhaps, they never were described with equal minuteness" (21).

5. Charles Brockden Brown, *Edgar Huntly*, 3. Further references will be cited parenthetically within the text.

6. Ziff, *Writing in the New Nation*, 180.

7. The Historical Society of Pennsylvania's collection of Brown's later notebooks reveals the extent of his concern in his last years with the nation's political and economic boundaries. In his "Book of Select Pieces Chiefly on Political Subject" (AM. 03399, vol. 2), for example, Brown transcribed news items dealing with the legislation and debates surrounding the protection of American interests at home and abroad. His "Commonplace Book" (AM. 03399, vol. 6) contains a series of copied articles critiquing Jefferson's leadership and citing threats of disunion from the West.

8. Axelrod, *An American Tale*, 3. Axelrod is one of the only critics to note the connection between the pamphlets and *Huntly*, although he reads the meaning of the connection largely in terms of the familiar psychological narrative, albeit one in which a crisis in national identity is mapped on to a narrative of psychological self-division and doublings (26–28). Looby reads the pamphlets as growing out of Brown's experiences in writing *Wieland* and that novel's "discouraged reflection on the tenability of the claim that a viable political order could be guaranteed by discursive reason without the aid of the unspoken loyalty and reverence that supported the legitimacy of previous states" (*Voicing America*, 193).

9. For the traditional account of the reception of the pamphlet, see Warfel, *Charles Brockden Brown*, 207–11. Most other accounts have relied on Warfel's contextualization. Warfel's extremely useful account has proved a troubling source for this material insofar as it overvalues the originality of Brown's rhetoric and underplays the stakes of the larger debate in which Brown is playing an explicitly partisan role. It has led to such dubious claims on behalf of the pamphlets as that of Bennett, who argues that they "entitle Brown to a place not among the crowd of polemicists whose writings troubled the time but to an honored place among the select company of political theorists intent on endowing the infant republic with an informing political philosophy" ("Brown: Man of Letters," 218); or Axelrod's claim that, if not for the success of Monroe's mission in Europe, Brown's "*Address* might have been instrumental in fomenting a war between France and the United States" (*An American Tale*, 3).

The fact is that Brown's pamphlet did capture much attention in the weeks following its publication, and it was used by some Federalist papers as evidence of the necessity of war, but by early February it had been discovered as a hoax, and even before its authorship was known, some Federalist papers were joining with the Republican press in denouncing it as a forgery. Its originality lay solely in its fiction of the French minister and the "discovered" pamphlet, and it was on the basis of this fiction that it attracted so much attention, as Federalists fought to prove the fiction true, while Republicans sought to undermine the entire Federalist position by proving the pamphlet a fiction. See *Aurora, and General Advertiser*, 26 and 28 January, and 2, 8, and 10 February 1803, for the attempts to prove the pamphlet a "forgery" in the face of widespread Federalist publicizing of its contents. For the standard Federalist line, see Ross, *Speeches*. This and other pamphlets show that neither Brown's arguments nor his rhetoric was original to himself; he was writing very much as a party-man.

10. *Aurora*, 28 January 1803, in an article speculating on the author of the "spurious pamphlet." It is ironic that Brown's pamphlet lost its front-page status the moment the *Aurora* disclosed his authorship; the very fact that Brown was a novelist proved grounds for the Republican paper to dismiss the political pamphlet as pure "romance": "The report goes that the celebrated pamphlet concerning Louisiana humerously [sic] attributed to a French *counsellor of state*—is the production of a *novel writer* of great celebrity in one of our capital cities—and this

brochure was issued—not with a serious view but to try the public taste in that *novel* walk of *Romance*" (10 February 1803). The *Aurora* enjoyed the joke sufficiently to repeat it several times throughout the issue, concluding by decisively pointing its finger at Brown, "the *Man at Home*; alias the counsellor of state"—an allusion to Brown's popular column in the *Weekly Magazine* of 1798.

11. *Aurora*, 28 January 1803. For a general overview of the Louisiana Crisis of 1803, see DeConde, *Affair of Louisiana.*

12. Charles Brockden Brown, *An Address*, 42–43.

13. A pamphlet by the colonizationist and jurist St. George Tucker identifies similar significance in the Louisiana territory. In *Reflections on the Cession of Louisiana* (1803), Tucker is especially pleased with the prospect the new territory provides of a thousand-mile "barrier" (13) between the United States and its enemies. Far from sharing Jefferson's expansionist ambitions for the territory, however, Tucker calls for a policy of *non*-settlement by which the land will be preserved as a place to relocate Indians, blacks, and "delinquents," while whites currently settled in the territory are invited to enter the United States and become citizens. By using the territory as a buffer and a "place of exile" (26) the nation is purged of all who are not "ready and willing to harmonize and become one people with us" (24). With this plan Tucker promises the end of the "the demon of discord" and the beginning of a true national identity (25).

14. James Morton Smith, *Freedom's Fetters*, 15.

15. For an account of the debates over naturalization that led up to the Naturalization Act of 1798, the most partisan citizenship act in the nation's history, see Kettner, *Development of American Citizenship*, ch. 8.

16. Marshall, *The Aliens*, 17.

17. The two most important European sources for the American promoters of anti-Illuminist hysteria were John Robison and the Abbé Barruel, both published in best-selling editions in the late 1790s. Robison himself was a former Mason who tells of the perversion of the Masonry by French philosophy such that now "AN ASSOCIATION HAD BEEN FORMED for the express purpose of ROOTING OUT ALL THE RELIGIOUS ESTABLISHMENTS, AND OVERTURNING ALL THE EXISTING GOVERNMENTS OF EUROPE" (*Proofs of a Conspiracy*, 14). The work was in a fourth edition in the United States one year after its publication in Britain. The best history of the Illuminati Crisis remains Stauffer, *The Bavarian Illuminati.*

18. Timothy Dwight, *Duty of Americans*, 19.

19. Quoted in Stauffer, *The Bavarian Illuminati*, 227.

20. Quoted in Miller, *Crisis in Freedom*, 6.

21. Anxieties about the effects of the revolt on Santo Domingo on the nation's slave population were not entirely paranoid, as Gabriel's Rebellion of 1800 would make clear. With the withdrawal of the British from the island in 1798, Adams and the Federalists backed Toussaint-Louverture against the French, but with strong reservations about the prospects of an independent black nation off the coast of the United States. From the earliest stages of the quasi war with France, political

leaders, especially from the slave-owning states, made uneasy connections between the state of relations with France and the security of America's slave system. The French understood this anxiety and did their best to fuel it (see Stinchombe, *The XYZ Affair*, 26–27, 112).

22. Harrison Gray Otis's rhetoric was characteristic as he argued that the government cannot allow "hordes of wild Irishmen . . . to come here with a view to disturb our tranquility, after having succeeded in the overthrow of their own Government" (quoted in James Morton Smith, *Freedom's Fetters*, 24). So vehement did anti-Irish sentiment grow during this period that a group of Irish leaders petitioned Congress for the repeal of the laws and measures that were being used to justify ethnic violence; see *The Plea of Erin* (1798). For an example of anti-Irish pamphlets circulating at the time, see Theodore Dwight's *An Oration*, in which he explicitly defines the Irish as the chief threat to national unity (30–31).

23. Quoted in Miller, *Crisis in Freedom*, 104–5.

24. Cobbett, *Detection of a Conspiracy*, 4. Cobbett's language in his tale of Irish "atrocities" borrows directly from the resurgent interest in the captivity narrative discussed in chapter 2.

25. Ibid., 24, 29.

26. As its first target for the Alien Friends Act, the administration chose the notorious French general Victor Collot, believed to be operating in disguise from within the country. Collot was a powerful symbol of all that the act sought to defend against: he was known to have performed extensive intelligence expeditions in the Louisiana Territory and was suspected of plotting with frontier citizens to establish an independent French state in the West. For an account of the administration's failure to successfully prosecute Collot under the Alien Act, see Miller, *Crisis in Freedom*, 189; and Kyte, "Detention of General Collot."

27. Cobbett called for "a sedition law to keep our own rogues from cutting our throats, and an alien law to prevent the invasion by a host of foreign rogues to assist them" (quoted in Miller, *Crisis in Freedom*, 55).

28. For an excellent discussion of Brown's understanding of the novel's public role, see Warner, *Letters of the Republic*, ch. 6; see also James D. Wallace, "Failure of Charles Brockden Brown," in *Early Cooper and His Audience*, 52–54, for an account of Brown's correspondence with Jefferson.

29. These concerns were not new for Brown. The *Weekly Magazine*, to which Brown was a regular contributing editor, closed its first volume (devoted in large measure to Brown's "Man at Home" series) with a lengthy appendix of documents surrounding the XYZ Affair, and volume 2 (in which Brown serialized *Arthur Mervyn*) closed with documents from the continuing debates on the crisis with France and the internal threats to U.S. security. Shirley Samuels has demonstrated *Wieland*'s engagement with the Alien and Sedition Acts, showing how Brown in his first novel works to complicate and challenge the fundamental precepts of the laws by "both blaming Carwin for introducing sexuality, disorder, and violence into the Wieland family, and explaining that introduction as nothing

more than an enhancement of sexual and familial tension already present. . . . Introduced as an external threat, the alien, Carwin, instead stands (in) for an internal one" ("*Wieland*: Alien and Infidel," 53). Although I would question the extent to which the novel's exploration of these concerns resolves into a "desire for the norm" (55), Samuels is persuasive in reading a novel often associated with Brown's high-Godwinism as a consideration of the period's anxieties about aliens and the inherent corruptibility of the American. In the end, Brown's first confrontation with these laws leaves him comfortable in his position as Republican critic, for as Samuels shows, the tragedy in the end "cannot finally be blamed on an alien intrusion; instead, the family-republic . . . is caught in the grip of transformations in which it discovers that the alien is already within" (60).

30. Krause, "Historical Essay," 298.

31. Larson writes, "The second part of *Arthur Mervyn* reflects the changes which occurred in Brown's thinking between his conception of the first part of the novel and his writing of the second part. The novels do not fit neatly together because they are not a unit; rather, the second part is a recasting of the themes Brown explored in the first part. . . . Brown's changing vision is revealed in *Edgar Huntly*; indeed, if *Arthur Mervyn, First Part* has an immediate sequel, it is *Edgar Huntly*" ("*Mervyn, Huntly* and the Critics," 208–9). Watts similarly marks the connection between the two novels in *The Romance of Real Life*, seeing *Huntly* as a study of "the psychological resonances of [the] momentous shift" toward liberalism narrated in *Mervyn* (115).

32. In fact, this marks something of a return to an earlier position. As a law student at sixteen, Brown wrote a "decision" for his law club on the very issues with which the Sedition Acts would be concerned twelve years later, deciding in favor of the principles that would justify the Sedition Act, citing the need for a defense of the "public peace" over the "evil and convenience of a single individual." For a transcription of Brown's "judgment" in this case, see Paul Allen, *Life of Brown*, 38–39.

33. Slotkin, *Regeneration through Violence*, 256. For an account of the printing history and a copy of the narrative, see Vail, "The Panther Captivity."

34. Kornfeld similarly notes the novel's equation of "savage" panther with the Indians ("Encountering 'the Other,'" 293).

35. The uncharacteristically descriptive passage is made even more striking by the rare pains Brown took in revising this passage from his original "Fragment." Compare page 29 of the "Fragment" with page 184 of *Huntly*.

36. Charles Brockden Brown, *Ormond*, 134; "Carwin the Biloquist," 279; "Stephen Calvert," 71. We of course never find out why Calvert has gone to live in the wilderness with the Indians, as the story was not completed. With regards to Carwin's discovery of his ventriloquist powers through the imitation of the Indian, it is interesting to note that the infamous con man Stephen Burroughs also reported in his biography of 1798 that he had first discovered his remarkable talents for creating false identities through the imitation of Indians (*Memoirs*, 24–25).

37. "Account of a Singular Change."

38. Brown's *Monthly Magazine* published "Another Instance of a Negro Turning White": "The change of colour which Harry Moss has, within a few years, undergone, from black to white, has been published so often that few curious persons are ignorant of it. In the town of North-Hempstead, something of the same kind is now to be seen. . . . The change is not the dead white of the *Albinos,* but is a good wholesome carnation hue. . . . How additionally singular it would be, if instances of the spontaneous disappearance of this sable mark of distinction between slaves and their masters were to become frequent!"

39. As Fiedler notes, Indians in this novel, except for Queen Mab, are mute (*Love and Death,* 160).

40. Crèvecoeur, *Letters,* 80.

41. Quoted in Warfel, *Charles Brockden Brown,* 63–64.

42. Quoted in Clark, *Pioneer Voice of America,* 195.

43. *Clara Howard* and *Jane Talbot* (both 1801).

44. *New-York Evening Post,* 24 January 1803. In this issue of the *Post,* Brown's pamphlet is brought before the public as proof of the necessity of immediate militancy action: "In speaking on the momentous subject of New-Orleans and Louisiana, in the former numbers of this paper, we have endeavoured to address the public to the necessity of *immediate active* measures to secure to us the important right of freely navigating the river Mississippi. We have shewn that the right is *ours.* . . . A pamphlet, which we have just received by a friend, from Philadelphia, has given new edge to that keen and anxious solicitude that we feel to what so deeply concerns the honor and prospects of the United States." This and the next four issues of the paper excerpted vast portions of the pamphlet, presenting it as if the "discovered" document was genuine.

45. Ross, *Speeches,* 39.

46. Charles Brockden Brown, *Monroe's Embassy,* 34.

47. Charles Lee, *Defence of the Alien and Sedition Laws,* 8–9.

CHAPTER 4: Cooper's Vanishing American Act

1. Irving, "Rip Van Winkle," in *History, Tales and Sketches,* 783.

2. Wallace, *Early Cooper and His Audience*: "At the outset of his own career, Cooper had Brown's failure very much in mind. . . . It was clear that ambition and genius could not guarantee success in the American market, but it was not at all clear what would" (63). Cooper makes a disparaging reference to Brown in *The Pilot* (1823), where he writes, "we manifestly reject the prodigious advantage of being thought a genius, by perhaps foolishly refusing the mighty aid of incomprehensibility to establish such a character" (94).

3. Cooper, *The Spy,* 31–32.

4. Ibid., 32.

5. House, *Cooper's Americans,* 73. House is one of the few critics to ad-

dress this aspect of Cooper's writing; see chapter 4. See also Spiller, "Cooper's Defense."

6. For a recent example, see Bradfield's *Dreaming Revolution,* ch. 3, in which he reads the novel as an attempt to resolve the guilt and instability brought about by Revolutionary fathers.

7. See, for example, Charles Hansforth Adams, *"Guardian of the Law,"* and Patterson, *Authority, Autonomy, and Representation.*

8. For example (although this characterization applies in some measure to much Cooper scholarship), see McWilliams, *Political Justice,* which reads *The Pioneers* in terms of the gradations of society described in Locke's *Second Treatise* (102); Dekker, in *American Historical Romance,* similarly reads the Tales against a "stadialist" theory of progress, formulated by Scottish philosophical historians, which charts four stages of society (ch. 3); and Brook Thomas opens his important essay on representations of the law in *The Pioneers* by claiming, "Few would argue with the statement that *The Pioneers* is a novel about the transformation of America from wilderness to civilization" ("Sources of American Legal History," 86).

9. That a chapter focusing on the Leatherstocking Tales of the 1820s reads *The Pioneers* and *The Prairie* while largely passing over *The Last of the Mohicans* demands explanation. My concern here is with those of Cooper's novels that are explicitly engaging the aspects of the early national period discussed in the previous two chapters. In many ways, *Mohicans* operates out of a somewhat different logic in its deployment of the Vanishing American, insofar as it is specifically concerned with America's prehistory and the earliest stirrings in the colonies of a *national* identity. Thus, there the Indian functions in more conventional terms: vanishing that his claims may be rightfully inherited by the Americans. What is happening in *The Prairie* and *The Pioneers,* I argue below, is different insofar as the Indian's vanishing is more carefully orchestrated to confront social, political, and racial challenges of the early national period. Nevertheless, it has been argued convincingly by Tompkins and Romero that *Mohicans* is similarly invested in concerns over the debates over slavery in the 1820s.

10. Jefferson, *Writings,* 1434.

11. Tompkins, *Sensational Designs,* 97–98.

12. Railton, *Fenimore Cooper,* 75–76.

13. Kelly, *Plotting America's Past,* 42.

14. Cooper, *The Pioneers,* 6. Further references will be cited parenthetically in the text.

15. Cooper, *Letters and Journals,* 4:75.

16. It was as the sheriff was seizing his father's estate in 1822 that he wrote *The Pioneers.* James Cooper, setting out to become the American man of letters, could ill afford to fail. As James Franklin Beard writes, "When he began the book in November or December 1821, James Cooper was, nominally at least, a man of substance. . . . When *The Pioneers* was finally published . . . on 1 February 1823, the author had been reduced to the status of mere novelist, stripped of his

properties and responsible, as a man of honor, for thousands of dollars of debts . . . entirely dependent on his writing to support his wife and four small children" ("Historical Introduction," xix).

17. Cheyfitz, "Literally White, Figuratively Red," 85.

18. We find in Lydia Maria Child's *Hobomok* (1824) a similar revolution. Here too the second generation must restore the structures and forms the parents had overthrown, as the Episcopalian Brown comes to marry the daughter of the fiercest Puritan in the land, in order that she might be "restored to her original rank, and shining amid the loveliest and proudest of the land" (73). And similarly it is the Vanishing American who finally brings this reconciliation about, renouncing his own claims on Mary—the claims of marriage—and disappearing into the wilderness so as to bring together the daughter of the Puritan tyrant and the sworn defender of British tradition in America. As Hobomok says upon his departure from the scene: "Hobomok will go far off among some of the red men in the west. They will dig him a grave, and Mary may sing the marriage song in the wigwam of the Englishman" (139).

19. Ringe, *James Fenimore Cooper*, 33.

20. For example, *Red Rover* and *Lionel Lincoln* both bring about the union of the British noble and American maiden after the dark villain—a pirate in one case and a psychotic old Briton in the other—has been removed from the scene.

21. Orians, *Cult of the Vanishing American*, 3; Heckewelder, *History, Manners and Customs*. Heckewelder's is a passionate cry for justice for the Indians, one that even goes so far as to compare the Indians favorably with whites on the subject of savagery (ch. 44). But his *History* is the history of a "vanished" people, one that allows the reader to mourn without having to make any active recompense.

22. See, for example, Romero, "Vanishing Americans"; Tompkins, *Sensational Designs*, 94–121.

23. Dippie, *Vanishing American*, 10–11.

24. See Drinnon, *Facing West*, ch. 10; Rogin, *Fathers and Children*.

25. For a history of this kind of rhetoric and the calculation of slave representation, see Simpson, "Political Significance of Slave Representation."

26. Quoted in Moore, *Missouri Controversy*, 19; I am indebted to Moore for my understanding of the Missouri Crisis.

27. Jefferson, *Writings*, 1449.

28. Moore, *Missouri Controversy*, 92.

29. King, *Substance of Two Speeches*, 25.

30. Hillhouse, *Pocahontas*, 3.

31. Quoted in Livermore, *Twilight of Federalism*, 96.

32. Timothy Dwight, *Travels in New England*, 1:121.

33. Jefferson said as much at the time, in an angry letter to Gallatin in which he pointed out how geographical divisions were being exploited, especially by the North, in the absence of the former divisions between Federalist and Republican:

"The Federalists compleatly put down, and despairing of ever rising again under the old division of whig and tory, devised a new one, of slave-holding, & non-slave-holding states, which, while it had a semblance of being Moral, was at the same time Geographical, and calculated to give them ascendancy by debauching their old opponents to a coalition with them" (*Writings*, 1448–49).

34. Cooper, *Notions*, 235.

35. Ibid., 240–41.

36. Cooper wrote, "I never was among the Indians. All that I know of them is from reading and hearing my father speak of them" (quoted in Spiller, *Critic of His Times*, 3).

37. Cooper, *Notions*, 241–42.

38. Most arguments on behalf of colonization, for example, saw very different numbers at work. The author of *A Few Facts Reflecting the American Coloniza-tion Society* (1830), for example, produces figures very different from those in Cooper's *Notions*, supporting anxieties regarding the increase in the freed slave population (9). Cooper's logic does find parallel in a much later violently racist work by J. H. Van Evrie, *Negroes and Negro "Slavery"* (1861), dedicated "To the White Men of America": "The free negro, in the American Union, is destined to extinction. It is only a question of time, when this doom will be accomplished. The census returns, and the universal experience, recognize this deplorable truth; but beyond them, and independent of any demonstration whatever, their extinction is a necessity" (309).

39. Cooper, *Notions*, 483.

40. In a recent essay, James D. Wallace reads in *Notions* evidence to refute the argument, first spelled out by Leslie Fiedler, that "miscegenation is the key to all Cooper's writing about race" ("Race and Captivity," 189). Wallace's primary claim, and one with which the whole of this chapter is necessarily in argument, is that "Cooper's racial discourse lacks any elements of genetics or any other science of race" (193). His claims about *Notion*'s supposedly "moderate" attitudes on race rely centrally on two passages: one in which the narrator suggests the possibility that, in the future and if removed from all contact with white civilization, Indians might one day be able to develop a civilization of their own; the second being a suggestion that racist attitudes must be overcome "ere any extensive intercourse can occur between the blacks and the whites." That such changes might theoret-ically occur is allowed by the book, but it is a stretch to claim from this evidence that Cooper treats racial attitudes as "rather a matter of custom than of essential difference, since it is based on our habitual recognition of likeness, and it *could* be overcome" (198). Wallace is correct in claiming that *Notions* expresses "abso-lutely no qualms about the 'horrors of miscegenation'" (199), but precisely be-cause the logic of the Bachelor's reasoning throughout these chapters works to demonstrate that there is no real *possibility* of miscegenation, as the vast majority of his evidence works to prove.

I would also point to a very odd passage in Cooper's *Sketches of Switzerland*

[Part One] (1836), based on travels he completed not long after the publication of *Notions,* in which Cooper encounters a "race of miserable objects called *Crétins"* (*Gleanings,* 270). Cooper corrects himself shortly after by noting that terming these unfortunates a "race" is not "rigidly true, as most of them are the offspring of ordinary parents" (270), but he goes on to speculate as to what would occur "did any accidental concurrence of circumstances permit the formation of a race of such beings! The perpetuation of physical and mental peculiarities cannot be doubted, and it would not be difficult to construct a genealogy for some of the equivocal animals of Africa, through the theories to which such premises give rise" (271). Such "theories" further demonstrate that Cooper is indeed engaging in a discourse of race, however incoherent, that has a "genetics."

41. Cooper, *The Prairie,* 183. Further references will be cited parenthetically in the text.

42. James P. Elliott, "Historical Introduction," xvii.

43. Cooper, *Notions,* 539.

44. St. George Tucker, *Reflections,* 24.

45. A notable exception to this tendency in Cooper novels is *Red Rover,* in which the black sailor, Scipio Africanus, is portrayed in relatively sympathetic and noble terms. But it is precisely his "nobility" that necessitates his death toward the end of the novel, vanishing from the community in a tragic scene very similar to Chingachgook's death scene.

46. Cooper, *The Spy,* 65–66.

47. Cooper, *Notions,* 484.

48. King, *Substance of Two Speeches,* 24. Such ingenious arithmetic is not unique to King; Joseph Blunt similarly argued that "the ten slave-holding states, containing a population of 2,272,000 free persons, and yielding a revenue of $8,602,381, $6,000,000 less than the revenue of New-York alone, send 19 more representatives than the same number of freemen in the middle or eastern states" (*An Examination,* 21). It was also picked up in the press as one of the most potent arguments in favor of the Missouri Bill: "The argument against the admission of slavery in the new states, arising from [the three-fifths] rule, is fully displayed by Mr. King; and the historical details connected with it, shewing the probable grounds upon which the rule itself was founded, are among the most valuable portions of Mr. King's pamphlet. By this rule, a disproportionate power is granted to the states possessing slaves" ("Slavery and the Missouri Question," 159).

49. Quoted in Horsman, *Race and Manifest Destiny,* 118.

50. Caldwell, *Original Unity,* 106. Popular interest in the subject of polygenism grew throughout the 1820s. The *North American Review,* for example, reported in 1823 a renewed fascination with the subject in response to the *Lectures on . . . the Natural History of Man* (1819) by the English racial theorist William Lawrence, which argued, without fully embracing polygenism, on behalf of natural racial hierarchies (17 [1823]: 13, 19).

51. Caldwell voiced arguments about the infertility of racial "hybrids": "It is

even asserted, as the result of observation, that when the descendants of mulattos continue to intermarry, for a few generations, the offspring ceases at length to be productive, and the breed becomes extinct. This is evidence direct and strong against the hypothesis of the unity of man" (*Original Unity*, 42).

52. Lawrence, *Classic American Literature*, 60.

53. "Slavery and the Missouri Question," 158.

54. Wright's Owenite community at Nashoba practiced, fairly openly, principles of free love and miscegenation. Not surprisingly, the community came under vicious attack and folded in 1828; see Eckhardt, *Fanny Wright*, chs. 5 and 6. The colonization movement found its origins in Gabriel's Rebellion of 1801 and fears of black violence, but it gained momentum in 1819 when the American Society for the Colonizing of Free People of Color was given authority under the Slave Trade Act to begin "returning" freed slaves, resulting in the founding of Liberia in 1823. It is important to remember, as Staudenraus points out in *The African Colonization Movement*, that the colonization effort was motivated not only by the desire to rid the nation of blacks, but also by the ambition of establishing a foreign colony.

55. Both Kammen and Walters describe the 1820s in these terms. Kammen writes, "What is most interesting about the 1820s, perhaps, is the fact that many Americans became engaged, in various ways, upon a quest for political order, social stability, and national identity" (*Season of Youth*, 43). Walters argues that the impulse behind such disparate social phenomena of the period as proslavery, anti-Masonry, colonization, and nativism was the perception that "old values were being lost and something or someone was to blame. Whatever was at fault had to be eliminated or controlled if America was to fulfill its destiny" (*American Reformers*, 10).

56. "Review of *Symmes's Theory*," 237.

57. There is debate over the actual identity of the author of *Symzonia*. I have for years been content to accept it as Symmes's own work according to J. O. Bailey's attribution, but my recent correspondence with Robert Schadewald on the subject has led to increasing skepticism about this attribution. For the sake of my present argument, however, the question of the text's author is secondary; I am here interested in how Symmes's theories of an internal world provide a potent landscape for the work of this utopian science fiction and Swiftian satire.

58. [Symmes?], *Symzonia*, 21.

59. Alexander Mitchell, *Vindication of Symmes's Theory*, 5, 24.

60. Irving Wallace, *Square Pegs*, 223–26.

61. See Bailey, "An Early American Utopian Fiction."

62. Symmes, *Light Gives Light*.

63. George Tucker, *Voyage to the Moon*, 9.

64. Ibid., 55. In *Notes*, Jefferson meditates at some length on this "evidence": "We know that among the Romans . . . the condition of their slaves was much more deplorable than that of the blacks in the continent of America. . . . Yet

notwithstanding these and other discouraging circumstances among the Romans, their slaves were often their rarest artists. . . . Epictetus, Terene, and Phaedrus, were slaves. But they were of the race of whites. It is not their condition then, but nature, which has produced the distinction" (*Writings*, 267–68). Tucker devoted much of his career to considering the subject of slavery, beginning with a pamphlet on the subject in 1801, *Letter . . . on . . . the late conspiracy of the slaves*, which advocated colonization as the only solution to the growing crisis of black violence (McLean, *George Tucker*, 180). Early in his career Tucker was an opponent of slavery and Jefferson's theories, but, according to McLean, after 1820 he became a virulent defender of slavery as the cornerstone of southern independence. Clearly, by 1827 he had come fully to accept Jefferson's logic as well.

65. George Tucker, *Voyage to the Moon*, 55.

66. Cooper, *The Monikins*, 266, emphasis added.

67. Cooper, *Letters*, 6:208–9.

CHAPTER 5: Poe's "Incredible Adventures and Discoveries Still Farther South"

1. Poe, *Letters*, 1:7–8.

2. For many of my insights into Poe's biography, I am indebted to Silverman, *Mournful and Never-Ending Remembrance*.

3. Poe, *Imaginary Voyages*, 192. All further citations from *Pym* will be to this edition, cited parenthetically in the text.

4. Poe, *Poetry and Tales*, 198.

5. Ibid., 189.

6. In addition to his well-known disparaging references to Lowell's abolitionism, see also his review of Robert Bird's *Sheppard Lee* in the *Messenger* of 1836, in which he celebrates Bird's "excellent chapters on abolition and the exciting effects of incendiary pamphlets and pictures, among our slaves in the South. This part of the narrative closes with a spirited picture of a negro insurrection, and with the hanging of Nigger Tom" (Poe, *Essays and Reviews*, 399).

7. Marchand, "Poe as Social Critic," 33–34.

8. This was done mainly on the basis of the work of William Doyle Hull's 1941 University of Virginia dissertation, "A Canon of the Critical Reviews of Edgar Allan Poe."

9. Rosenthal, "Poe, Slavery."

10. Morrison, *Playing in the Dark*, 32.

11. Fiedler writes in 1966, "Insofar as *Gordon Pym* is finally a social document as well as a fantasy, its subject is slavery; and its scene, however disguised, is the section of America which was to destroy itself defending that institution. It is, indeed, to be expected that our first eminent Southern author discover that the proper subject for American gothic is the black man, from whose shadow we have

not yet emerged" (*Love and Death*, 397). Indeed, despite the claims of recent critics to the contrary, Pym's proslavery ideology and his southern sympathies was analyzed frequently and well in some of the earliest criticism of the *Pym* revival. Levin in *The Power of Blackness* reads the novel through the "Southern self-consciousness of the author" (120) and finds in it a "consciousness of guilt and a fear of retribution" (122) with regards to the slave system. In his 1960 "Introduction to *Pym*," Kaplan offered an extended interpretation of the scenes in Tsalal in terms of Poe's antipathy toward blacks. And in his introduction to the Penguin edition of *Pym*, Beaver takes Kaplan's and Fiedler's arguments still further in suggesting specific historical developments in the debate over slavery to which Poe may have been responding in his novel, especially Nat Turner's revolt of 1831.

12. Nelson, *Word in Black and White*, 91.

13. Bradfield, *Dreaming Revolution*, 80 and 121 n.27, in which he cites the "Review" as Poe's without any comment as to the disputed authorship.

14. Dayan, "Amorous Bondage," 239–40. This essay is largely a reworking of a more muted version of the same argument found in "Romance and Race." Rowe makes a similar claim in "Poe, Ante-bellum Slavery," suggesting a critical tradition of "repress[ing] the subtle complicity of literary Modernism with racist ideology, which now Poe may be said to represent both in his ante-bellum historical context and his 'modern' revival" (136). Rowe refers here to a shared aesthetic project in both Poe and modernism (and its postmodern heirs): a poetic language "demand[ing] a special literacy, a competency of poetic reading and writing that would develop into the sorts of *institutions* of sophisticated interpretation that have their origins in aesthetic modernism" (137).

15. As Whalen usefully cautions, in his study of race in Poe's writing, "denunciation can easily take the place of criticism" ("Subtle Barbarians," 175).

16. Poe, *Letters*, 1:77; *Essays and Reviews*, 978.

17. In a letter dated 30 May 1835, in which Poe comes to terms with White as to his new role as unofficial editor of the *Messenger*, he concludes, "The high compliment of Judge Tucker is rendered doubly flattering to me by my knowledge of his literary character" (*Letters*, 1:60).

18. Quoted in Horsman, *Race and Manifest Destiny*, 123.

19. Dew, "An Address," 277.

20. Ibid., 278. For a similar argument see Upshur, "Domestic Slavery."

21. Tise, *Proslavery*, 308.

22. Quoted in ibid., 345; emphasis added.

23. Upshur, "Partisan Leader," 73.

24. "Slavery," 337.

25. For example, "The Shadow—a Parable" (1835), contains all three: "the boding and the memory of Evil"; "the shadow was vague, and formless, and indefinite"; "a dark and undefined shadow" (Poe, *Poetry and Tales*, 218–20); see

Pollin, *Word Index.* "Berenice," published the same year, closely mirrors the review's use of "vague" to describe yet another "shadow": "vague, variable, indefinite, unsteady."

26. Poe, *Letters,* 1:90. I remain unconvinced by Rosenthal's argument that the letter refers to another, earlier proslavery review by Tucker, and I continue to read the letter as referring to Tucker's primary authorship of the "Slavery" review.

27. There is nothing surprising in his doing so—as editor, Poe frequently revised much of the prose in the magazine that he did not write, and Tucker thought well enough of Poe's literary abilities to grant him freedom to edit his essay as he saw fit. That Poe would not need approval of such changes is made clear in a letter in which Tucker promises to send some poetry for the *Messenger* on the "condition" that Poe, whose taste and opinion he highly valued, "judge them candidly, and reject them if they do not come up to either my standard or yours" (Poe, *Complete Works,* 12:24).

28. See *Southern Literary Messenger* 2 (1836): 342. Further evidence of Poe's willingness to claim this review is supplied by the fact that he later worked to distance himself from another anonymous piece in the *Messenger* by Tucker, a review of Dickens widely attributed to Poe. In his "Chapter on Autography," Poe writes, "We have reason to believe [the review] was from the pen of Judge Beverley Tucker. We take this opportunity of mentioning the subject," he goes on, as "it is a burthen we are not disposed and never intended to bear. The review appeared in March, we think, and we had retired from the *Messenger* in the January preceding" (*Autography,* 40). That Poe must here expose his former patron as the author of this piece of criticism is due to his need to keep his own judgment above reproach. That he feels no corresponding need to point toward Tucker's hand in the "Slavery" review suggests his willingness to benefit from the anonymous conditions of the literary marketplace when they happen to work to his advantage.

29. Further, James Kirke Paulding, whose proslavery work is extolled in the highest terms in the review, was at this time Poe's contact at Harper's, publishers of *Pym.*

30. Poe, *Poetry and Tales,* 322.

31. Ibid., 320. See also Gillian Brown, "Poetics of Extinction," in which she reads "Usher" as sharing the age's obsession with extinction. Brown usefully describes Poe's ambition to locate and perpetuate an "indelible legibility," an ambition born out of the "anthropological imperative of Poe's exercises in terror" (333).

32. "Slavery," 338. Apparently Poe found such scenes overdone and took the liberty of excising one. In his letter to Tucker, Poe writes, "One very excellent passage in relation to the experience of a sick bed has been, necessarily, omitted altogether" (*Letters,* 1:90).

33. "Slavery," 338.

34. See Hungerford, "Poe and Phrenology," 1–23.

35. Horsman, *Race and Manifest Destiny,* 121.

36. Poe, *Essays and Reviews,* 329.

37. Poe, *Letters,* 1:184–85.

38. Poe, *Essays and Reviews,* 329.

39. Quoted in Gould, *Mismeasure of Man,* 50.

40. Gould, *Mismeasure of Man,* 51.

41. Morton, *Crania Americana,* 2–3.

42. Ibid., 260. Morton adds, "The *Caucasians* were, with a single exception, derived from the lowest and least educated class of society" (261). For a reconsideration of Morton's measurements and conclusions, see Gould, *Mismeasure of Man,* 50–69, in which he describes the "juggling" Morton engaged in to arrive at the conclusions he and his readers expected to find.

43. Morton, *Crania Americana,* 267, 277.

44. Morton, *Crania Aegyptiaca,* 1.

45. Morton's "true" Caucasians, the "Pelasgic" family, measure 88 cubic inches; whereas the Semitic, Egyptian, and Negroid measure 82, 80, and 79 cubic inches, respectively.

46. Morton, *Crania Aegyptiaca,* 17.

47. Lindsly, "Differences in Intellectual Character," 616; emphasis added.

48. Ibid., 616. And not simply to other whites: "The superiority of the whites, is almost universally felt and acknowledged by the other races. . . . And indeed this consciousness of inferiority is the only rational mode of explaining the docility and patience with which the blacks submit to slavery" (617–18).

49. John T. Irwin, *American Hieroglyphics,* 43.

50. See, for example, A. Robert Lee, " 'Impudent and ingenious fiction.' " Lee argues that the novel is "neither quite fiction of fact nor quite factual fiction, . . . at once drawing us in while at the same time actually encouraging readerly circumspection and doubt" (125). See also Kennedy, "The Invisible Message," where he argues that "the hoax apparently embodied [Poe's] conception of man's relationship to the phenomenal world; the pursuit of meaning confirms only the deceptiveness and inaccessibility of truth" (126); and *"Pym* Pourri," where Kennedy focuses on images of decomposition as Poe's trope for the violation of literary taboos and conventions. Spengemann suggests, "Like Pym's hallucinations, the hoax implies, Poe's wild imaginings are just as real and just as consequential as anything else—perhaps even more so" (*Adventurous Muse,* 141–42).

51. Rowe, *Through the Custom House,* 93.

52. Kennedy, *Poe, Death, and the Life of Writing,* 147.

53. As Rowe writes, "The hidden textuality of Pym's voyage gradually emerges from the darkness to enter the body of the work" (*Through the Custom House,* 99). For John T. Irwin, *Pym* provides the most subtle portrayal of the "myth of hieroglyphic doubling as the simultaneous origin of man and language," and the novel's final lesson is that the "real self is the written self" (*American Hieroglyphics,* 64, 120). For Kennedy, "inscription opens an alternative to oblivion,

ensuring the remembrance of the one who writes" (*Poe, Death, and the Life of Writing*, 176).

54. Rowe, *Through the Custom-House*, 95.

55. Rowe, "Poe, Ante-bellum Slavery," 117.

56. For the definition of a grampus as a killer whale, or orca, see Pollin, "Notes and Comments," 225, note 2.2A.

57. But, as we are told by Pym a short time later, in one of the narrator's characteristic amnesiac gaps, Augustus had composed his note on the back of a letter forged as an excuse to Pym's family for his long absence while at sea. Therefore the blank "back" of the message should have revealed to Pym his own forgery.

58. Williams, *World of Words*, 126.

59. Rowe, *Through the Custom House*, 101. For Rowe, "What is in fact inscribed at the heart of the island is the doubleness of writing, . . . a major theme of the work" (106).

60. See Pollin, "Notes and Comments," 244, note 4.3G.

61. See, for example, the description of Toby in "The Journal of Julius Rodman" (1840), in a scene in which a tribe of Indians are shocked by the black man's appearance: "Toby . . . was as ugly an old gentleman as ever spoke—having all the peculiar features of his race; swollen lips, large white protruding eyes, flat nose, long ears, double head, pot-belly, and bow legs" (*Imaginary Voyages*, 569). See also the description of Pompey in "The Pysche Zenobia": "He was three feet in height. . . . He had bow-legs and was corpulent. His mouth should not be called small, nor his ears short. His teeth, however, were like pearl, and his large full eyes were deliciously white. Nature had endowed him with no neck, and had placed his ankles (as usual with that race) in the middle of the upper portion of the feet" (*Poetry and Tales*, 289). In the *Gentleman's Magazine* (1837) we find another similar passages, which Poe likely saw, in yet another article on "White Negroes": "The Albinos themselves possess the usual peculiarities of the negro formation; their heads are square or flat-sided—their hair is wooly and frizzled—their noses are short, broad, and flat—their lips are large and projecting, and their shins most decidedly curved" (220).

62. See, for example, the description of the murder of the mate's guard: "Peters . . . seized him by the throat, and, before he could utter a single cry, tossed him over the bulwarks" (108).

63. I am indebted to Pollin for the observation: "Pym gives us minute and exact particulars; yet he does not see anything so striking as 'the name upon her stern,' which they had been scrutinizing" ("Notes and Comments," 272 note 10.7A).

64. Hoffman, *Poe Poe Poe Poe Poe Poe Poe*, 276.

65. Quoted in Horsman, *Race and Manifest Destiny*, 141. Others writing in the wake of Morton were still less tentative on this issue; for example, the author of *The Negro: What Is His Ethnological Status?* (1840), who seeks to prove that

the Negro is not a descendant of Ham or of Adam and Eve, but a different species altogether: "God has set a line of demarcation so ineffaceable, so indelible besides color, and so *plain*, between the children of Adam and Eve whom he endowed with immortality, and the negro who is of this earth only, that none can efface" (44). He claims by the end to have proved "that the negro being created before Adam, consequently he is a *beast* in God's nomenclature; and being a beast, was under Adam's rule and dominion, and, like all other beasts or animals, has no soul," and "that God destroyed the world by a flood, for the crime of the amalgamation, or miscegenation of the white race . . . with negroes" (45). The author, "Ariel," concludes with an apocalyptic prophecy not unlike that found at the end of *Pym*: "The people of the United States have now thrust upon them, the question of negro equality, social, political and religious. How will they decide it? If they decide it one way, then they will make the *sixth* cause of invoking God's wrath, once again against the earth" (47–48).

66. Kaplan, "Introduction to *Pym*," 155. As Kaplan demonstrates, more indeed could be translated from these terms, as most of the words found in Tsalal turn out to be derived from Hebrew words for darkness: Tsalal = to be dark; Klock-Klock = to be black; Too-wit = to be dirty, etc.

67. John T. Irwin, "Quincuncial Network," 184.

68. Poe, *Essays and Reviews*, 1232.

69. Quoted in Stanton, *United States Exploring Expedition*, 25. I am indebted to Stanton for my understanding of Reynolds's relationship to the expedition.

70. Poe, *Essays and Reviews*, 1241.

71. Stanton, *United States Exploring Expedition*, 53.

72. Hall, "Natural History of Man," lxxii.

73. Pickering, *Races of Man*, 3–4.

74. Ziff, *Literary Democracy*, 82.

75. Jones, "Literary Prospects of America," 267.

76. See Hungerford, "Poe and Phrenology," 6–7.

77. Poe, *The Brevities*, 129.

78. Poe, *Autography*, 13.

79. So severe was Poe's criticism of those works he thought to be unworthy of inclusion in American letters—even those by such undisputed luminaries as Cooper and Irving—that he early became known for his "savagery." The image of Poe as a literary "savage" circulated as early as 1836, and Poe himself helped to popularize the image by reprinting notices in the *Messenger* that defined him in these terms: "Woe seize on the luckless wights who feel the savage skill with which the editor uses his tomahawk and scalping knife," wrote the *Cincinnati Mirror* in a review appended to the magazine's "Supplement" (Thomas and Jackson, *Poe Log*, 201). As his reputation for "savagery" followed him throughout his career, he found himself labeled "the Comanche of literature" and "our literary Mohawk." This last reference is from a poem by a minor satirist, A. J. Duganne, that accompanied a woodcut portraying Poe as an Indian with tomahawk in one

hand and scalping knife in the other. The caption reads, "With tomahawk up-raised for deadly blow,/Behold our literary Mohawk, Poe" (quoted in Reilly, "Poe in Pillory," 9).

80. Thomas and Jackson, *Poe Log,* 346.

81. Ibid., 351.

82. It is a common mistake, one corrected to some degree in recent criticism, to consider Poe as standing outside the concerns of the literary nationalism of his time. Poe was indeed openly contemptuous of the narrow-minded patriotism that dictated the positive critical reception of even failed American works, and throughout his career Poe lambasted "the gross paradox of liking a stupid book the better, because . . . its stupidity is American" (Poe, *Essays,* 506). But Poe's distaste for American critical and publication practices did not undermine his commit-ment to the idea of a truly great *American* literature, one freed from the jingoism endemic in the 1830s and '40s. In the mid-1840s, as McGill has shown, Poe even aligned himself, uncomfortably but productively, with the Young Americans, a literary nationalist movement that shared his disaffection for much of what passed as "American Literature" ("Poe, Literary Nationalism"). This unlikely alliance was motivated in large measure by a common frustration with the conditions under which authors worked as a result of the lack of an international copyright law and the intricate system of piracy and puffery in American magazines.

83. Poe, *Autography,* 12. The series was originally published in *Graham's Magazine* in November and December 1841. An "Appendix of Autography" followed in January 1842.

84. Poe, *Essays and Reviews,* 1252; emphasis added.

85. Poe, *Autography,* 82.

86. On his death bed in 1849, Poe called out for Reynolds. Or so the story goes. For a version of this apocryphal ending to Poe's career, see Quinn, *Poe,* 640.

CHAPTER 6: Douglass and the Rewriting of American Race

1. Olney compares the autobiographical projects of Franklin and Douglass to demonstrate the unique burdens facing Douglass (" 'Born a Slave,' " 155).

2. Stepto, "Distrust of the Reader," 300, 303.

3. Douglass, *Papers,* 1:16.

4. Roper, *Narrative,* 13.

5. See, for example, Douglass's letter of "thanks" to A. C. C. Thompson for his public denunciation of the *Narrative* on the basis of Thompson's previous "knowledge" of Douglass when a slave. As Douglass points out, this act of denun-ciation serves as an ironic testimonial to his own claims regarding his past. See the letter to Garrison, 27 January 1846, in Douglass, *Life and Writing,* 1:133.

6. Grimes, *Life,* 95.

7. Roper, *Narrative,* 1.

8. Grimes, *Life,* 120.

9. Andrews, *To Tell a Free Story,* 81.

10. Douglass, *Narrative,* 39. Further references will be cited parenthetically in the text.

11. See Gates, "From Wheatley to Douglass," 52.

12. Bingham, *Columbian Orator,* 295.

13. Quoted in Gates, "Preface to Blackness," 52.

14. Ibid., 45.

15. Grimes describes a similar scene of conflict over writing, when he is severely whipped for "mak[ing] impressions with my fingers, such as letters" on the wet mortar of a new oven (*Life,* 74).

16. Douglass, *Papers,* 1:8.

17. Baker, "Autobiographical Acts," 247.

18. Stepto, *From behind the Veil,* 20.

19. The quote is from Olney, "'Born a Slave,'" 158.

20. Moses, "Writing Freely," 67.

21. As Olney glosses this move, "I write my self down in letters, I underwrite my identity and my very being, as indeed I have done in and all through the foregoing narrative that has brought me to this place, this moment, this state of being" ("'Born a Slave,'"157).

22. Letter to Garrison, 27 January 1846, in Douglass, *Life and Writings,* 1:133.

23. Douglass, *Life and Writings,* 1:34.

24. Douglass, *Papers,* 2:101.

25. Letter to Charles Sumner, 2 September 1852, in Douglass, *Life and Writings,* 2:210.

26. "Our Paper and Its Prospects," *North Star,* 3 December 1847, in Douglass, *Life and Writings,* 1:281.

27. Douglass, *Life and Writings,* 1:352.

28. "Change of Opinion Announced," *North Star,* 23 May 1851, in ibid., 2:156.

29. "What to the Slave Is the Fourth of July?" in Douglass, *Papers,* 2:362.

30. Douglass, *Life and Writings,* 1:59.

31. Douglass frequently told a story "on the subject of the supposed inferiority of the black man" about an incident in which he was riding in a carriage one night and entered into conversation with some of his traveling companions. It being dark, they did not know he was black, and he found himself treated with great "deference and respect" for his learning and his eloquence. At this time, Douglass recounts, "he wished . . . that it was perpetual night in America." But with the dawn, the visual signs are restored, "as the sun's rays burst forth, dispelling the darkness, one of the gentlemen beside him happened to observe the crisp of his hair, and he called out to his companions . . . 'God!—it's a Nigger!'" This account is from Douglass, *Life and Writings,* 1:101–2.

32. Douglass offers an early attack on racial science in an 1850 debate with a proponent of the American School, Professor Grant; see ibid., 2:238–42.

33. "The Claims of the Negro Ethnologically Considered: An Address Delivered in Hudson, Ohio, on 12 July 1854," in ibid., 2:503.

34. Gates, "Binary Oppositions," 230.

35. Sundquist, *To Wake the Nations*, 85.

36. These articles are pasted to the inside cover of the copy of *Claims of the Negro, Ethnologically Considered* at Grinnell College's Burling Library. Their sources and the identity of the original owner of the pamphlet are unrecorded.

BIBLIOGRAPHY

"Account of a Remarkable Alteration of Colour in a Negro Woman." *American Museum* 4 (1788): 501–2.

"Account of a Singular Change of Colour in a Negro." *Weekly Magazine* 1 (1798): 110–11.

Adams, Charles Hansforth. *"The Guardian of the Law": Authority and Identity in James Fenimore Cooper*. University Park, Penn.: Penn State University Press, 1990.

Adams, John. *The Political Writings of John Adams: Representative Selections*. Edited by George A. Peek Jr. New York: Macmillan, 1985.

Adams, John, and Thomas Jefferson. *The Adams-Jefferson Letters: The Complete Correspondence between Thomas Jefferson and Abigail and John Adams*. Edited by Lester J. Cappon. Chapel Hill: University of North Carolina Press, 1959.

Adams, John, and Benjamin Rush. *The Spur of Fame: Dialogues of John Adams and Benjamin Rush, 1805–1813*. Edited by John A. Schultz and Douglass Adair. San Marino, Calif.: Huntington Library, 1966.

Adventures of Jonathan Corncob Loyal American Refugee. 1787. Edited by Noel Perrin. Boston: Godine, 1976.

The Affecting History of the Dreadful Distresses of Frederic Manheim's Family. Philadelphia: Mathew Carey, 1794.

Allen, Ethan. *The Narrative of Colonel Ethan Allen*. 1779. Edited by Brooke Hindle. New York: Corinth Books, 1961.

Allen, Paul. *The Life of Charles Brockden Brown*. 1815. Dunbar, N.Y.: Scholar's Facsimiles & Reprints, 1975.

Almy, Robert F. "J. N. Reynolds: A Brief Biography with Particular Reference to Poe and Symmes." *Colophon* 2 (1937): 227–45.

American in Algiers, or the Patriot of Seventy-Six in Captivity. A Poem, in Two Cantos. New York: J. Buel, 1797.

American Museum 1 (1787) – 10 (1791).

American Quarterly Review 1 (1827) – 22 (1837).

Analectic Magazine 1 (1813) – 10 (1817).

Anderson, Benedict. *Imagined Communities: Reflections on the Origin and Spread of Nationalism*. Revised edition. London: Verso, 1991.

Andrews, William. *To Tell a Free Story: The First Century of Afro-American Autobiography, 1760–1865*. Urbana: University of Illinois Press, 1986.

"Another Instance of a Negro Turning White." *Monthly Magazine* 3 (1800): 392.

The Arabian Nights Entertainment . . . The First American Edition, Freely Transcribed from the Original Translation. 2 vols. Philadelphia: H. & P. Rice, 1794.

[Ariel]. *The Negro: What Is His Ethnological Status?* 1840. Reprint, Cincinnati, 1867.

Arner, Robert D. "The Connecticut Wits." In *American Literature 1764–1789: The Revolutionary Years,* edited by Everett Emerson. Madison: University of Wisconsin Press, 1977.

Axelrod, Alan. *Charles Brockden Brown: An American Tale.* Austin: University of Texas, 1983.

Baepler, Paul. "The Barbary Captivity Narrative in Early America." *Early American Literature* 30 (1995): 95–120.

Bailey, J. O. "An Early American Utopian Fiction." *American Literature* 14 (1942): 285–93.

Bailyn, Bernard. *The Ideological Origins of the American Revolution.* Cambridge, Mass.: Harvard University Press, 1967.

Baker, Houston A., Jr. "Autobiographical Acts and the Voice of the Southern Slave." In *The Slave's Narrative,* edited by Davis and Gates.

Balibar, Etienne. "Culture and Identity (Working Notes)." In *The Identity in Question,* edited by John Rajchman. New York: Routledge, 1995.

Barnby, H. G. *The Prisoners of Algiers: An Account of the Forgotten American-Algerian War, 1785–1797.* London: Oxford University Press, 1966.

Barruel, Abbé. *Application of Barruel's Memoirs of Jacobinism to the Secret Societies of Ireland and Great Britain.* London, 1798.

Bartram, William. *Travels of William Bartram.* 1791. New York: Dover, 1955.

Beard, James Franklin. "Historical Introduction." In *The Pioneers,* by James Fenimore Cooper.

Beaver, Harold. "Introduction." *The Narrative of Arthur Gordon Pym.* New York: Penguin, 1975.

Belknap, Jeremy. *The Foresters, An American Tale; Being a Sequel to the History of John Bull the Clothier.* 1792. Upper Saddle, N.J.: Literature House, 1970.

Bennett, Charles E. "Charles Brockden Brown: Man of Letters." In *Critical Essays on Charles Brockden Brown,* edited by Rosenthal.

Bercovitch, Sacvan. *The American Jeremiad.* Madison: University of Wisconsin, 1978.

Berkhofer, Robert F. *The White Man's Indian: Images of the American Indian from Columbus to the Present.* New York: Knopf, 1978.

Berlant, Lauren. *The Anatomy of National Fantasy: Hawthorne, Utopia, and Everyday Life.* Chicago: University of Chicago Press, 1991.

Bhabha, Homi K., ed. *Nation and Narration.* New York: Routledge, 1990.

Bingham, Caleb. *The Columbian Orator: Containing a Variety of Original and Selected Pieces. . . .* 6th ed. Troy, N.Y.: Parker and Bliss, 1815.

Bleecker, Ann Eliza. *The History of Maria Kittle.* 1797. Reprinted in *The Garland*

Library of North American Indian Captivities, edited by Wilcolm E. Washburn. 311 vols. New York: Garland, 1978.

Bloch, Ruth H. *Visionary Republic: Millennial Themes in American Thought, 1756–1800.* Cambridge: Cambridge University Press, 1985.

Blunt, Joseph. *An Examination of the Expediency and Constitutionality of Prohibiting Slavery in the State of Missouri.* New York: C. Wiley, 1819.

Bontemps, Arna. "The Slave Narrative: An American Genre." In *Great Slave Narratives,* edited by Arna Bontemps. Boston: Beacon Press, 1969.

Brackenridge, Hugh Henry. *Modern Chivalry.* 1792. Edited by Lewis Leary. New Haven, Conn.: College and University Press, 1965.

Bradfield, Scott. *Dreaming Revolution: Transgression in the Development of American Romance.* Iowa City: University of Iowa Press, 1993.

Brennan, Timothy. "The National Longing for Form." In *Nation and Narration,* edited by Bhabha.

Brown, Charles Brockden. *An Address to the Government of the United States, on the Cession of Louisiana to the French; and on the Late Breach of Treaty by the Spaniards.* Philadelphia: John Conrad, 1803.

——. *Arthur Mervyn or Memoirs of the Year 1793.* 1799–1800. Kent, Ohio: Kent State University Press, 1980.

——. *Edgar Huntly or Memoirs of a Sleep-Walker.* 1799. Edited by Sydney J. Krause and S. W. Reid. Kent, Ohio: Kent State University Press, 1984.

——. "Fragment." *Monthly Magazine* 1 (1799): 21–44.

——. "Memoirs of Carwin the Biloquist." In *Wieland, or the Transformation Together with Memoirs of Carwin the Biloquist,* edited by Fred Lewis Pattee. New York: Harcourt Brace Jovanovich, 1926.

——. "Memoirs of Stephen Calvert." In *Alcuin, a Dialogue/Memoirs of Stephen Calvert,* edited by Sydney J. Krause, S. W. Reid, and Robert D. Arner. Kent, Ohio: Kent State University Press, 1987.

——. *Monroe's Embassy, or, the Conduct of the Government, in Relation to Our Claims to the Navigation of the Mississippi.* Philadelphia: John Conrad, 1803.

——. *Ormond or the Secret Witness.* 1799. Edited by Sydney J. Krause, S. W. Reid, and Russell B. Nye. Kent, Ohio: Kent State University Press, 1982.

——. *The Rhapsodist and Other Uncollected Writings.* Edited by Harry R. Warfel. New York: Scholars' Facsimiles & Reprints, 1943.

Brown, Gillian. "The Poetics of Extinction." In *The American Face of Edgar Allan Poe,* edited by Rosenheim and Rachman.

Brown, William Hill. *The Power of Sympathy.* 1789. Albany: New College and University Press, 1970.

Budd, Louis J., and Edwin H. Cady. *On Poe: The Best from American Literature.* Durham, N.C.: Duke University Press, 1993.

Buel, Richard, Jr. *Securing the Revolution: Ideology in American Politics, 1789–1815.* Ithaca, N.Y.: Cornell University Press, 1972.

Burns, James MacGregor. *The Vineyard of Liberty.* New York: Knopf, 1982.

Burroughs, Stephen. *Memoirs of the Notorious Stephen Burroughs of New Hampshire.* 1798. New York: Dial Press, 1924.

Butler, James. *Fortune's Foot-ball: or, the Adventures of Mercutio. Founded on Matters of Fact.* 2 vols. Harrisburg, Penn.: John Wyeth, 1797–98.

Caldwell, Charles. *Thoughts on the Original Unity of the Human Race.* New York: E. Bliss, 1830.

Carey, Matthew. *A Short Account of Algiers.* Philadelphia: M. Carey, 1794.

Carson, Ada Lou, and Herbert L. Carson. *Royall Tyler.* Boston: Twayne, 1979.

Castronovo, Russ. *Fathering the Nation: American Genealogies of Slavery and Freedom.* Berkeley: University of California Press, 1995.

Cathcart, James Leander. *The Captives: Eleven Years a Prisoner in Algiers.* Edited by J. B. Newkirk. La Porte, Ind.: Herald Print, 1897.

——. "The Diplomatic Journal and Letter Book of James Leander Cathcart, 1788–1796." *Proceedings of the American Antiquarian Society* 64 (1954): 303–436.

Chase, Richard. *The American Novel and Its Tradition.* 1957. Baltimore: Johns Hopkins University Press, 1980.

Cheyfitz, Eric. "Literally White, Figuratively Red: The Frontier of Translation in *The Pioneers.*" In *James Fenimore Cooper: New Critical Essays,* edited by Robert Clark. Totawa, N.J.: Barnes & Noble, 1985.

Child, Lydia Maria. *Hobomok & Other Writings on Indians.* 1824. Edited by Carolyn L. Karcher. New Brunswick, N.J.: Rutgers University Press, 1986.

Clark, David Lee. *Charles Brockden Brown: Pioneer Voice of America.* Durham, N.C.: Duke University Press, 1952.

Cobbett, William. *Detection of a Conspiracy, Formed by the United Irishmen, with the Evident Intention of Aiding the Tyrants of France in Subverting the Government of the United States of America.* Philadelphia: Wm. Cobbett, 1798.

Columbian Magazine; or Monthly Magazine 1 (1786–87).

Cooper, James Fenimore. *Gleanings in Europe: Switzerland.* 1836. Edited by Robert E. Spiller and James F. Beard. Albany: State University of New York Press, 1980.

——. *The Letters and Journals of James Fenimore Cooper.* Edited by James Franklin Beard. 6 vols. Cambridge, Mass.: Belknap Press, 1968.

——. *Lionel Lincoln; or, The Leaguer of Boston.* 1825. Edited by Donald A. Ringe and Lucy B. Ringe. Albany: State University of New York Press, 1984.

——. *The Monikins.* 1835. Edited by James S. Hedges. Albany: New College and University Press, 1990.

——. *Notions of the Americans: Picked up by a Travelling Bachelor.* 1828. Edited by Gary Williams. Albany: State University of New York Press, 1991.

——. *The Pilot; a Tale of the Sea.* 1823. Edited by Kay Seymour House. Albany: State University of New York Press, 1986.

——. *The Pioneers, or the Sources of the Susquehanna; a Descriptive Tale.* 1823. Edited by James Franklin Beard. Albany: State University of New York Press, 1980.

——. *The Prairie: A Tale.* 1827. Edited by James P. Elliott. Albany: State University of New York Press, 1985.

——. *Red Rover; a Tale.* 1827. Edited by Thomas and Marianne Philbrick. Albany: State University of New York Press, 1991.

——. *The Spy: A Tale of the Neutral Ground.* 1821. Edited by James H. Pickering. New Haven, Conn.: College and University Press, 1971.

Crèvecoeur, J. Hector St. John de. *Letters from an American Farmer and Sketches of Eighteenth-Century America.* 1782. Edited by Albert E. Stone. New York: Penguin, 1981.

"The Curses of Slavery: Treatment of American Prisoners at Algiers." *Rural Magazine* 1 (1795): 118–22.

Daniels, Roger. *Coming to America: A History of Immigration and Ethnicity in American Life.* New York: Harpers, 1990.

Dauber, Kenneth. *The Idea of Authorship in America: Democratic Poetics from Franklin to Melville.* Madison: University of Wisconsin Press, 1990.

Dauer, Manning J. *The Adams Federalists.* Baltimore: Johns Hopkins University Press, 1953.

Davidson, Cathy N. *Revolution and the Word: The Rise of the American Novel.* New York: Oxford University Press, 1986.

Davis, Charles T., and Henry Louis Gates Jr., eds. *The Slave's Narrative.* New York: Oxford University Press, 1985.

Dayan, Joan. "Amorous Bondage: Poe, Ladies, and Slaves." *American Literature* 66 (1994): 239–73.

——. "Romance and Race." In *The Columbia History of the American Novel,* edited by Emory Elliot. New York: Columbia University Press, 1991.

DeConde, Alexander. *This Affair of Louisiana.* New York: Scribner's, 1976.

Defoe, Daniel. *The Life and Strange Surprizing Adventures of Robinson Crusoe.* 1719. Edited by J. Donald Crowley. New York: Oxford University Press, 1981.

Dekker, George. *The American Historical Romance.* Cambridge: Cambridge University Press, 1987.

Dennis, Larry R. "Legitimizing the Novel: Royall Tyler's *The Algerine Captive.*" *Early American Literature* 9 (1974): 71–80.

Dew, Thomas R. "An Address, on the Influence of the Federative Republican System of Government upon Literature and the Development of Character." *Southern Literary Messenger* 2 (March 1836): 277–78.

Diggins, John P. "Slavery, Race, and Equality: Jefferson and the Pathos of Enlightenment." *American Quarterly* 28 (1976): 206–28.

Dippie, Brian W. *The Vanishing American: White Attitudes and U.S. Indian Policy.* Lawrence: University of Kansas Press, 1982.

Douglass, Frederick. *Claims of the Negro, Ethnologically Considered. An Address, Before the Literary Societies of Western Reserve College.* Rochester, N.Y.: Lee, Mann & Co., 1854.

——. *The Frederick Douglass Papers, Series One: Speeches, Debates, and Interviews.* Edited by John W. Blassingame. 5 vols. New Haven, Conn.: Yale University Press, 1979.

——. *The Life and Writings of Frederick Douglass.* Edited by Philip S. Foner. 5 vols. New York: International Publishers, 1950.

——. *The Narrative of the Life of Frederick Douglass, An American Slave. Written by Himself.* 1845. Edited by Houston A. Baker Jr. New York: Penguin, 1982.

Drinnon, Richard. *Facing West: The Metaphysics of Indian-Hating and Empire Building.* Minneapolis: University of Minnesota Press, 1980.

Dwight, Theodore. *An Oration, Spoken at Hartford, in the State of Connecticut, on the Anniversary of American Independence, July 4th, 1798.* Hartford, Conn.: Hudson and Goodwin, 1798.

Dwight, Timothy. *The Duty of Americans, at the Present Crisis, Illustrated in a Discourse, Preached on the Fourth of July, 1798.* New Haven, Conn.: Thomas and Samuel Green, 1798.

——. *Travels in New England and New York.* 1821. 4 vols. Cambridge, Mass.: Harvard University Press, 1969.

Eckhardt, Celia Morris. *Fanny Wright: Rebel in America.* Cambridge, Mass.: Harvard University Press, 1984.

Elliott, Emory. *Revolutionary Writers: Literature and Authority in the New Republic 1725–1810.* New York: Oxford University Press, 1982.

Elliott, James P. "Historical Introduction." In *The Prairie: A Tale,* by James Fenimore Cooper.

Engell, John. "Narrative Irony and National Character in Royall Tyler's *Algerine Captive.*" *Studies in American Fiction* 17 (1989): 19–32.

A Few Facts Reflecting the American Colonization Society and the Colony at Liberia. Washington D.C.: Way & Gideon, 1830.

Fiedler, Leslie. *Love and Death in the American Novel.* New York: Stein & Day, 1966.

Fields, Barbara Jeane. "Slavery, Race and Ideology." *New Left Review* 181 (1990): 95–118.

Fisher, Dexter, and Robert Stepto, eds. *Afro-American Literature: The Reconstruction of Instruction.* New York: MLA Press, 1979.

Fishkin, Shelley Fisher. "Interrogating 'Whiteness,' Complicating 'Blackness': Remapping American Culture." *American Quarterly* 47 (1995): 428–66.

Fliegelman, Jay. *Prodigals and Pilgrims: The American Revolution against Patriarchal Authority, 1750–1800.* New York: Cambridge University Press, 1982.

Foss, John. *Journal of the Captivity and Suffering of John Foss.* 2d edition. New-buryport, Mass.: A. March, 1798.

Foster, Frances Smith. *Witnessing Slavery: The Development of Ante-bellum Slave Narratives.* 2d edition. Madison: University of Wisconsin Press, 1994.

Franklin, Benjamin. *Writings.* Edited J. A. Leo Lemay. New York: Library of America, 1987.

Franklin, Wayne. *Discoverers, Explorers, Settlers: The Diligent Writers of Early America.* Chicago: University of Chicago Press, 1977.

——. *The New World of James Fenimore Cooper.* Chicago: University of Chicago Press, 1982.

Freehling, William W. "The Founding Fathers and Slavery." *American Historical Review* 77 (1972): 81–93.

Gates, Henry Louis, Jr. "Binary Oppositions in Chapter One of *Narrative of the Life of Frederick Douglass, an American Slave, Written By Himself.*" In *Afro-American Literature,* edited by Fisher and Stepto.

——. "From Wheatley to Douglass: The Politics of Displacement." In *Frederick Douglass,* edited by Sundquist.

——. "Preface to Blackness: Text and Pretext." In *Afro-American Literature,* edited by Fisher and Stepto.

Gelles, Edith B. "Gossip: An Eighteenth Century Case." *Journal of Social History* 22 (1989): 667–84.

Gellner, Ernest. *Nations and Nationalism.* Oxford: Basil Blackwell, 1983.

Gentleman's Magazine (1837–38).

Gossett, Thomas F. *Race: The History of an Idea in America.* New York: Schocken, 1963.

Gould, Stephen Jay. *The Mismeasure of Man.* New York: Norton, 1981.

Grabo, Norman. *The Coincidental Art of Charles Brockden Brown.* Chapel Hill: University of North Carolina Press, 1981.

Graham's Magazine (1840–45).

Greene, John C. *American Science in the Age of Jefferson.* Ames: Iowa State University Press, 1984.

Grimes, William. *The Life of William Grimes . . . Written by Himself.* 1825. In *Five Black Lives: The Autobiographies of Venture Smith, James Mars, William Grimes, The Rev. G. W. Offley, James L. Smith,* edited by Arna Bontemps. Middletown, Conn.: Wesleyan University Press, 1971.

Gustafson, Thomas. *Representative Words: Politics, Literature, and the American Language, 1776–1865.* New York: Cambridge University Press, 1992.

Hall, John Charles. "An Analytical Synopsis of the Natural History of Man." Preface to *The Races of Man,* by Pickering.

Hamilton, Alexander, John Jay, and James Madison. *The Federalist Papers.* 1787. Edited by Clinton Rossiter. New York: Mentor, 1961.

Heckewelder, Rev. John. *History, Manners and Customs of the Indian Nations who Once Inhabited Pennsylvania and the Neighbouring States.* 1819. Reprint, Philadelphia: Historical Society of Pennsylvania, 1881.

Hietala, Thomas R. *Manifest Design: Anxious Aggrandizement in Late Jacksonian America.* Ithaca, N.Y.: Cornell University Press, 1985.

Hillhouse, William. *Pocahontas; a Proclamation: with plates.* New Haven, Conn.: J. Clyme, 1820.

History of Constantius and Pulchera; or Constancy Rewarded. Salem, Mass.: T. C. Cushing, 1795.

History of the Captivity and Sufferings of Mrs. Maria Martin, Who Was Six Years a Slave in Algiers . . . Written by Herself—With a History of Algiers. Boston: W. Creary, 1806.

Hobsbawm, E. J. *Nations and Nationalism since 1780.* Cambridge: Cambridge University Press, 1990.

Hoffman, Daniel. *Poe Poe Poe Poe Poe Poe Poe.* New York: Doubleday, 1972.

Horsman, Reginald. *Expansion and American Indian Policy, 1783–1812.* East Lansing: Michigan State University Press, 1967.

———. *Race and Manifest Destiny: The Origins of American Racial Anglo-Saxonism.* Cambridge, Mass.: Harvard University Press, 1981.

House, Kay Seymour. *Cooper's Americans.* Columbus: Ohio State University Press, 1965.

Howe, John R., Jr. "Republican Thought and the Political Violence of the 1790s." In *National Unity on Trial, 1781–1816,* edited by E. James Ferguson. New York: Random House, 1970.

Hudson, Nicholas. "From 'Nation' to 'Race': The Origin of Racial Classification in Eighteenth-Century Thought." *Eighteenth Century Studies* 29 (1996): 247–64.

Hughes, Philip Russell. "Archetypal Patterns in *Edgar Huntly.*" *Studies in the Novel* 5 (1973): 176–90.

Hull, William Doyle. "A Canon of the Critical Review of Edgar Allan Poe." Ph.D. diss., University of Virginia, 1941.

Humphreys, David, et al. *The Anarchiad: A New England Poem.* 1786–87. Edited by William K. Bottorff. Gainesville, Fla.: Scholars' Facsimiles & Reprints, 1967.

Hungerford, Edward. "Poe and Phrenology." In *On Poe,* edited by Budd and Cady.

Hunt, Alfred N. *Haiti's Influence on Antebellum America: Slumbering Volcano in the·Caribbean.* Baton Rouge: Louisiana State University Press, 1988.

Irving, Washington. *History, Tales and Sketches.* Edited by James W. Tuttleton. New York: Library of America, 1983.

Irwin, John T. *American Hieroglyphics: The Symbol of the Egyptian Hieroglyphics in the American Renaissance.* Baltimore: Johns Hopkins University Press, 1980.

———. "The Quincuncial Network in Poe's *Pym.*" In *Poe's Pym,* edited by Kopley.

Irwin, Ray W. *The Diplomatic Relations of the United States with the Barbary Powers.* Chapel Hill: University of North Carolina Press, 1931.

Jefferson, Thomas. *Writings.* Edited by Merrill D. Peterson. New York: Library of America, 1984.

Jones, John Beauchamp. "Thoughts on the Literary Prospects of America." *Burton's Gentleman's Magazine* 5 (1839): 267.

Jordan, Winthrop D. Introduction to *An Essay on the Causes of the Variety of Complexion and Figure in the Human Species,* by Samuel Stanhope Smith. 1810. Cambridge, Mass.: Harvard University Press, 1965.

——. *White over Black: American Attitudes toward the Negro, 1550–1812.* Chapel Hill: University of North Carolina Press, 1968.

Kammen, Michael. *A Season of Youth: The American Revolution and the Historical Imagination.* Oxford: Oxford University Press, 1978.

Kaplan, Sidney. "Introduction to *Pym.*" In *Poe: A Collection of Critical Essays,* edited by Robert Regan. Englewood Cliffs, N.J.: Prentice Hall, 1969.

Kelly, William P. *Plotting America's Past: Fenimore Cooper and the Leatherstocking Tales.* Carbondale: Southern Illinois University Press, 1983.

Kennedy, J. Gerald. "The Invisible Message: The Problem of Truth in Pym." In *The Naiad Voice: Essays on Poe's Satiric Hoaxing,* edited by Dennis W. Eddings. Port Washington, N.Y.: Associated Faculty Press, 1983.

——. *Poe, Death, and the Life of Writing.* New Haven, Conn.: Yale University Press, 1987.

——. "*Pym* Pourri: Decomposing the Textual Body." In *Poe's Pym,* edited by Kopley.

Kettner, James H. *The Development of American Citizenship 1608–1870.* Chapel Hill: University of North Carolina Press, 1975.

King, Rufus. *Substance of Two Speeches, Delivered in the Senate of the United States, On the Subject of the Missouri Bill.* New York: Kirk & Mercein, 1819.

Kopley, Richard, ed. *Poe's Pym: Critical Explorations.* Durham, N.C.: Duke University Press, 1992.

Kornfeld, Eve. "Encountering 'the Other': American Intellectuals and Indians in the 1790s." *William & Mary Quarterly* 3d ser., 52 (1995): 287–314.

Kramer, Michael P. *Imagining Language in America: From the Revolution to the Civil War.* Princeton, N.J.: Princeton University Press, 1992.

Kramnick, Isaac. "The 'Great National Discussion': The Discourse of Politics in 1787." *William and Mary Quarterly* 3d ser., 45 (1988): 3–32.

Krause, Sydney. "*Edgar Huntly* and the American Nightmare." *Studies in the Novel* 13 (1981): 294–302.

——. "Historical Essay." In *Edgar Huntly,* by Charles Brockden Brown.

Kyte, George W. "The Detention of General Collot: A Sidelight on Anglo-American Relations, 1798–1800." *William and Mary Quarterly* 3d ser., 6 (1949): 628–30.

Larson, David M. *"Arthur Mervyn, Edgar Huntly* and the Critics." *Essays in Literature* 15 (1988): 206–19.

Lawrence, D. H. *Studies in Classic American Literature.* New York: Viking, 1961.

Lee, A. Robert. "'Impudent and ingenious Fiction': Poe's *The Narrative of Arthur Gordon Pym of Nantucket.*" In *Edgar Allan Poe: The Design of Order,* edited by A. Robert Lee. Totowa, N.J.: Barnes & Noble, 1987.

Lee, Charles. *Defence of the Alien and Sedition Laws, Shewing their entire consistency with the Constitution of the United States. . . .* Philadelphia: Fenno, 1798.

Levin, Harry. *The Power of Blackness.* New York: Knopf, 1958.

Lewis, R. W. B. *The American Adam: Innocence, Tragedy, and Tradition in the Nineteenth Century.* 1955. Chicago: University of Chicago Press, 1968.

Lindsly, Harvey. "Differences in the Intellectual Character of the Several Varieties of the Human Race." *Southern Literary Messenger* 5 (1839): 616–20.

Lipsitz, George. "The Possessive Investment in Whiteness: Racialized Social Democracy and the 'White' Problem in American Studies." *American Quarterly* 47 (1995): 369–87.

Livermore, Shaw. *The Twilight of Federalism: The Disintegration of the Federalist Party 1815–1830.* Princeton, N.J.: Princeton University Press, 1962.

Looby, Christopher. *Voicing America: Language, Literary Form, and the Origins of the United States.* Chicago: University of Chicago Press, 1996.

Lycurgus [Josiah Meigs]. "The History of White Negroes." *New-Haven Gazette, and Connecticut Magazine* 1 (April 13, 1786): 65–67.

Madison, James. *The Papers of James Madison. Vol. 15: 24 March 1793–20 April 1795.* Edited by Thomas A. Mason, Robert A. Rutland, and Jeanne K. Sisson. Charlottesville: University Press of Virginia, 1985.

Marchand, Ernest. "Poe as Social Critic." In *On Poe,* edited by Budd and Cady.

Markoe, Peter. *The Algerine Spy in Pennsylvania: or, Letter Written by a Native of Algiers on the Affairs of the United States of America, From the Close of the Year 1783 to the Meeting of the Convention.* Philadelphia: Prichard & Hall, 1787.

Marshall, Humphrey. *The Aliens: A Patriotic Poem.* Philadelphia, 1798.

Massachusetts Magazine 1 (1789) – 8 (1796).

McGill, Meredith L. "Poe, Literary Nationalism, and Authorial Identity." In *The American Face of Edgar Allan Poe,* edited by Rosenheim and Rachman.

McLean, Robert Colen. *George Tucker: Moral Philosopher and Man of Letters.* Chapel Hill: University of North Carolina Press, 1961.

McWilliams, John P., Jr. *Political Justice in a Republic: James Fenimore Cooper's America.* Berkeley: University of California Press, 1972.

Michaels, Walter Benn. *Our America: Nativism, Modernism, and Pluralism.* Durham, N.C.: Duke University Press, 1995.

——. "'You Who Never Was There': Slavery and the New Historicism, Deconstruction and the Holocaust." *Narrative* 4 (1996): 1–16.

Miller, John C. *Crisis in Freedom: The Alien and Sedition Acts*. Boston: Little, Brown, 1951.

Mitchell, Alexander. *A Treatise on Natural Philosophy in Vindication of Symmes's Theory of the Earth Being a Hollow Sphere*. Eaton, Ohio: Samuel Tizzard, 1826.

Monthly Anthology, and Boston Review 1 (1803) – 10 (1811).

Monthly Magazine 1 (1799) – 3 (1800).

Moore, Glover. *The Missouri Controversy 1819–1821*. Lexington: University of Kentucky Press, 1953.

Morgan, Edmund S. "Slavery and Freedom: The American Paradox." *Journal of American History* 59 (1972): 5–29.

Morrison, Toni. *Playing in the Dark: Whiteness and the Literary Imagination*. Cambridge, Mass.: Harvard University Press, 1992.

Morrow, Nancy V. "The Problem of Slavery in the Polemic Literature of the American Enlightenment." *Early American Literature* 20 (1986): 236–55.

Morton, Samuel George. *Crania Aegyptiaca; or, Observations on Egyptian Ethnography, derived from Anatomy, History and the Monuments*. Philadelphia: John Pennington, 1844.

——. *Crania Americana; or, a comparative view of the skulls of various aboriginal nations of North and South America*. Philadelphia: John Pennington, 1839.

Moses, Wilson J. "Writing Freely?: Frederick Douglass and the Constraints of Racialized Writing." In *Frederick Douglass*, edited by Sundquist.

Nagel, Paul C. *This Sacred Trust: American Nationality 1798–1898*. New York: Oxford University Press, 1971.

Nelson, Dana D. *The Word in Black and White: Reading "Race" in American Literature, 1638–1867*. New York: Oxford University Press, 1992.

New-Haven Gazette 1 (1784) – 2 (1786).

New York Magazine; or, Literary Repository 1 (1790) – 3 (1792).

North American Review 1 (1815) – 22 (1826).

"Observations on the Gradation in the Scale of Being between the Human and Brute Creation." *Columbian Magazine* 2 (1788): 14–22, 70–75.

Olney, James. "'I Was Born a Slave': Slave Narratives, Their Status as Autobiography and as Literature." In *The Slave's Narrative*, edited by Davis and Gates.

Orians, G. Harrison. *The Cult of the Vanishing American*. Toledo, Ohio: H. J. Chittenden, 1934.

Patterson, Mark R. *Authority, Autonomy, and Representation in American Literature, 1776–1865*. Princeton, N.J.: Princeton University Press, 1988.

Peale, Charles Willson. "Account of a Negro, or a very dark Mulatto, turning White." *Massachusetts Magazine* 3 (1791): 744.

Pearce, Roy Harvey. *Savagism and Civilization: A Study of the Indian and the American Mind*. 1953. Revised edition. Berkeley: University of California Press, 1988.

Pease, Donald E. *Visionary Compacts: American Renaissance Writings in Cultural Context.* Madison: University of Wisconsin Press, 1987.

Petter, Henri. *The Early American Novel.* Columbus: Ohio State University Press, 1971.

Pickering, Charles. *The Races of Man; and Their Geographical Distribution.* 1848. Revised edition. London: George Bell, 1876.

The Plea of Erin, or The Case of the Natives of Ireland in the United States . . . Addressed by them to the Congress of the Year 1798. Philadelphia: Freeman's Journal, 1798.

Pocock, J. G. A. *The Machiavellian Moment: Florentine Political Thought and the Atlantic Republican Tradition.* Princeton, N.J.: Princeton University Press, 1975.

Poe, Edgar Allan. *The Brevities: Pinakidia, Marginalia, Fifty Suggestions and Other Works.* Edited by Burton R. Pollin. New York: Gordian Press, 1985.

——. *A Chapter on Autography.* 1841–42. Edited by Don C. Seitz. New York: Dial Press, 1926.

——. *The Complete Works of Edgar Allan Poe.* Edited by James A. Harrison. 12 vols. New York: Thomas Y. Crowell, 1902.

——. *Essays and Reviews.* Edited by G. R. Thompson. New York: Library of America, 1984.

——. *The Imaginary Voyages: The Narrative of Arthur Gordon Pym, The Unparalleled Adventure of One Hans Pfaal, The Journal of Julius Rodman.* Edited by Burton R. Pollin. Boston: Twayne, 1981.

——. *The Letters of Edgar Allan Poe.* Edited by John Ward Ostrom. 2 vols. New York: Gordian Press, 1966.

——. *Poetry and Tales.* Edited by Patrick F. Quinn. New York: Library of America, 1984.

Pollin, Burton R. "Notes and Comments." In *The Imaginary Voyages,* by Edgar Allan Poe.

——. *Word Index to Poe's Fiction.* New York: Gordian Press, 1982.

Porte, Joel. *The Romance in America: Studies in Cooper, Poe, Hawthorne, Melville, and James.* Middletown, Conn.: Wesleyan University Press, 1969.

Prucha, Francis Paul. *The Indians in American Society: From the Revolutionary War to the Present.* Berkeley: University of California Press, 1985.

Pudaloff, Ross J. "Cooper's Genres and American Problems." *ELH* 50 (1983): 711–27.

Quinn, Arthur Hobson. *Edgar Allan Poe: A Critical Biography.* New York: Appleton-Century-Crofts, 1941.

Railton, Stephen. *Fenimore Cooper: A Study of His Life and Imagination.* Princeton, N.J.: Princeton University Press, 1978.

Reilly, John E. "Poe in Pillory: An Early Version of a Satire by A. J. H. Duganne." *Poe Studies* 6 (1973): 9–12.

"Review of *Symmes's Theory of Concentric Spheres: Demonstrating that the Earth is Hollow. . . .*" *American Quarterly Register* 1 (1827): 235–53.

Richardson, Lyon N. *A History of Early American Magazines, 1741–1789.* New York: Thomas Nelson and Sons, 1931.

Ringe, Donald A. *American Gothic: Imagination and Reason in Nineteenth-Century Fiction.* Lexington: University of Kentucky Press, 1982.

——. *James Fenimore Cooper.* New York: Twayne, 1962.

Robinson, Donald L. *Slavery in the Structure of American Politics 1765–1820.* New York: Harcourt Brace Jovanovich, 1971.

Robison, John. *Proofs of a Conspiracy Against all the Religions and Governments of Europe, Carried on in the Secret Meetings of Free Masons, Illuminati, and Reading Societies.* 4th ed. New York: George Forman, 1798.

Roediger, David R. *The Wages of Whiteness: Race and the Making of the American Working Class.* London: Verso, 1991.

Rogin, Michael Paul. *Fathers and Children: Andrew Jackson and the Subjugation of the American Indian.* New York: Vintage, 1975.

Romero, Laura. "Vanishing Americans: Gender, Empire, and New Historicism." *American Literature* 63 (1991): 385–404.

Roper, Moses. *A Narrative of the Adventures and Escape of Moses Roper, from American Slavery.* 1838. New York: Negro University Press, 1970.

Rosenheim, Shawn, and Stephen Rachman, eds. *The American Face of Edgar Allan Poe.* Baltimore: Johns Hopkins University Press, 1995.

Rosenthal, Bernard. "Poe, Slavery and the *Southern Literary Messenger*: A Reexamination." *Poe Studies* 7 (December 1974): 29–38.

——, ed. *Critical Essays on Charles Brockden Brown.* Boston: G. K. Hall, 1981.

Ross, James. *The Speeches of Mr. Ross and Mr. Morris . . . relative to the free navigation of the river Mississippi.* Philadelphia: Bronson, 1803.

Rowe, John Carlos. "Poe, Ante-bellum Slavery and Modern Criticism." In *Poe's Pym,* edited by Kopley.

——. *Through the Custom House: Nineteenth-Century American Fiction and Modern Theory.* Baltimore: Johns Hopkins University Press, 1982.

Rowson, Susanna. *Charlotte Temple: A Tale of Truth.* 1791. Albany: New Co'lege and University Press, 1964.

——. *Slaves in Algiers; or, A Struggle for Freedom: A Play.* Philadelphia: Wrigley and Berriman, 1794.

Rush, Benjamin. "Observations Intended to Favour a Supposition that the Black Color (as it is called) of the Negroes is Derived from the LEPROSY." *Transactions of the American Philosophical Society* 4 (1799): 289–97.

Samuels, Shirley. "*Wieland*: Alien and Infidel." *Early American Literature* 25 (1990): 46–66.

Sanders, Ronald. *Lost Tribes and Promised Lands: The Origins of American Racism.* Boston: Little, Brown, 1978.

Saxton, Alexander. *The Rise and Fall of the White Republic: Class Politics and Mass Culture in Nineteenth-Century America.* London: Verso, 1990.

Schmitt, Cannon. *Alien Nation: Nineteenth-Century Gothic Fictions and English Nationality.* Philadelphia: University of Pennsylvania Press, 1997.

Schulz, Dieter. "*Edgar Huntly* as Quest Romance." *American Literature* 43 (1971–72): 323–35.

Seaborn, Capt. Adam [John Cleves Symmes?]. *Symzonia: A Voyage of Discovery.* 1820. Gainesville, Fla.: Scholars' Facsimiles & Reprints, 1965.

Sheehan, Bernard W. *Seeds of Extinction: Jeffersonian Philanthropy and the American Indian.* Chapel Hill: University of North Carolina Press, 1973.

Shuffleton, Frank, ed. *A Mixed Race: Ethnicity in Early America.* New York: Oxford University Press, 1993.

Sieminski, Greg. "The Puritan Captivity Narrative and the Politics of the American Revolution." *American Quarterly* 42 (1990): 35–56.

Silverman, Kenneth. *Edgar A. Poe: Mournful and Never-Ending Remembrance.* London: Weidenfeld, 1992.

Simpson, Albert F. "The Political Significance of Slave Representation, 1787–1821." *Journal of Southern History* 7 (1941): 315–42.

Simpson, David. *The Politics of American English, 1776–1850.* New York: Oxford University Press, 1986.

Slaughter, Thomas P. *The Whiskey Rebellion: Frontier Epilogue to the American Revolution.* New York: Oxford University Press, 1986.

"Slavery." *Southern Literary Messenger* 2 (1836): 336–39.

"Slavery and the Missouri Question." *North American Review and Miscellaneous Journal* 10 (1820): 137–68.

Slotkin, Richard. *Regeneration through Violence: The Mythology of the American Frontier, 1600–1860.* Middletown, Conn.: Wesleyan University Press, 1973.

Smith, James Morton. *Freedom's Fetters: The Alien and Sedition Laws and American Civil Liberties.* Ithaca, N.Y.: Cornell University Press, 1956.

Smith, Samuel Stanhope. *An Essay on the Causes of the Variety of Complexion and Figure in the Human Species.* Philadelphia: Aitken, 1787.

Smollett, Tobias. *The Adventures of Roderick Random.* 1748. New York: New American Library, 1964.

Sollors, Werner. *Beyond Ethnicity: Consent and Descent in American Culture.* New York: Oxford University Press, 1986.

"Some Account of a Motley Coloured, or Pye Negro Girl, and mulatto boy, exhibited before the American Philosophical Society, in the Month of May, 1784, for their examination." *American Museum* 3 (1788): 37–39.

Sommer, Doris. *Foundational Fictions: The National Romances of Latin America.* Berkeley: University of California Press, 1991.

Southern Literary Messenger 1 (1834) – 11 (1845).

"Speech of an Indian." *American Museum* 3 (1788): 256–57.

Spengemann, William C. *The Adventurous Muse: The Poetics of American Fiction, 1789–1900.* New Haven, Conn.: Yale University Press, 1977.

Spiller, Robert E. *Fenimore Cooper: Critic of His Times.* New York: Minton, Blach, 1931.

——. "Fenimore Cooper's Defense of Slave-Owning America." *American Historical Review* 35 (1930): 575–82.

Stanton, William. *The Great United States Exploring Expedition of 1838–1842.* Berkeley: University of California Press, 1975.

——. *The Leopard's Spots: Scientific Attitudes toward Race in America, 1815–1859.* Chicago: University of Chicago Press, 1960.

Stark, Aubrey. "Poe's Friend Reynolds." *American Literature* 11 (1939): 152–59.

Starling, Marion Wilson. *The Slave Narrative: Its Place in American History.* 1946. Boston: G. K. Hall, 1981.

Staudenraus, P. J. *The African Colonization Movement 1816–1865.* New York: Columbia University Press, 1961.

Stauffer, Vernon. *New England and the Bavarian Illuminati.* 1918. New York: Russell & Russell, 1967.

Stepto, Robert B. "Distrust of the Reader in Afro-American Narratives." In *Reconstructing American Literary History,* edited by Sacvan Bercovitch. Cambridge, Mass.: Harvard University Press, 1986.

——. *From behind the Veil: A Study of Afro-American Narrative.* Urbana: University of Illinois Press, 1979.

Stinchombe, William C. *The XYZ Affair.* Westport, Conn.: Greenwood Press, 1980.

Stineback, David. "Introduction." In *Edgar Huntly,* by Charles Brockden Brown. New Haven, Conn.: College and University Press, 1973.

Sundquist, Eric J., ed. *Frederick Douglass: New Literary and Historical Essays.* New York: Cambridge University Press, 1990.

——. "Slavery, Revolution and the American Renaissance." In *The American Renaissance Reconsidered,* edited by Walter Benn Michaels and Donald E. Pease. Baltimore: Johns Hopkins University Press, 1985.

——. *To Wake the Nations: Race and the Making of American Literature.* Cambridge, Mass.: Harvard University Press, 1993.

Symmes, John Cleves. *Light Gives Light, To Light Discover—Ad Infinitum.* St. Louis [Missouri Territory], 1818.

Szatmary, David. *Shays's Rebellion: The Making of an Agrarian Rebellion.* Amherst: University of Massachusetts Press, 1980.

Takaki, Ronald. *Iron Cages: Race and Culture in Nineteenth-Century America.* New York: Oxford University Press, 1990.

Tanselle, G. Thomas. "The Editing of Royall Tyler." *Early American Literature* 9 (1974): 83–95.

——. *Royall Tyler.* Cambridge, Mass.: Harvard University Press, 1967.

Thomas, Brook. "*The Pioneers,* or the Sources of American Legal History: A Critical Tale." *American Quarterly* 36 (1984): 86–111.

Thomas, Dwight, and David K. Jackson. *The Poe Log: A Documentary Life of Edgar Allan Poe 1809–1849.* Boston: G. K. Hall, 1987.

Tise, Larry E. *Proslavery: A History of the Defense of Slavery in America, 1701–1840.* Athens: University of Georgia Press, 1987.

Tompkins, Jane. *Sensational Designs: The Cultural Work of American Fiction, 1790–1860.* New York: Oxford University Press, 1985.

Tucker, George. *A Voyage to the Moon.* 1827. Boston: Gregg Press, 1975.

Tucker, Nathaniel Beverley. *The Partisan Leader: A Tale of the Future.* 1836. Chapel Hill: University of North Carolina Press, 1971.

Tucker, St. George. *Reflections, on the Cession of Louisiana to the United States.* Washington, D.C.: Samuel Harrison Smith, 1803.

Tyler, Mary Palmer. *Grandmother Tyler's Book: The Recollections of Mary Palmer Tyler (Mrs. Royall Tyler, 1775–1866).* Edited by Frederick Tupper and Helen Tyler Brown. New York: G. P. Putnam, 1925.

Tyler, Royall. *The Algerine Captive or, The Life and Adventures of Doctor Updike Underhill: Six Years a Prisoner Among the Algerines.* 1797. Edited by Don L. Cook. New Haven, Conn.: College and University Press, 1970.

——. *The Contrast, a Comedy.* 1787. In *Representative American Plays,* edited by Arthur Hobson Quinn. New York: Century, 1917.

——. *The Prose of Royall Tyler.* Edited by Marius B. Peladeau. Montpellier: Vermont Historical Society, 1972.

Underhill, John. *Newes From America; or, A New and Experimentall Discoverie of New England; Containing, a True Relation of their War-like Proceedings these Two Yeares Last Past.* 1638. New York: Da Capo, 1971.

Universal Asylum; and Columbian Magazine 1 (1786) – 9 (1792).

Upshur, A. P. "Domestic Slavery, as it Exists in our Southern States with Reference to its Influence upon Free Government." *Southern Literary Messenger* 5 (1839): 677–87.

——. "The Partisan Leader." *Southern Literary Messenger* 3 (1837): 73–89.

Vail, R. W. G. "The Abraham Panther Indian Captivity, with a Bibliographic Introduction." *American Book Collector* 2 (August–September 1932): 165–72.

VanDerBeets, Richard. *The Indian Captivity Narrative: An American Genre.* Landham, Md.: University Press of America, 1984.

Van Evrie, J. H. *Negroes and Negro "Slavery": The First an Inferior Race: The Latter Its Normal Condition.* New York: Van Evrie, Horton, 1861.

Vincent, Philip. *A True Relation of the Late Battel Fought in New-England, between the English and the Pequet Salvages.* 1638. Reprinted in *Collections of the Massachusetts Historical Society* 3d ser., 6 (1837): 29–43.

Walker, I. M., ed. *Edgar Allan Poe: The Critical Heritage.* London: Routledge & Kegan Paul, 1986.

Wallace, Irving. *The Square Pegs: Some Americans Who Dared to Be Different.* New York: Knopf, 1957.

Wallace, James D. *Early Cooper and His Audience.* New York: Columbia University Press, 1986.

——. "Race and Captivity in Cooper's *The Wept of Wish-ton-Wish.*" *American Literary History* 7 (1995): 189–209.

Walters, Ronald. *American Reformers 1815–1860.* New York: Hill & Wang, 1978.

Warfel, Harry R. *Charles Brockden Brown: American Gothic Novelist.* Gainesville: University of Florida Press, 1949.

Warner, Michael. *The Letters of the Republic: Publication and the Public Sphere in Eighteenth-Century America.* Cambridge, Mass.: Harvard University Press, 1990.

Watts, Steven. *The Romance of Real Life: Charles Brockden Brown and the Origins of American Culture.* Baltimore: Johns Hopkins University Press, 1994.

Weekly Magazine 1 (1798) – 4 (1799).

Whalen, Terence. "Subtle Barbarians: Poe, Racism, and the Political Economy of Adventure." In *Styles of Cultural Activism: From Theory and Pedagogy to Women, Indians, and Communism,* edited by Philip Goldstein. Newark: University of Delaware Press, 1994.

"White Negroes." *Gentleman's Magazine* 1 (1837): 220.

Williams, Michael J. S. *A World of Words: Language and Displacement in the Fiction of Edgar Allan Poe.* Durham, N.C.: Duke University Press, 1988.

Winthrop, John. *Winthrop's Journal: "History of New England" 1630–1649.* 2 vols. New York: Scribner's Sons, 1908.

Wood, Gordon. *The Creation of the American Republic, 1776–1787.* Chapel Hill: University of North Carolina Press, 1967.

Worcester Magazine 1 (1786) – 4 (1788).

Yates, Abraham. "History of the Movement for the United States Constitution." 1789. In *Class Conflict, Slavery, and the United States Constitution,* by Staughton Lynd. Indianapolis, Ind.: Bobbs-Merrill, 1967.

Ziff, Larzer. *Literary Democracy: The Declaration of Cultural Independence in America.* New York: Viking, 1981.

——. *Puritanism in America: New Culture in a New World.* New York: Viking, 1973.

——. *Writing in the New Nation: Prose, Print, and Politics in the Early United States.* New Haven, Conn.: Yale University Press, 1991.

INDEX

Library of Congress Cataloging-in-Publication Data

Gardner, Jared.
Master plots : race and the founding of an American literature.
1787–1845 / Jared Gardner.
p.   cm.
Includes bibliographical references (p.   ) and index.
ISBN 0-8018-5813-5 (alk. paper)
1. American literature—1783–1850—History and criticism.
2. Literature and society—United States—History—19th century.
3. Literature and society—United States—History—18th century.
4. National characteristics, American, in literature.   5. Afro-
Americans in literature.   6. Slavery in literature.   7. Indians in
literature.   8. Race in literature.   I. Title.
PS208.G37   1998
810.9′355—dc21   97-40732
                                                            CIP